Politics and Cult
in Wartime Jap

POLITICS AND CULTURE IN WARTIME JAPAN

BEN-AMI SHILLONY

CLARENDON PRESS · OXFORD

Oxford University Press, Walton Street, Oxford OX2 6DP

Oxford New York Toronto
Delhi Bombay Calcutta Madras Karachi
Petaling Jaya Singapore Hong Kong Tokyo
Nairobi Dar es Salaam Cape Town
Melbourne Auckland
and associated companies in
Berlin Ibadan

Oxford is a trade mark of Oxford University Press

Published in the United States by
Oxford University Press, New York

First published 1981
First issued in paperback with corrections 1991

British Library Cataloguing in Publication Data
Shillony, Ben-Ami
Politics and culture in wartime Japan.
1. Japan—Politics and government
—1912–1945
I. Title
320.9′52   JQ1615
ISBN 0–19–821573–8
ISBN 0–19–820260–1 (Pbk)

Printed and bound in
Great Britain by Bookcraft Ltd,
Midsomer Norton, Bath

To my Father and Mother

Preface

The Pacific War was the most traumatic collective experience of the Japanese in modern times. Looking back at the war with China, the alliance with Germany, the attack on the US, the exploitation of fellow Asians, the maltreatment of prisoners of war, the suppression of freedom, the shrill patriotism, the false euphoria, the suffering, the destruction, the loss of life, and the humiliating defeat, the present-day Japanese cannot but feel ashamed and angered. Much of postwar Japanese writing about that period has therefore been emotive and polemic. The war was a 'dark valley' (*kurai tanima*), into which the country had been dragged by irresponsible militarists, and out of which it was rescued at the last moment. The only plausible purpose for writing about the wartime years was to learn how to avoid similar pitfalls in the future; and the proper way of treating the subject was in a tone of moral outrage. The result was a distorted image of a docile nation manipulated by a few fanatics in uniform.

As the events of the early 1940s recede into the past, it becomes easier, especially for an outsider, to evaluate them in a more dispassionate manner. By doing so, one may discover that the wartime regime of Japan, repressive as it was, was very different from the totalitarian states of that time in other places. When one realizes how tenuous and frail democracy is elsewhere in the world, and how strong is the tendency towards arbitrary rule, one may conclude by wondering not why democracy failed in Japan, but rather how, despite the undemocratic tradition and the pressures of war, a totalitarian dictatorship did not evolve there.

The political values of wartime Japan were part of a wider cultural milieu, in which traditional concepts had already been deeply modified by Western attitudes. Confrontation with the West in a bloody and protracted war created a cultural dilemma which could not be solved.

The present study tries to examine the political and cultural contours of wartime Japan: how was the regime established; what were its characteristics and limitations; how did the emperor, the bureaucracy, and the politicians act; how was the Prime Minister deposed in the midst of the war; what kind of regime existed under his successors; what was the role of the press; how did the intellectuals fare; and what were the prevailing attitudes towards various aspects of the West? Any attempt to encompass such a wide subject necessarily leaves out other areas not directly connected with it. Hence I have not gone into the social and economic sides of the war, which have already been treated by Western historians; into local history; or into the treatment of other nationals, topics which deserve a study of their own.

The sources upon which this book draws are numerous and diverse: documents, diaries, books, magazines, newspapers, biographies, monographs, general histories, and memoirs, both from wartime and postwar years. As the period under discussion is still within the living memory of many Japanese, the volume of materials about it is immense and expanding, and I do not dare to claim that I have exhausted them all.

This book was prepared and written in three different countries, and I would like to thank the persons and institutions that helped me in my work. A grant from the Japan Foundation enabled me to go to Japan in 1975 for the initial research. A fellowship from St. Antony's College presented me with the opportunity to spend a fruitful year at Oxford in 1976–7. The Harry S. Truman Research Institute of the Hebrew University of Jerusalem provided me with generous assistance and suitable environs in which to complete the book.

I would like to thank in particular Professor Emeritus Oka Yoshitake of Tokyo University; Professor Hosoya Chihiro of Hitotsubashi University; Professor Itō Daiichi of Hokkaidō University; Mr Hata Ikuhiko, then Chief Historian of the Finance Ministry; Mr G. R. Storry and Dr Brian Powell of the University of Oxford; Dr Charles D. Sheldon of the University of Cambridge; Dr Gordon Daniels of the University of Sheffield; Professor John J. Stephan of the University of Hawaii; Professor Marius B. Jansen of Princeton University; Professor Thomas R. H. Havens of Connecticut College; Professor Donald Roden of

Rutgers College; Mr Frank J. Shulman of the McKeldin
Library, University of Maryland; Professor Harold Z. Schiffrin
and Dr Albert A. Altman of the Hebrew University of Jerusalem; who have helped me in many and different ways towards
the completion of this book.

I am indebted to Mrs Sondra Frisch who made important
stylistic suggestions, and to Mrs Helga Low and Mrs Etti
Shalem who took great care in typing the manuscript. My
warmest thanks go to my wife Lena, who in addition to her own
teaching and research has provided me with constant inspiration and thoughtful advice.

B.S.
Jerusalem, October 1980

Contents

xii *Contents*

Introduction

Japan was never a true democracy before 1945, although progress had been made towards that goal in many fields. The Imperial Constitution of 1889 established the rule of law, granted limited civil liberties, and set up a partially representative legislation, although sovereignty remained vested in the emperor, the government was not responsible to the Diet, and the military was not subordinate to the cabinet. Nevertheless, during the decade following World War I, party cabinets came into existence, an independent press developed, liberal and socialist ideas were expressed, and the trade-union movement developed.

The Manchurian Incident of 1931 reversed that trend. Cabinets lost their party complexion and were headed primarily by bureaucrats or military men, free speech was curbed, nationalism replaced liberalism as the predominant ideology, and the military became the dominant group in the state. The rise of anti-liberal regimes in Europe strengthened those who advocated greater government intervention and the establishment of a strong 'national defence state'. Their goal was partly achieved in the late 1930s, not through constitutional or institutional changes, but as a result of the pressures of the China War and preparations for an even larger conflagration.

The man who presided over Japan's shift towards totalitarianism was a soft-spoken politician, Prince Konoe Fumimaro, who was Prime Minister from June 1937 until January 1939, and again from July 1940 until October 1941. Coming from one of the noblest families in Japan and being, at the same time, the youngest prime minister in the twentieth century (he assumed office at the age of forty-seven), Konoe was popular with both conservatives and reformists. The imperial court, the military, the bureaucracy, the politicians, and the business leaders all supported him and expected him to provide the country with the stability and leadership it had been lacking for a long time.[1]

But in July 1937, only one month after Konoe became Prime Minister, the Marco Polo Bridge (Lukouchiao) Incident erupted, plunging Japan into a protracted war with China. Konoe, who had never held a government position before, made no serious attempt to restrain the army which pressed for a show of force, and the incident quickly escalated into a war. After an initial hesitation, Konoe endorsed the military solution, that called for a crusade to crush the 'traitorous Chiang Kai-shek regime'. The war was officially labelled a 'holy war' (*seisen*) and in November 1938 its goal was declared to be a 'new order in East Asia' (*Tōa shin'chitsujo*), an expression that sounded similar to Hitler's slogan of a 'New Order' in Europe. The new order was to be a political, military, and economic bloc of the three 'liberated' nations of East Asia, Japan, China, and Manchoukuo, including the two Japanese colonies of Korea and Taiwan.

In April 1938 the Diet passed the National Mobilization Law (*Kokka sōdōin*) that empowered the government to control manpower, resources, production, prices, and wages, and to suppress undesired meetings and publications. Although the law had been enacted on the understanding that it would not be applicable to the war with China, most of its stipulations were put into effect shortly after its promulgation.

In January 1939 Konoe resigned and was appointed President of the Privy Council, replacing Baron Hiranuma Kiichirō, who assumed the premiership. This precipitated a new period of cabinet instability which lasted for a year and a half. The three short-lived cabinets, headed respectively by a civilian, an army man, and a navy man, underlined the need for a strong government that could lead the country at a difficult time. Once again, the choice fell on Prince Konoe. Konoe had been preparing for his return to office by launching, in June 1940, a movement for the establishment of a New Political Order (*shin taisei*), which meant dissolution of the political parties, strengthening of the authority of the cabinet, and consolidation of the nation behind the war effort. Such a new order would have enhanced the power of the government, as well as Konoe's position *vis-à-vis* the military.

Konoe's appeal for the dissolution of the parties was received enthusiastically by the politicians, who were disappointed by their own ineffectiveness. Within a short time, from 6 July to 15 August, all the parties in the Diet dissolved themselves voluntarily. But, as Gordon Berger has pointed out, this did not mean political suicide. The politicians continued to maintain their grip on the Diet as well as on their local political machines, and they expected the New Order to provide them with even more power than they had before.[2]

However, the meaning of the New Political Order was vague, and each group interpreted it in its own way. The army chiefs were interested in a mass movement, which would provide the military with popular support, but the politicians wanted a mere amalgamation of the existing parties, in which they would remain the leading figures. The bureaucracy was opposed to any mass movement that might undermine its authority. Konoe vacillated between the conflicting views in his continuous attempts to work out a compromise formula.

The new political structure which eventually emerged was not a party but a 'public organization' (*kōji kessha*), called the Imperial Rule Assistance Association (IRAA, *Taisei yokusankai*). It was inaugurated on 12 October 1940, as a loose framework for uniting the people behind the government through various volunteer organizations. Far from being a mass movement, the new body was a tool of the authorities used to mobilize public support. The Prime Minister was, ex officio, the President (*sōsai*) of the Association, and the local governors and mayors functioned as its branch chiefs. Konoe's attempt to increase his own power was not successful. Although he was the head of the IRAA, its members did not owe him personal allegiance. He had to share his authority with a Vice-President (*fuku sōsai*) from the military (first Reserve General Yanagawa Heisuke and later Reserve General Andō Kisaburō); a board of eleven directors; and an advisory committee composed of the vice-ministers, the chiefs of the Military and Naval Affairs Bureaux, the secretaries of both Houses and other high-ranking officials. There was little popular enthusiasm for the New Order. A survey conducted by the *Bungei shunjū* magazine in December 1941 showed that out of 685 peopled polled, 600 did not understand what it was all about.[3]

The bureaucracy's domination of the New Political Order was demonstrated by the organization of neighbourhood asso-

ciations. Konoe and the army wanted to achieve the regimentation of society into residential and occupational corporations
that would constitute the 'integrated state'. But such a
structure, reminiscent of European fascism, could create new
nuclei of power that would challenge existing authority. To
forestall that danger the Home Ministry announced, a month
before the inauguration of the IRAA, the creation of neighbourhood, borough, and hamlet associations under its own
control. These associations were to distribute rationed food,
collect contributions, drill for civil defence, circulate official
announcements, send soldiers off to the front, and watch for
saboteurs and spies.

   Every ten households formed a neighbourhood association
(*tonarigumi*, also called *rimpohan*), and representatives of
neighbourhood associations formed a borough (*chōkai* or
chōnaikai), or a hamlet association (*burakukai*). But above that
level, the authority remained with the government officials.
Since membership in a *tonarigumi* was a prerequisite for
obtaining rationed food, a great majority of the people were
embraced by it. So in April 1941, seven months after the system
was established, the Home Ministry could announce that there
were already 1.1 million *tonarigumi* in Japan, encompassing
most of the population.[4]

   Resentment against *laissez-faire* capitalism had existed in
various circles in Japan throughout the 1930s. 'Reformist'
military officers and 'revisionist' bureaucrats advocated
government control of the economy, to ensure better living-
standards for peasants, and to mobilize more resources for war.
Under the wartime conditions, which developed after 1937,
these plans could be carried out. In August 1939, the Diet
passed the Major Industries Association Ordinance, which
empowered the government to set up 'control associations'
(*tōseikai*) in vital industries. The government's control of
industry, like the control of the population at large, was to be
exercised through a mechanism of self-supervision. The *tōseikai*
was a compulsory cartel, under the 'guidance' of a government
ministry, for allocating raw materials and setting production
quotas for its members. The outbreak of the Pacific War
accelerated this process, and by the end of 1942, most of Japan's
industries had been organized into 'control associations'. Each

tōseikai was headed by a prominent businessman in that field, so that the grip of the large financial concerns (*zaibatsu*) on the national economy was not basically changed. But there was no central authority to co-ordinate the various cartels, which remained under the jurisdiction of different ministries. The Cabinet Planning Board lacked power to enforce its recommendations, and the authority of the Prime Minister to interfere in the affairs of other ministries was always limited.[5]

To marshal the support of the people for the war effort, the government conducted an extensive propaganda campaign. Already in August 1938, the first Konoe cabinet, with General Araki Sadao as Education Minister, declared a 'spiritual mobilization' (*seishin sōdōin*). Education, culture, entertainment, and the media were to raise morale and to consolidate public support for the government. Slogans like 'One hundred million hearts beating as one' (*ichioku isshin*) and 'The eight corners of the world under one roof' (*hakkō ichiu*) were widely displayed and quoted. In November 1940 the 2,600th anniversary of the legendary founding of Japan in 660 BC was celebrated with great fanfare. In April 1941 the school system was reformed. The elementary schools (*shōgakkō*) were transformed into National Schools (*kokumin gakkō*), in which more emphasis was put on 'national' subjects such as Japanese history, geography, morals, and language.

All these reforms were introduced and accepted as emergency measures, to help win the war against China. Yet the war dragged on with no end in site, straining Japan's economy and precipitating the much bigger confrontation with the US and Britain in 1941.

Konoe supported the army's view that a show of force would depose Chaing Kai-shek, and that a military alliance with Germany would deter the US and Britain from interfering with Japan. He agreed with the military that Hitler's successes in Europe presented Japan with a historic opportunity to establish her own political and economic sphere in East and Southeast Asia. But although the military were ready to risk war with the US and Britain to attain that goal, Konoe was not. He supported the tough line as long as the fighting was only against the Chinese, but he balked at the prospect of a showdown with the Western powers.

On 22 September 1940 Japanese troops, with the advance permission of the Vichy government, entered northern Indo-China. Five days later Germany, Japan, and Italy signed the Tripartite Pact, which recognized East Asia as a Japanese sphere of influence. On 13 April 1941 a Neutrality Pact with the Soviet Union was signed in Moscow, and in July of that year Japanese troops entered southern Indo-China. These moves, which were initiated by the army and endorsed by the Konoe cabinet, were aimed at strengthening Japan's position in Southeast Asia and guaranteeing her the lion's share in the spoils of the apparently crumbling European powers in that area. But coming as they did in the wake of the German advances in Europe, they frightened the US to such a degree that war with Japan became an imminent probability.[6]

1

The Wartime Regime

It will take a long time to weld Japan into a completely totalitarian state.

Foreign Minister Matsuoka Yōsuke, July 1940

I. POLITICAL REPRESSION

Decision-making had always been a complicated and exhausting process in prewar Japan, and no single individual could dispose of matters by himself. As a rule, military affairs were in the hands of the general staffs of the army and navy, which in July 1937 had joined to form the Imperial Headquarters (*daihon'ei*). Both chiefs of staff were under the command of the emperor and had direct access to him. Since the emperors of Japan did not, customarily, exercise their right of command, the armed services in fact enjoyed a high degree of autonomy.

After the outbreak of the war with China, a co-ordinating body, the Imperial Headquarters and Cabinet Liaison Conference (*daihon'ei seifu renraku kaigi*), was established. It was made up of the Prime Minister, the Foreign Minister, the two service ministers, the two chiefs of staff, and other officials. When major decisions had to be made, the conference convened in the imperial palace in the presence of the emperor. On such occasions it acted as an Imperial Conference (*gozen kaigi*) and its decisions, reached by consensus, were final and binding. But even these decisions had ultimately to be approved by the cabinet and the Imperial Headquarters in order to make them operational.

Nominating prime ministers was the prerogative of the emperor, which he exercised, like his other prerogatives, only on the advice of a lower authority. In the Meiji and Taishō periods, that authority was the *genrō* (Elder Statesmen), a select group of people so designated for their contribution to the Meiji Restoration. After the death of Yamagata Aritomo in 1922, Prince Saionji Kimmochi remained the only *genrō*, and he advised the emperors on the nomination of prime ministers for the next sixteen years. But as the Prince grew old, new people were brought into the selecting process. When Prime Minister Abe resigned in January 1940, the ninety-one-year-old Saionji refused to make a recommendation of his own. Instead, Lord Keeper of the Privy Seal Yuasa Kurahei convened the senior statesmen (*jūshin*), a title given to former prime ministers, with the President of the Privy Council, and they selected Admiral Yonai. Prince Saionji then approved the selection and the Lord Keeper conveyed it to the emperor. When the Yonai cabinet resigned in July 1940, Marquis Kido Kōichi, who had become Lord Keeper in the previous month, convened the *jūshin* and they selected Prince Konoe to be Prime Minister for the second time. Although Konoe's candidacy was not approved by Saionji, Kido recommended it to the emperor and Konoe was appointed Prime Minister.[1] Prince Saionji died in November 1940.

When Konoe resigned in October 1941, because of differences with the militant Army Minister General Tōjō Hideki, Kido convened the *jūshin* in the imperial palace in order to select a successor. After several names had been mentioned and discussed, Kido proposed the candidacy of Army Minister Tōjō who, in his opinion, was the only man capable of ensuring full co-operation between the army and the navy. Kido also suggested that Tōjō should retain his portfolio as Army Minister and therefore remain a general on the active list. Although most of the *jūshin* were civilians, Kido's arguments carried weight. After some deliberation, the proposal was unanimously adopted and conveyed to the emperor. Tōjō himself took no part in that decision, and it came as a surprise to him.[2]

The Tōjō cabinet was not a military cabinet in the technical sense of the word. Beside Tōjō and Navy Minister Admiral Shimada Shigetarō, most other ministers were civilian bureaucrats: Foreign Minister Tōgō Shigenori, Finance Minister Kaya Okinori, Commerce and Industry Minister Kishi Nobusuke, and Chief Cabinet Secretary Hoshino Naoki. But there were no party politicians in this cabinet, unlike the previous ones, and General Tōjō was the dominant figure in it.

After the establishment of the new cabinet on 18 October

negotiations with the US were resumed, but on 26 November Secretary of State Cordell Hull informed the Japanese that the American embargo on their country would be lifted only when Japan withdrew its forces from 'China and Indochina'. This far-reaching demand was interpreted in Tokyo as an outright rebuff. On 1 December the Imperial Conference met, with all cabinet members attending, and decided to go to war against the US, Britain, and the Netherlands. A week later, Japanese naval planes attacked Pearl Harbor.[3]

Had the civilian ministers, who took part in that conference, opposed the decision to start a war, they might have delayed it, because resolutions had to be reached unanimously. But no one voiced any objection. All participants seemed to be convinced that war was preferable to accepting the American demands, and that the military could seize the new territories and defend them, as they had done in previous wars.

Prime Minister General Tōjō Hideki, who now headed the war cabinet, was neither the supreme leader nor the commander-in-chief. The direction of the campaign remained in the hands of the Imperial Headquarters and the front commanders. Tōjō's task was to provide over-all co-ordination between the services, and between them and the government. For this purpose he was well suited. He had been Commander of the Military Police in Manchuria from 1935 until 1937, Chief of Staff of the Kwantung Army from 1937 to 1938, Vice-Minister of the Army for seven months during the first Konoe cabinet, and Inspector-General of Army Aviation from 1938 to 1940.

Tōjō was known as a thorough and strict administrator, ready to make decisions and stick by them, features for which he had gained the nickname 'razor' (*kamisori*).[4] When Konoe constructed his second cabinet in July 1940, Tōjō was chosen to be the Army Minister, and he remained in that office until July 1944. Tōjō wielded power in the army, but he was never its 'boss'. His peers, who had recommended him for the cabinet post, remained influential in the Army Ministry and in the General Staff. It was an established custom that senior officers rotated every few years, and if Tōjō had not succeeded Konoe in October 1941, it is conceivable that another general would have been selected for that post.

Tōjō was the first person to be Prime Minister and Army Minister concurrently. This combination of portfolios gave him considerable power in both military and civilian affairs. In addition, during the first four months of his cabinet, Tōjō was also Home Minister and, as such, in charge of internal security during the crucial first months of the war. He also held other portfolios for short periods, and from November 1943 he was Munitions Minister. This concentration of power made Tōjō into the strongest Prime Minister in Japan in the twentieth century but, as historians have already pointed out, it was not enough to make him into a dictator.

The principle of the 'independence of the supreme command' (*tōsuiken dokuritsu*), as established by the Meiji Constitution, not only prevented civilian control over the armed forces, but also enabled both chiefs of staff to remain independent of each other as well as of their service ministers, all four being equally and directly subordinate to the emperor. As a result, Tōjō's control over the navy was never more than tenuous, and even within the army he could not interfere with operational decisions. As Prime Minister and Army Minister, Tōjō was the first among equals, but he was expected to consult his colleagues, some of whom were his seniors or previous superiors. Generals Terauchi Hisaichi, Hata Shun'roku, and Sugiyama Hajime preceded him in rank and had been Army Ministers before him. (When Sugiyama was Army Minister in the first Konoe cabinet, Tōjō was his deputy.)

Tōjō's status and popularity were much lower than those of the German, Italian, Russian, or Chinese dictators of that time. He was not accorded any special title, no one pledged personal allegiance to him, there was no particular faction behind him, and no brain trust or personal coterie around him. All expressions of loyalty were directed solely towards the emperor, and never toward Tōjō. As teamwork, collective leadership, consensus, and loyalty to a sacred monarchy had long been the political standards, dictatorship by a prime minister was strongly discouraged.

After the initial victories in the Pacific War, Tōjō took advantage of the jubilant mood to enhance his public image. He addressed rallies, inspected factories and schools, reviewed troops, chatted with people in the street, and drove in open cars.

But he knew well that any attempt to build a personality cult would backfire. Therefore he took care to assure everyone that he harboured no personal ambitions. Appearing before the House of Representatives' Committee on the Special Wartime Administration Bill in February 1943, he said:

The interpellation has used the term 'dictatorial government'. This is a point on which I wish to make myself perfectly clear. Führer Adolf Hitler, Duce Benito Mussolini, Premier Joseph Stalin, President Franklin D. Roosevelt, and Prime Minister Winston Churchill have been mentioned. But my position in the Japanese state is essentially different from theirs. In my humble way, I am serving His Majesty, at His Majesty's August Command, as Prime Minister. In that capacity I am the leader of the nation, but as an individual, I am but one of His Majesty's humble servants. In this respect I am not different from any one of you . . . It is this that makes the Prime Minister of Japan entirely different from the European dictators.[5]

Such expressions of humility and self-effacement might have been hypocritical, but the fact that Tōjō found it necessary to make them in the first place, and to resort to the image of the humble servant, sets him apart from the other wartime leaders.

Tōjō was not a dictator, but there was little freedom in Japan by the end of 1941, and even less after the Pacific War broke out. The Peace Preservation Law (*Chian ijihō*) of 1925, amended in 1928, banned any action, speech, or writing that advocated the abolition of private property, or of the imperial regime (*kokutai*, translated also as national polity). This outlawed the communist party and any communist propaganda. A far-reaching amendment of the law, passed in March 1941, stipulated the death penalty in the more severe cases and empowered the authorities to keep in 'preventive detention' (*yobō kōkin*) people who constituted a risk to public peace.[6]

Censorship, first confined to preventing disrespectful language concerning the imperial family or the revelation of military secrets, was expanded in the 1930s to prevent criticism of the armed forces. The National Defence Security Law (*Kokubō hōanhō*) of May 1941 imposed the death penalty for the revelation of any 'strategic information' which could benefit the enemy.[7] The emergency situation created by the outbreak of the Pacific War made it easy for the government to introduce stricter measures to curb speech and assembly. On 17

December 1942, the Diet passed a Special Emergency Act, prohibiting political assemblies without permission from the local police, and imposing heavy penalties on the spreading of 'malicious rumours'. The authorities could now crack down on any political organization which they did not like.[8]

One of the constant fears of the wartime regime was the ressurection of the long-suppressed communist party. The 1941 secret report of the Police Bureau (*keiho-kyoku*) claimed that communists were trying to exploit the economic hardships caused by the war with China, and to incite the people against the government. The 1942 report claimed that after the outbreak of the Pacific War, communist agents succeeded in infiltrating the new patriotic associations.[9]

At the Imperial Conference of 1 December 1941, which preceded the war, Tōjō, in his capacity as Home Minister, declared: 'We have strengthened our control over those who are anti-war and anti-military, such as communists, rebellious Koreans, certain religious leaders, and others who we fear may be a threat to the public order. We believe that in some cases we might have to subject some of them to preventive arrest.'[10] When the war broke out, many suspected pacifists were arrested on directions issued by Tōjō. Addressing the Diet on 1 February 1943, Tōjō said:

I am sure of victory in this war. I never think about defeat. Defeat can come only in two ways. One is if our imperial army or navy are defeated. Of this I have no fear. The other is if our country breaks from within. To counter that danger, we shall act thoroughly to stop any speech or action which might harm our internal unity.[11]

How pervasive were the political arrests? From the first round-ups of communists in 1928 until the outbreak of the Pacific War in 1941, about 74,000 persons were arrested on charges of violating the Peace Preservation Law. During the Pacific War, about 2,000 more people were arrested on these charges. In addition about 1,500 people were arrested for violating the speech, publication, and assembly regulations, 250 were arrested for spreading 'malicious rumours', and about 50 were put under 'preventive detention'. However, most of those arrested did not remain behind bars, but were released after interrogation. Only about 5,000 people were prosecuted for

violating the Peace Preservation Law during the seventeen
years between 1928 and the end of the Pacific War.[12] Although
that law provided for death penalties in certain cases, only two
men were sentenced to death for violating it, the Soviet master-
spy Richard Sorge and his Japanese accomplice Ozaki
Hotsumi. The remaining members of the spy-ring received
prison sentences. The traditional policy was to bring the
'political offenders' back to the fold, rather than to punish them.
When the war ended, there were only about 2,500 political
prisoners behind bars, including the leadership of the communist party and spy suspects.[13]

The political arrests silenced opposition, spread fear, and put
thousands of people in gaol for their views. But compared with
the mass arrests, deportations, and killing of millions in
countries like Germany or the Soviet Union, oppression in
Japan was relatively mild. There were no concentration camps,
and those who recanted were either released or received short
prison terms. Nevertheless, life behind bars was grim, and
torture was often used in interrogation. In the last year of the
war, hundreds of prisoners died of malnutrition, maltreatment,
or in air raids.[14]

Political oppression did not spare religion. The religious
federations, such as the Great Japan Buddhist Association (*Dai
Nihon bukkyōkai*, formed in March 1941), and the Great Japan
Wartime Religious Association (*Dai Nihon senji shūkyō hōkoku-
kai*, formed in October 1944), supported the government and
the war.[15] But some of the more independent religious sects
refused to conform. The 1941 Police Bureau report complained
that the *Tenrikyō*, *Seichō-no-ie*, *Nichirenshū*, and *Tendai* sects had
not kept their pledge to change their curriculum according to
the new regulations of the Ministry of Education. The report
noted that among Christians, the Catholic Church co-operated
with the authorities, whereas certain Protestant denominations, 'under the influence of enemy countries', were propagating 'anti-Japanese and anti-war ideas'. A similar complaint
appeared in the Bureau's report for 1942. It stated that 'some
narrow-minded Protestant sects ... founded by Jewish-like
Christians' were still propagating pacifism and cosmopoli-
tanism. In September 1943 thirty-two Christian priests and
missionaries of the Seventh Day Adventists sect were arrested;

in June 1944 the sect, which had 1,000 believers and eighteen churches, was charged with maintaining secret contacts with the US and consequently outlawed.[16] In July 1943 the *Sōka kyōiku gakkai* (mother of the present-day *Sōka gakkai*) was outlawed, and twenty-two of its leaders, including the founder Makiguchi Tsunesaburō, were arrested. Makiguchi died in prison in November 1944.[17] Altogether about 1,800 persons were arrested in Japan during the war for offences connected with religion. Of these, 210 were Christians.

The agency charged with the enforcement of the Peace Preservation Law and other laws of political nature was the Special Higher Police (*Tokubetsu kōtō keisatsu*, abbreviated as *tokkō*), which was established in 1911 after the alleged attempt on the emperor's life by Kōtoku Shūsui and his fellow anarchists. During the 1920s and 1930s the *tokkō* carried out the arrests and interrogations of communists, socialists, suspicious Koreans, certain religious leaders, and, occasionally, right-wing extremists. It had branches in all police precincts and was responsible to the Police Bureau of the Home Ministry.[18]

Prosecution of political offenders (or 'thought criminals', *shisō hanzaisha*, as they were called) was carried out by the Thought Section (*shisōbu*) of the Justice Ministry. There were special Thought Procurators (*shisō kenji*) at the district-court. appeal-court, and Supreme-Court level, assigned to the task of prosecuting political offenders. They were kept up to date on political and ideological developments among left-wing and right-wing adherents, and were periodically summoned to Tokyo for briefings.[19]

Another agent of political repression was the Military Police (*kempei*). This branch, which was basically in charge of police functions within the ranks, expanded its vigilance in the late 1930s to include anything which might endanger the war effort. Since pacifism, liberalism, and sympathy for the US or Britain were considered to be obstacles to victory, the Military Police were determined to suppress them. There were only about 7,500 *kempei* in Japan during the war, but they were dreaded everywhere.[20] Tōjō had a special relationship with the Military Police, dating from the time he had served as Commander of the Kwantung Army's *kempei*. In July 1941 he appointed his friend Major-General Katō Hakujirō as Chief of Staff of the Military

Police, and in August 1942 his former deputy, Colonel Shikata Ryōji, became Chief of the Tokyo Military Police. After the outbreak of the Pacific War, Major-General Katō made an appeal to the public. Speaking on the national radio, he said: 'In some quarters Military Policemen are feared and suspected as a kind of secret police. I positively assure you . . . that you need not fear them.' The *kempei*, however, remained Tōjō's most trusted instrument against dissenters and opponents, spying on them, and trying to intimidate them.[21]

Yet the *tokkō* and the *kempei* could not suppress the opposition to Tōjō among politicians and senior statesmen. When the military setbacks increased and Tōjō lost the support of the emperor's advisers and some of his own peers, neither the Special Higher Police nor the Military Police could keep him in office.

Unlike totalitarian countries, there was no central, powerful, and independent secret police in wartime Japan, on the model of the Gestapo or the NKVD. The *tokkō* was subordinate to the Home Ministry and functioned as part of the metropolitan and local police. Yet the home minister who controlled it did not acquire extraordinary power, and home ministers were changed as often as other ministers.[22]

The *kempei* were subordinate to the Army Ministry (the navy had no military police of its own) and could not act independently of it. During the Pacific War, four different officers held the post of commander-in-chief of the Military Police (*kempei shireikan*), but none of them became particularly powerful in it.[23] The *tokkō* and the *kempei* suppressed political dissent, but they did not owe allegiance to any single leader or chief.

Wartime Japan is often referred to as a totalitarian or fascist state.[24] These labels are meaningful only if understood in their broadest and pejorative senses, as nicknames for highlighting the repressive and aggressive character of the state. But if we accept more rigorous definitions of totalitarianism and fascism, then wartime Japan certainly cannot fall into these categories.

Jacob Talmon has defined totalitarianism as a regime that lays claim to a sole and exclusive political truth,[25] but Japan possessed neither an official dogma nor an omniscient leader to interpret the truth. Hannah Arendt has stressed the central role that unrestricted terror and a powerful secret police play in totalitarian regimes.[26] While there was certainly oppression in wartime Japan, it never reached the level of unrestricted terror and there was nothing comparable to the concentration camps and wholesale bloodshed of Nazi Germany or Soviet Russia. The Special Higher Police and the Military Police were instruments of repression, but lacked the power and authority of the secret police organizations in totalitarian states. Most of the political prisoners, including unrepentant communists, survived the war.

Franz Neumann has pointed out that a totalitarian regime is characterized by the total politicization of society, carried out by an exclusive mass party.[27] However, in Japan social, communal, and occupational loyalties continued to exist independently of the state, and no mass party could abolish them. Even if we followed the broader definition of totalitarianism offered by Karl Popper, i.e. a closed society that attempts to carry out social engineering,[28] it would still be difficult to apply it to Japan. Wartime Japan *was* a closed society, but with little social engineering. The social changes that took place were the result of the levelling phenomenon common to societies engaged in total war, when class distinctions are eroded and more egalitarian modes of behaviour arise.

Marxist historians refer to prewar and wartime Japan as fascist because, in their view, she was a capitalist state that was trying to stem revolution by recourse to repression at home and aggression abroad.[29] But there is no evidence that capitalists dominated the state or pulled the wires behind the scenes. The *zaibatsu* had more personal and ideological links with the political parties than with the military, and they had given more support to the liberal cabinets of the 1920s than they did to the military-dominated cabinets of the 1930s and 1940s.

European fascism employed quasi-revolutionary slogans to combat communism,[30] but Japan, although definitely anti-Marxist, did not concoct a revolutionary ideology to win over the masses. The Japanese leaders did not identify themselves with the regimes of their European allies; there were no Japanese replicas of Hitler or Mussolini, and the government remained on the whole conservative.

2. THE WARTIME DIET

The Imperial Diet (*teikoku gikai*) of Japan, which was established in 1890, was composed of two houses: a House of Peers of hereditary and nominated members, and a House of Representatives, which, from 1928, was elected by all adult males. The Diet possessed the power to pass laws, approve the state budget, deliberate on national policy, and question the cabinet. It was not sovereign, and could not appoint or dismiss the government, powers which were reserved for the emperor. But it could prevent budget increases, stop bills, ask embarrassing questions, and petition the emperor. These limited privileges had given the Diet, from the beginning, leverage for consolidating its power and for becoming one of the important élites in prewar Japan.[31]

Every Prime Minister was obliged to reach an accommodation with the House of Representatives, in order to secure the passage of his legislation and budgets. This was done by inviting party members to serve in the cabinet, or by the prime ministers themselves becoming leaders of those parties. From 1918 until 1922, and from 1924 until 1932, party presidents served as prime ministers, bringing the political system of Japan close to that of a parliamentary democracy. After the assassination of Prime Minister Inukai Tsuyoshi in May 1932, no party politician served as prime minister until 1945, but those who held that position were nevertheless compelled to secure the co-operation of Diet politicians. This was usually done by inviting politicians from both parties to join the cabinet. The patriotic mood that developed after the Manchurian Incident, and, to an even greater degree, after the outbreak of the China War, made that co-operation easier, since no politician wished to be branded as an opponent of the war. The Diet hailed the military actions in China and approved the great war budgets. However, parliamentary support of the government was not automatic and it always required pressure as well as persuasion.[32]

Diet members enjoyed freedom of speech on the floor, though in the dense patriotic conformism of the 1930s only a few dared to make use of it. Thus, in May 1936 Saitō Takao of the *Minseitō* blamed the army for the 26 February Incident of that year.[33] But when in January 1937 Hamada Kunimatsu of the same party accused the army of trying to set up a dictatorship in Japan, the irritated War Minister, General Terauchi Hisaichi, demanded an apology. Hamada stuck to his words and called on the War Minister to commit *seppuku* (hara-kiri) to atone for his lies. The only way for Terauchi to oust Hamada from the Diet was to bring down the cabinet and force a general election. He therefore resigned and refused to recommend a successor. Prime Minister Hirota then had to resign and the emperor nominated General Hayashi as Prime Minister. Hayashi dissolved the Diet and called a general election. But in that election, which was held in April 1937, Hamada's party, the *Mineseitō*, came out first with 179 seats of a total of 446; the *Seiyūkai* was second with 175; the left-wing *Shakai taishūtō* received 37; while the military-backed *Kokumin dōmei* gained only 11. Both Saitō and Hamada were re-elected.[34]

Hayashi's position became untenable and his failure in the polls obliged him to resign in June. He was replaced by Prince Konoe Fumimaro, then President of the House of Peers. Konoe enjoyed the support of the Diet and appointed party politicians to his cabinet, as did his successor Baron Hiranuma Kiichirō. When General Abe Nobuyuki became Prime Minister in August 1939, relations with the Diet again deteriorated. Although three politicians served in Abe's cabinet, the Prime Minister's inability to cope with the economic and international problems of Japan cost him the support of the parties. In January 1940, 276 Diet members signed a petition of no confidence in the cabinet. Formally this did not oblige the cabinet to step down, but Abe drew the appropriate conclusion and resigned. Thus between 1937 and 1940 two cabinets had to resign because of failure in the Diet.[35]

Although Diet members enjoyed immunity for things they did or said in the House, the Diet could expel a member for misbehaviour. The first such case in the Shōwa period occurred in March 1938, when Nishio Suehiro of the Social Mass Party, in a speech about the National Mobilization Bill, called on Prime Minister Konoe to learn from Hitler, Mussolini, and Stalin how to organize a state in a time of emergency. The reference to Stalin sounded preposterous to the military and their supporters in the Diet, and so the Discipline Committee of the Diet decided to expel Nishio. The next case occurred in

February 1940, when Saitō once again spoke out against the
army, criticizing the war in China and the burdens suffered by
the people at home. The army accused Saitō of 'blemishing the
holy war' and the Discipline Committee resolved to expel him.
In November 1941 the businessman and former member of the
Minseitō, Miyazawa Taneo, criticized the military budget and
was also obliged to resign his Diet seat. Yet no further sanctions
were applied against these critics and they were allowed to
stage a political comeback. Nishio was returned to the Diet
following a by-election in Osaka in June 1939, and Saitō was
re-elected to his parliamentary seat in the general election of
April 1942.[36]

The dissolution of the parties in 1940 did not affect the
composition of the Diet. The party labels were gone, but all
members retained their seats. The prestige of the House was
even enhanced by the dissolution, as the Diet appeared now to
have a national, rather than a partisan, orientation. Nevertheless, the government still needed to group the Diet members in
some organization that would enable it to control them. In the
first session after the dissolution which convened in December
1940, most members joined the Diet Members' Club (*Giin
kurabu*). But, as Gordon Berger has shown, Konoe's plan to
turn this organization into a political party under his leadership
failed because of the politicians' opposition to such a plan.[37]

In September 1941, a Diet Members' Imperial Assistance
League (*Yokusan giin dōmei*) was formed, under the auspices of
the IRAA. Three hundred and twenty-six, or 70 per cent of the
House of Representatives, joined it. However, some parliamentary groups refused to join. The largest of these was the *Dōkōkai*
(Association of the Like-Minded), led by Hatoyama Ichirō, a
former Minister of Education. Most of its thirty-seven members
were known for their moderate and liberal inclination. Among
them were Kita Reikichi, the younger brother of Kita Ikki
(executed in 1937 for assisting the 26 February rebels); Inukai
Ken, the son of the late Prime Minister Inukai Tsuyoshi (assas-
sinated in 1932); Katayama Tetsu, a former socialist; Ashida
Hitoshi, president of the *Japan Times*; and the former *Seiyūkai*
politician Ōno Bamboku. The most illustrious member of that
group was Ozaki Yukio, the eighty-three-year-old politician
who had been elected to the House of Representatives in every

election since the establishment of the Diet in 1890. Throughout his life, Ozaki had been an outspoken critic of government oppression. In 1913 he had accused the Katsura Cabinet of hiding behind the throne and using imperial edicts to suppress the people. In 1937 he admitted to a reporter: 'I am always thinking how to die for the emperor, the country and the people. The reason that I speak so boldly in the Diet is that I am not afraid of death anymore. . . . It is better for me to die for the cause of justice than to die in a hospital under the care of nurses.'[38]

Another group that did not join the Assistance League was the *Kōa giin dōmei* (League for Strengthening Asia) which had twenty-seven members, including the former socialist Nishio Suehiro and the former leader of the *burakumin* liberation movement Matsumoto Jiichirō. Two other such groups were the *Giin kurabu* (Diet Members Club) with eleven members, and the *Dōnin kurabu* (Comrades Club) with eight members, both of which included former members of the Social Mass Party.[39]

The Pacific War did not alter the basic functions of the Diet. Unlike Nazi Germany, where the Reichstag was never convened during the war, the Japanese Diet continued to meet regularly. Each year the regular (*tsūjō*) session started on 26 December and lasted for three months. The Diet was also convened for five extraordinary (*rinji*) sessions and one special (*tokubetsu*) session during the war. These latter sessions, which lasted only a few days, were called to approve urgent budgets and legislation.[40]

Nevertheless, after the outbreak of war the character of the Diet's work changed. There was now less time for deliberations or interpellations, and the government insisted on speedy passage of its bills. Censorship was strict. Diet members had to clear their speeches in advance with the cabinet, and whole passages were deleted by the censors from the protocol. In the 84th regular session, which lasted from December 1943 until March 1944, eighty-four items were struck off the record.[41]

Externally, the government paid great respect to the Diet. Each session was opened by the emperor, and the proceedings received front-page coverage in the newspapers. Tōjō and other members of the cabinet appeared regularly before the Diet to report on the situation and to explain the war aims, but nobody expected the Diet to block the bills which were brought before it. The first major bill presented after the outbreak of the Pacific War was the Press, Publication, Assembly, and Association Special Control Law (*Genron, shuppan, shūkai, kesshatō rinji torishimarihō*), which banned unauthorized convocations and publications. It was approved on 17 December 1941, after only one day of deliberation. Another important bill, instituting a far-reaching administrative reform, was passed on 29 October 1943, after only three days of deliberation.[42] Budgets were approved in similar haste. The wartime Diet followed the example of Diets during previous wars and always approved budgets presented to it by the government.

The House of Representatives, elected in April 1937, was expected to be dissolved in the spring of 1941, when the maximum period of four years had passed. But the Konoe cabinet decided in 1941 that the tense international situation of that year was not the right time for holding a general election, and it asked the Diet to postpone the election for one year. However, the situation instead of improving developed into a general war. Tōjō did not regard the war as a bad time for elections: on the contrary, he believed that the patriotism stimulated by the war would help him to change the composition of the Diet, so that it would be more favourable to the government. In January 1942 the cabinet announced that a general election would be held at the end of April. In a speech before the Diet on 18 February Tōjō explained: 'The reason for holding the general election while the War of Great East Asia is being fought, is that it presents a good opportunity for consolidating our national strength. . . . It is also hoped that by this election, a fresh and stronger Diet will be formed.'[43]

Since there was no political party which could present a list of candidates, and the government was prevented by law from doing so, Tōjō 'privately' summoned thirty-three prominent persons and asked them to form a group which would prepare a list of 'patriotic candidates'. The group which was thus established declared itself the Imperial Rule Assistance Political Structure Association (*Yokusan seiji taisei kyōgikai*, abbreviated as *Yokkyō*). It included the vice-president of the IRAA Andō Kisaburō, the president of the Chamber of Commerce Fujiyama Aiichirō, and the seventy-nine-year-old commentator Tokutomi Sohō. Formally it was an unofficial body for recommending candidates, but in fact nobody could overlook its official links. Former Prime Minister Reserve General Abe Nobuyuki was elected as its president.[44]

The *Yokkyō* scanned the country for suitable candidates through the local branches of the IRAA. In doing so, it had to face the fact that the local political machines of incumbent Diet members were still strong and could not be ignored. The main difficulty was that in order to introduce 'new faces' into the Diet, it was necessary to enlist the support of the existing politicians. When the list was finally completed in early April, it included the names of 235 incumbent Diet members, 18 former Diet members, and 213 new candidates; altogether 466 names.[45]

The government wanted these candidates to be elected, but it could not prevent others from challenging them. Incumbent Diet members who did not find themselves in that list, or new aspirants who had not been recommended, registered their candidacies as independents. Consequently, 613 independent candidates ran for the Diet, including 132 incumbents, 49 former Diet members, and 432 new aspirants. The total number of 1,079 candidates was the highest ever registered in Japan. In Tokyo alone, 100 candidates competed for thirty-two parliamentary seats.[46]

Among the unrecommended candidates were Diet members who had not joined the *Yokusan giin dōmei*, like Ozaki, Kita, Inukai, Katayama, Ashida, and Nishio. They ran as independents and did not form any joint list. Ozaki even went as far as addressing a letter to Tōjō in which he accused him of illegal intervention in the polls.[47]

The only group that put up a separate list, of forty-six candidates, was the right-wing *Tōhōkai* (Society of the East) established in 1936 by Nakano Seigō, a former liberal and Pan-Asianist who had become an admirer of Hitler and Mussolini. Nakano founded his organization on a fascist model, complete with black shirts, rallies, marches, and himself as the charismatic leader. In the general election of 1937, the *Tōhōkai* gained eleven seats in the House of Representatives. It was formally dissolved in 1940, together with the other parties, and Nakano even joined the board of directors of the IRAA. But when he

discovered that the IRAA was not going to become the totalitarian party he had wanted, he left it in protest in March 1941
and re-established his group. Since he was a right-wing
opponent of the regime, Nakano was less vulnerable to government attack than were the liberals. He could accuse Tōjō of
betraying the 'spontaneous patriotism' of the people and of
relying on bureaucratic oppression, without being branded a
traitor. Nakano's idea was that Japan should emulate the fascist
models of Europe which, in his opinion, expressed the popular
wills of the Italian and German peoples. As the anti-American
and anti-British activities of the *Tōhōkai* suited the official
propaganda, the authorities did not prevent Nakano and his
comrades from conducting a vociferous election campaign and
from nominating forty-six candidates of their own for the
general election.[48]

The government could not officially interfere in the election
campaign, but behind the scenes it exerted pressure to secure
the election of the recommended candidates. Tōjō secretly
arranged to give each of them 5,000 yen from the army's 'special
funds'.[49] The Home Ministry instructed the police to suppress
any critical comments about the regime, the war, or the legality
of the recommended list. During one day of the campaign, 15
August, six rallies were suspended in Tokyo and fifty-six
speakers were warned. In rural areas, where villages usually
voted in blocks, less pressure was needed to obtain the desired
results.[50]

Covert interference by the government also took other forms.
The state radio urged the people to vote for 'patriotic figures',
while the government-controlled press called openly for
electing the recommended candidates. Semi-official organizations, like the reservists, the IRAA, the neighbourhood associations, and women's and youth groups, conducted their own
campaign in favour of 'patriotic candidates'.[51] The most
militant of these organizations was the Great Japan Imperial
Rule Assistance Young Men's Corps (*Dai Nihon yokusan
sōnendan*, abbreviated as *Yokusō*), which had been founded in
January 1942 with the army's support. Based on the model of
the Nazi storm troopers, it enlisted men above the age of
twenty-one for activities intended to spur the people to greater
patriotic efforts in production, in the raising of funds, and in

supporting the armed forces. The corps staged rallies and parades in favour of the recommended candidates, and intimidated the unrecommended ones.[52]

The army was trying to establish, through the Young Men's Corps, the Nazi-like mass party that it had failed to achieve through the IRAA. The man who led this drive was Brigadier-General Mutō Akira, the head of the powerful Bureau of Military Affairs at the Army Ministry since 1939. But the bureaucrats and politicians who had thwarted the army's machinations in 1940 succeeded in doing the same in 1942. Bowing to pressure from members of his cabinet, such as Finance Minister Kaya, State Minister Suzuki, and Chief Cabinet Sectretary Hoshino, Tōjō finally gave in, and on 20 April, ten days before the general election, Mutō was transferred from his post and appointed Commander of the Imperial Guards Division, Tōjō's friend, Major-General Satō Kenryō, was named as the new bureau chief.[53]

Although it was not considered very patriotic to run as an independent candidate, more than 600 people dared to do so. One of them was Saitō Takao, who had been expelled from the Diet in 1940 for criticizing the army. When the police confiscated Saitō's campaign material in his native Hyōgo Prefecture, he went to Tokyo and after arguing with the Home Ministry officials was allowed to reprint his material in a censored form. But in Nagasaki Prefecture the campaign aides of an unrecommended candidate were arrested; and in Kagoshima Prefecture independent candidates were prevented from renting halls for their campaign speeches.[54]

Two unrecommended candidates were temporarily arrested during the election campaign. One of them was the elderly Ozaki Yukio, who ran as an independent in Mie Prefecture. On 12 April, while campaigning in Tokyo for a friend, also an unrecommended candidate, Ozaki quoted in his speech an old *senryū* (comic short poem) which said: 'A house for sale, writes the third generation in an elegant Chinese style' (*Karayō de uriie to kaku sandaime*). By referring to this image, Ozaki was deploring the new generation of leaders who, in his opinion, were dissipating the achievements of their Meiji predecessors. The police claimed that Ozaki had ridiculed 'the august reign of the present emperor', who was the third generation after

Emperor Meiji, and Ozaki was charged with *lèse-majesté*. Another member of the *Dōkōkai*, Ashida Hitoshi, was arrested because he had expressed some praise for the United States' humane treatment of prisoners of war. Both politicians were freed by the day of election. Ozaki was later prosecuted, but no charges were pressed against Ashida.[55]

This was not the first time that the Japanese had gone to the polls during a war. General elections had been held during the First Sino-Japanese War (1894) and twice during World War I (1915 and 1917). Yet those wars were not total wars, and several political parties were always allowed to compete for the public vote. Now, for the first time in modern Japanese history, no such competition existed. Official intervention in elections had occurred on previous occasions with only limited success for the government. In 1892 twenty-five people died and nearly four hundred were injured, when Home Minister Shinagawa Yajirō ordered local governors to use the police against the popular parties. But when the votes were counted, it became clear that these parties had won a victory. In 1915, the cabinet of the ostensibly liberal Ōkuma Shigenobu used threats and bribes on a large scale to assure the election of the *Dōshikai* candidates, but although that party received a majority, the opposition *Seiyūkai* retained almost a third of the Diet seats. In the first universal manhood suffrage election of 1928, the *Seiyūkai* cabinet of General Tanaka Giichi deployed private strong-man squads against its *Minseitō* rivals, yet the *Minseitō* received almost as many Diet seats as the ruling *Seiyūkai*.[56] In 1942 the government went to great lengths not to appear to be interfering with the freedom of elections, but by using the semi-official recommendation system, masterminding the propaganda campaign, and using various covert pressures, it in fact achieved a degree of intervention unsurpassed by previous cabinets.

The controlled election campaign did not arouse much public interest. All candidates supported the war, praised the armed forces, and called for a 'fight until victory'. Only a few criticized the government and these were quickly silenced. The one exciting event during the campaign was the Doolittle air raid on Tokyo, Yokohama, Nagoya, and Kobe on 18 April, in which fifty people were killed and about one hundred houses destroyed. The casualties were not reported and the raid was said to boost the morale of the people. The editorial in the *Miyako* on 21 April said: 'The enemy air raid on Japan has infused fresh vigour into the somnolent election campaign.' The editorial in *Nichi nichi* on the same day admitted: 'It is reported that thus far little enthusiasm is shown by the people towards the forthcoming elections, and only small numbers attend the campaign meetings.'[57] But on election day, 30 April, 12 million voters out of an electorate of 14.5 million turned up at the polls. This high turnout (82.7 per cent, the highest since 1930) can be attributed to emotional involvement with the war, as well as to official and neighbourhood pressure to vote.[58]

When the votes were counted, the recommended candidates had won a clear victory. They received 66.3 per cent of all valid votes, and gained 381 out of the 466 seats (81.8 per cent) in the House of Representatives. However, more than a third, i.e. 33.7 per cent, of the votes went to independent candidates, who received 85 seats in the House. Thus, Tōjō's hope for infusing 'new blood' into the Diet was only partially realized. In the new Diet, 247 members were incumbents, 20 were former Diet members, while 199 were new faces.[59] As in the previous cases of government interference in the election process, the government's success was not complete. As before, the authorities stopped short of coercion or the falsification of ballots, and the electorate did not find it particularly dangerous to vote for candidates disliked by the government.

Among the newly elected members were two cabinet ministers: Kishi Nobusuke, the Minister of Commerce and Industry, and Ino Hiroya, the Minister of Agriculture and Forestry. This corrected the previous anomaly in which no member of the Tōjō cabinet had held a parliamentary seat. Other new members included Reserve Colonel Hasihmoto Kingorō, who had been active in the military plots in the early 1930s; Akao Bin, a leading right-wing activist; and the political scientist Rōyama Masamichi, who had retired three years earlier from Tokyo Imperial University. The person who received the highest number of votes was a new candidate, retired General Shiōden Nobutaka, who had gained fame by his nationalistic and anti-Semitic speeches. He polled 76,250 votes in the fifth electoral district in Tokyo, which had traditionally elected socialist candidates.[60] Hashimoto, Rōyama, and Shiōden were recommended candidates, Akao was not.

Out of the thirty-seven members of the *Dōkōkai*, only nine were re-elected. Among them were Ozaki Yukio and Ashida Hitoshi, both of whom had been arrested during the election campaign, and Inukai Ken, who had been questioned for his alleged indiscretions. Out of the twenty-seven members of the *Kōa giin dōmei*, eleven were re-elected, including Nishio Suehiro. Saitō Takao, whose candidacy the government had tried to suppress, received the highest number of votes in his electoral district in Hyōgo Prefecture. Seven members of the *Tōhōkai* were also re-elected, including the outspoken Nakano Seigō, who came first in his electoral district in Fukuoka Prefecture.[61]

When the new Diet met in May, both the recommended and unrecommended members joined in a patriotic front behind the war effort. On 20 May, on the government's initiative, a new parliamentary body was formed, the Imperial Rule Assistance Political Association (IRAPA, *Yokusan seiji-kai*). Almost all the Diet members joined it in a demonstration of patriotism. The IRAPA comprised 98.3 per cent of the House of Representatives, and was headed by General Abe Nobuyuki, who was not himself a Diet member. There were now no more formal divisions in the Diet and the members were seated, for the first time in the history of the House, not according to their political affiliations but according to their home prefectures.[62] However, eight Diet members, including Ozaki Yukio, Inukai Ken, and Kita Reikichi, did not join the IRAPA. In June 1943 they were joined by six other members, including Hatoyama and Nakano. But the former parliamentary groups were not revived and all those who had left the IRAPA remained independents.[63]

The new parliamentary alignment helped the government to control the Diet, but it was still necessary to provide the politicians with a semblance of power in order to obtain their support. In June 1942 the government set up consultative committees for each ministry. Out of the 374 men who were selected to serve on these committees, 244 were members of the House of Representatives and 80 were members of the House of Peers. In April 1943 Tōjō brought in two politicians to join his cabinet. They were Yamazaki Tatsunosuke, formerly of the

Seiyūkai, who became Minister of Agriculture and Forestry; and Ōasa Tadao, formerly of the *Minseitō*, who became State Minister.[64]

The wartime Diet passed all the bills which the government introduced, but behind the scenes dissenting voices could sometimes be heard. On 26 December 1942 the *Asahi* reported that the government had withdrawn an amendment to the election law, 'in order to avoid friction with the Diet'. On 4 March 1943 the *Mainichi* revealed that there was still criticism in the Diet concerning the behaviour of the Young Men's Corps during the previous election. When the government introduced in March 1943 an amendment to the criminal law, thirty members of the House of Representatives dared to vote against it, claiming that the new law was too harsh. They included Hatoyama Ichirō, Nakano Seigō, and Miki Bukichi.[65]

Diet members used their right to present interpellations as a means of expressing discontent. During the election campaign, Baron Ōkōchi Masaharu of the House of Peers asked the Prime Minister pointedly whether the system of recommending candidates did not violate the constitution. Tōjō had to defend himself and promise that there would be no government interference in the election. Yamazaki Tatsunosuke of the House of Representatives asked Tōjō in February 1943, two months before joining the cabinet, whether the government planned to put further restrictions on the freedom of the people. Tōjō vowed that it did not. At the same session another Diet member, Kita Sōichirō, wanted to know if the Prime Minister was not already wielding dictatorial powers. Tōjō was compelled to express utter opposition to the idea of dictatorship and to declare that his sole aim in asking for more powers was to speed up war production.[66]

Despite these occasional queries, there was no meaningful opposition in the Diet during the war. Japan was fighting for her life and it was war, as well as repression, which produced a regimented vote on most issues. But repression was not total, and regimentation was not complete. The government depended on the Diet for the passage of bills and budgets, and most of the old politicians remained in the Diet throughout the war, hiding their discords behind the façade of wartime unity.[67] The prestige of the Diet as an imperial institution was preserved, and there was no attempt to abolish or suspend it. On the other hand, the constant concern of the Diet members to preserve their political power might have dissipated their energies, leaving them little motivation to oppose the war policies or suggest alternatives to them.

3. TŌJŌ AND THE BUREAUCRACY

Prewar Japan was run by an educated bureaucracy, recruited largely from the imperial universities. The bureaucrats were regarded as the cream of society, because they were representatives of the emperor rather than the servants of the people. Their professed paternalistic outlook, combined with an arrogant awareness of power, was reminiscent of the *samurai* in feudal Japan and of the oligarchs in the Meiji period. When the politicians were accused of being selfish and corrupt, the bureaucrats kept their image of honesty and devotion to duty. Only the military officers, who sacrificed their lives for the country, were regarded as representing a higher kind of duty to the emperor.

The bureaucracy functioned on the basis of laws, and officials were usually graduates of the law departments of the universities. The Meiji Constitution, which had established the rule of law in Japan, was never amended or abrogated. Unlike totalitarian countries, there was no constitutional break in Japan prior to 1945. Some laws, like the General Mobilization Law of 1938, may be regarded as having violated the spirit of the constitution, but they were passed as temporary measures in reponse to the necessities of war.

Constitutional continuity was paralleled by institutional stability. Most of the institutions that had functioned in the 1920s and 1930s continued to function throughout the war, although their relative power changed. Cabinet positions which in the 1920s were held by party politicians were held in the late 1930s by bureaucrats and military men. Despite the many changes in policy, there wːre no major purges in Japan prior to 1945. The bureaucrats continued to serve the state in time of war with the same zeal they had shown in time of peace.

The war substantially strengthened the power of the bureaucracy, but this power was not concentrated in the hands of a single man or institution. The cabinet remained a federation of ministries and agencies, each scrupulously guarding its privileges and autonomy. The Prime Minister was never the chief executive; he was the chief co-ordinator whose task was to ensure a united cabinet policy. He could neither dictate to the other ministers nor change them at will; replacing a minister was a complicated task which required both pressure and persuasion.

Policies were not decided by a single statesman, but were a result of long consultations among various power élites, like the general staffs of the army and navy, cabinet ministers, and palace officials. Decision-making remained, as it had always been, an exhausting process, even in time of war. Kishi Nobusuke, who served as Minister of Commerce and Industry and later as Vice-Minister of Munitions in the Tōjō cabinet, told a reporter in 1944:

It often takes two or three months for the Munitions Ministry to reach a decision on an important matter. Then the decision must be discussed at a meeting of the cabinet, which in turn issues an order to be executed at various government and industrial levels. Thus it may take half a year before the decision goes into effect. Even a wise decision is sometimes worthless by the time it is executed, for the situation by then has changed.[68]

The bureaucratic limits imposed on the Japanese government were noticed by contemporary observers. Herbert Norman wrote in 1940 that the 'almost anonymous but experienced bureaucracy' of Japan, which had snuffed out all signs of genuine democracy, was also blocking 'the victory of outright fascist forces'. Hillis Lory, having spent several years in Japan, observed in 1943 that Japan was not a one-man government: 'General Tōjō, the premier, has great power, but his authority in the Japanese government does not equal Roosevelt's in the United States nor Churchill's in England, to say nothing of Hitler's and Mussolini's dictatorships.'[69]

There were thirteen cabinet ministries at the outbreak of the war: Home, Finance, Foreign Affairs, Army, Navy, Justice, Education, Agriculture and Forestry, Commerce and Industry, Communication, Railways, Colonies, and Welfare. In addition, there were the Prime Minister's Office, the Chief Cabinet Secretariat, the Planning Board, and the cabinet bureaux of Legislation and Information. This structure proved cumber-

some when the need arose to make a decisive move, such as
increasing arms production. The Planning Board, for instance,
was only an advisory body which had no power to compel the
various ministries to implement its recommendations, and the
prime minister did not possess that power either.[70]

Only in March 1943, fifteen months after the outbreak of the
Pacific War, was an attempt made to increase the prime
minister's powers in this respect. A Special Wartime Administrative Law (*senji gyōsei shokken toku-reihō*), which was passed that
month, authorized the prime minister, for the first time, to issue
directives to the economic ministries on matters relating to war
production. But this was not enough to ensure central control,
since the various ministries continued to compete with each
other over budgets and raw materials. In November 1943 the
government set up the new Ministry of Munitions (*gunjūshō*),
which took over most of the functions of the Ministry of
Commerce and Industry, the Planning Board, and the
economic departments of the army and the navy. To stress the
authority of the new ministry, Tōjō himself assumed the office of
Minister of Munitions. Actual leadership there was wielded by
the outgoing Minister of Commerce and Industry, Kishi
Nobusuke, who became State Minister and Vice-Minister of
Munitions. The ministry itself employed both civilians and
officers from the army and the navy.[71]

These administrative changes bore some fruit. Production of
aeroplanes increased by three times between 1942 and 1944,
and outlays in munitions industries were doubled. But inter-
agency conflicts continued to plague the government. Shortly
afterwards, the growing shortages in raw materials caused by
the air and sea blockade, the lack of sufficient skilled labour,
and the devastation caused by the air raids, prevented further
increases in production. No exhortation from above, or resolution from below, could change that gloomy situation.[72]

The largest and most pervasive civilian branch of government was the Home Ministry (*naimushō*). It was in charge of
local government, elections, police, internal security, public
works, civil defence, rationing, publications, censorship, and
Shintō shrines. It also supervised the neighbourhood associations, the IRAA, and a host of other patriotic organizations. Its
officials, policemen, and agents represented, more than anyone

else, the government's authority in every locality, controlling the population and deciding about its essential needs. But, unlike the situation in totalitarian countries, no cabinet member built himself a power base in his capacity as Home Minister. Tōjō was Home Minister during the first two months of the war, and then turned the post over to a senior bureaucrat, Yuzawa Michio. Yuzawa, who orchestrated the general election of 1942 as well as the 'recommendation elections' for the town and village councils in May of that year, stayed in office for fourteen months.[73] Altogether, five different men served as Home Minister during the war and none of them became particularly powerful in that role.

As a corporate body the Home Ministry was strong and influential. It resented sharing power with the military or with other civilian branches, and prevented attempts to set up independent grass-roots organizations. For some time the IRAA, backed by the military, constituted a threat. But in March 1941 the radical wing of that organization was suppressed and the IRAA came under the control of the Home Ministry.[74] Once that organization was tamed, it was allowed to increase its authority. In May 1942 the IRAA was given control over most patriotic organizations, such as the Great Japan Industrial Patriotic Association, the Agricultural Patriotic Association, and the Great Japan Women's Association. In June, General Andō Kisaburō, IRAA Vice-President, joined the cabinet as a State Minister, and in April 1943 he replaced Yuzawa as Home Minister. On the other hand, a former Home Minister and bureaucrat, Gotō Fumio, replaced General Andō as Vice-President of the IRAA in April 1943. The subservience of the IRAA to the Home Ministry was now complete.[75] Previously in August 1942, the IRAA had been put in charge of the neighbourhood associations, a move which the Home Ministry had once tried to prevent. In February 1943 heads of the neighbourhood associations in big cities began to receive salaries from the Home Ministry, and in March that year membership in a neighbourhood association became compulsory.[76]

The Young Men's Corps, which was established in January 1942, proved more difficult to curb. It enjoyed the support of the army, and many of its leaders were reserve officers. During the election campaign of April 1942, the Young Men criticized both the 'old-fashioned politicians' and the 'selfish bureaucrats', in their drive for a national revival. These populist appeals, independence of action, and links with the army were resented by the Home Ministry, which feared the rise of a Nazi-model organization. Ultimately the Home Ministry was triumphant. In December 1943 the government forced the Corps to reshuffle its leadership and accept the hegemony of the IRAA.[77]

Unlike the Home Ministry, which was strengthened by the war, the Foreign Ministry lost power. This was the natural culmination of a process which had begun in the early 1930s, when the military became the arbiters of Japan's security, and the Foreign Ministry was relegated to the status of a propaganda office, entrusted with the task of explaining and justifying the acts of the military. After the outbreak of the Pacific War, the functions of the Foreign Ministry decreased as the embassies in Washington, London, and other Western capitals were closed down. The acquisition of East and Southeast Asia raised the question of which government branch would conduct relations with the 'sister countries' there. The Foreign Ministry, already in nominal charge of relations with Japan's client states in the area, Manchoukuo, Nanking China, and Thailand, demanded to be entrusted with the task. But the army, suspicious of the liberal-minded officials of the Foreign Ministry, insisted on the establishment of a special Great East Asia Ministry, which would handle relations with the 'liberated' countries in the area.

In personal terms, this was a confrontation between Foreign Minister Tōgō Shigenori, a veteran diplomat and former Ambassador to Berlin and Moscow, and Prime Minister Tōjō. Tōgō opposed the plan of setting up a new ministry, rejected the suggestion that he step down, and even called on Tōjō to resign. The deadlock was solved when Navy Minister Shimada informed Tōgō that the emperor was upset by the crisis and wanted to avoid the resignation of the entire cabinet. Tōgō resigned, but was not punished for his opposition to the Prime Minister. After leaving office he was appointed to the House of Peers.

The Great East Asia Ministry (*Daitōashō*), which was established in September 1942, incorporated the Ministry of Colonies, the Asia Affairs Bureau of the Foreign Ministry, the Bureau of Manchurian Affairs, and the Asia Development Board. Aoki Kazuo, a senior official in the Ministry of Finance who had served until then as a liaison officer with the army, was appointed as the first Minister of Great East Asia. The new Foreign Minister was a former diplomat, Tani Masayuki, who had been until then President of the Information Bureau. But Tani was resented by the bureaucrats of the Foreign Ministry, and after six months in office he had to resign. Tōjō realized that he had to select an official who would enjoy the support of the ministry. So Shigemitsu Mamoru, a former Ambassador to Moscow, London, and Nanking, was appointed Foreign Minister in April 1943.[78]

The Justice Ministry co-operated with the Home Ministry in suppressing dissent. Its prosecutors prepared the trials and its judges passed the sentences. However, unlike in many countries at war, no state of emergency was declared in Japan, and the police could not act arbitrarily. The great majority of those who were arrested had to be prosecuted or freed. There were no special tribunals for wartime offenders and every defendant faced the same judicial system. Although the judges were government officials and, together with other parts of the bureaucracy, helped to maintain the existing system, they enjoyed a higher degree of freedom than other officials. The constitution provided them with considerable independence: they were appointed for life; they could not be dismissed easily; and they could not be shifted at will.

Japanese judges tended not to impose severe sentences, in order to enable the offender to correct himself. Capital punishment was rare, and life imprisonment was imposed only in extreme cases. Although there were many offences for which a person could be sentenced to death in Japan, such as murder, arson, treason, rebellion, and certain violations of the Peace Preservation Law, only fifty-seven people were executed during the war for offences of any kind. This average of fifteen executions a years was considerably lower than that of twenty-eight a year in the liberal 1920s, or the twenty a year in the 1930s.[79]

The government exerted pressure on the judges to be more severe. In February 1944 judges from all over Japan were summoned to Tokyo, where Prime Minister Tōjō and Justice Minister Iwamura Michio called on them to be strict and to impose 'extraordinary sentences' in view of the circumstances. One of the judges present at the meeting, Hosono Nagao, President of the Hiroshima Court of Appeals, criticized that instruction, saying that it violated the autonomy of the judiciary; but he was not punished for his outspokenness. Another judge, Okai Tōshirō of Yokohama, went so far as to send a letter to Tōjō urging him to resign. He was put on trial for misdemeanour and obliged to resign, but he was not arrested.[80]

The independence of the judges was also apparent in the legal repercussions of the general election. Ozaki Yukio, who was charged with *lèse-majesté* during the election campaign, was defended by two prominent lawyers, Unno Fukichi and Uzawa Sōmei. Uzawa was a member of the House of Peers and in 1936 had defended Lieutenant-Colonel Aizawa Saburō, who had murdered Major-General Tetsuzan. At his trial, Ozaki was permitted to accuse Tōjō of violating the constitution and of suppressing the freedom of the people. The verdict was given in December 1942: the eighty-four-year-old politician was found guilty and sentenced to eight months in prison, but the judges ruled that because of Ozaki's age the punishment be postponed for two years, apparently in the hope that he would die in the meantime. Ozaki appealed to the Supreme Court, where the case remained for almost two years. Then on 27 June 1944 the Supreme Court dismissed the verdict of the lower court and acquitted the defendant. Ozaki outlived the wartime leaders of Japan; he died in 1954, at the age of ninety-five.[81]

Another trial that resulted from the 1942 elections was related to their very legality. Four unrecommended candidates from the Second District in Kagoshima Prefecture, who had lost in the elections, appealed to the Supreme Court to nullify the election results in their district, on the grounds that there had been official interference. The plaintiffs, led by Tomiyoshi Eiji, a former Diet member from the Social Mass Party, claimed that the Governor, Susukida Yoshitomo, had urged teachers and policemen to help recommend candidates to be elected. Their attorney was Diet member Saitō Takao, who had been elected despite the government's efforts to suppress him. The Supreme Court treated the complaint seriously and appointed one of its members, Judge Yoshida Hisashi, to investigate it. The government tried to persuade Yoshida to dismiss the case, but he did not succumb to pressure. Yoshida went to Kago-shima, and after an investigation which lasted almost three years, he ruled on 1 March 1945 that the plaintiffs were right: the Governor had interfered in the elections. Therefore the election results in the district were declared null and void, and new elections were held in the district on 20 April. By this time, however, the Prefecture of Kagoshima was already subject to American air raids, and fewer people were concerned with the elections. The recommended candidates were re-elected, but whereas in the 1942 election they had each received between 17,000 and 25,000 votes, this time they received only between 8,700 and 13,000 votes each. The unrecommended candidates, who had received about 4,000 votes each in 1942, polled about 7,000 votes each in 1945.[82]

Thus, the same bureaucracy which had constituted an obstacle for the development of democracy before the war proved to be a barrier to the development of dictatorship during the war.

4. THE EMPEROR AND THE WAR

The Great East Asia War was declared by Emperor Hirohito on 8 December 1941, and was ended by his edict on 14 August 1945. During the war the emperor remained the supreme leader of the nation and the focus of its loyalty and devotion.

According to the constitution of 1889, the emperor was the chief commander of the armed forces and had the right to declare war and make peace, and in the exercise of these functions he was not bound by the Diet or the cabinet. He was the direct superior of the chiefs of staff of the army and the navy and could appoint or dismiss them at will. Every major military move required his approval and both chiefs of staff reported to him regularly in times of peace and even more often in war time. In practice, however, the emperors of modern Japan did not use the powers that the constitution invested in them. Following the tradition of detached 'sons of heaven', and influenced by Western models of constitutional monarchy, they seldom interfered in politics or administration. The cabinet and the military chiefs, which were supposed to advise the emperor and carry out his orders, were in fact the arbiters of policy, since the emperor always sanctioned their collective advice. The emperor's power to appoint prime ministers, chiefs of staff, and other senior officials was compromised by the custom that in these matters too he should heed the counsel of advisers, such as the Elder Statesmen (*genrō*), the Lord Keeper of the Privy Seal (*naidaijin*), or the out-going officials themselves.[83]

When the Pacific War broke out, Emperor Hirohito was forty years old and had already been emperor for fifteen years. Unlike his illustrious grandfather and sickly father, he was a shy person with a scholarly interest in marine biology, but his sense of duty was strong, and he greatly admired his famous grandfather, whose sayings he frequently repeated. On the whole, he followed the principle that a monarch should sanction the decisions of the duly constituted organs of state.[84]

This did not mean that the emperor was a mere rubber stamp or robot. In audiences with senior officials or military commanders, he used to ask questions, give general instructions, and express his pleasure or displeasure with what he had heard. When he appointed General Abe Nobuyuki as Prime Minister in August 1939, the emperor instructed him to avoid a confrontation with the US and Britain. In 1940 Prince Konoe complained to a friend, 'Whenever a new cabinet is formed these days, the emperor warns the new premier on these points: respecting the provisions of the constitution, avoiding any upheavals in the business world, and co-operating with the Anglo-American powers. . . . But politics in Japan today cannot be run in accordance with these imperial wishes.'[85] Such instructions were mere exhortations which did not carry the weight of an imperial command. The official imperial statements and edicts were drafted by the cabinet or the military and had to be approved by the Privy Council (*sūmitsuin*) before the emperor signed them.

On several occasions before the war, the emperor's personal intervention decided an issue. Hirohito's displeasure with Prime Minister Tanaka Giichi over the assassination of Chang Tso-lin in 1928 brought down the Tanaka cabinet. During the 26 February Incident of 1936, the rebels were unsuccessful because of the emperor's uncompromising opposition. In 1938 his objection to war with Russia prevented the Changkufeng Incident on the Soviet–Manchurian border from escalating into a war.[86] In all these cases the emperor threw his weight in favour of the more moderate line. But he intervened only when the opinions of his advisers were divided. There was no case in which he vetoed a collective recommendation by the cabinet or the supreme command.

The Imperial House Law (*kōshitsu tempan*) of 1889, amended in 1917 and 1918, granted the court full autonomy in running its affairs. The appointments and budget of the imperial house were outside the jurisdiction of the cabinet or the Diet, and the Minister of the Imperial Household (*kunai daijin*) was not a cabinet member. The emperor stood at the head of the imperial family (*kōshitsu*), which was composed of his brothers and sons, as well as the male representatives of specially designated family branches. All male members of the imperial family carried the title of Imperial Prince (*miya*), could succeed the emperor or serve as regents under special circumstances, and had direct access to the throne. By the outbreak of the Pacific War there were sixteen imperial princes: the emperor's three brothers, Prince Chichibu, Tamakatsu, and Mikasa; his two sons Akihito (aged 8) and Masahito (aged 6, later Prince Hitachi); the heirs to the two old imperial families Fushimi and Kan'in; and the heads of nine new imperial families, which had branched out of the Fushimi family between the years 1864 and 1906, namely Yamashina, Nashimoto, Kitashirakawa, Kuni, Kaya, Higashifushimi, Takeda, Higashikuni, and Asaka.[87]

Most of the imperial princes served as career officers in the army or the navy, exemplifying the links between the armed services and the throne. Prince Kan'in Kotohito (born into the Fushimi family but adopted by the Kan'in family in 1872) served as the Army Chief of Staff from December 1931 until October 1940. When the war broke out he was seventy-six years old and held the position of Military Councillor (*gunji sangiin*), a prestigious title with little power. His nephew, Prince Fushimi Hiroyasu, who had served as the Navy Chief of Staff from October 1933 until April 1941, was also a Military Councillor. Both were relatives of the emperor: one of Kan'in's brothers, Prince Yamashina, had married a sister of the late Emperor Meiji, while another brother, Prince Kuni Asahiko, was the grandfather of the empress. Prince Fushimi's daughter was married to the empress's brother.

The three Imperial Princes Nashimoto, Asaka, and Higashikuni, all sons of Prince Kuni Asahiko (and therefore uncles of the empress), were Military Councillors by the outbreak of the Pacific War. General Prince Higashikuni Naruhiko was also Chief of the Home Defence (*bōei sōshirekan*) from December 1941 until April 1945. Both he and Prince Asaka were married to sisters of Emperor Taishō (and were therefore uncles of the emperor). In October 1943, Prince Higashikuni's eldest son, Morihiro, married the emperor's eldest daughter, Shigeko. Prince Higashikuni's close family relations with the emperor gave him a most important position in the palace, and his interest in politics made him a favourite with activists and power-seekers of all kinds.[88]

The emperor's three younger brothers served as officers but, because of their age, had not attained important positions. Prince Chichibu, Hirohito's first brother, was an army colonel. However, his position at the palace had suffered from the involvement of some of his former friends among the Young Officers in the 26 February rebellion. Furthermore, according to Hirohito's secret monologue in 1946 to a group of close advisers, as recorded by Terasaki Hidenari of the Ministry of Foreign Affairs and discovered only in 1990, Prince Chichibu infuriated the emperor in 1939 when he tried, on behalf of the army, to pressure Hirohito and the government to join the Axis.[89] In 1940, at the age of thirty-eight, he retired because of tuberculosis and spent the war years with his wife at Gotemba near Mount Fuji. Prince Takamatsu, Hirohito's second brother, was stationed as a navy commander in Tokyo. The youngest brother, Prince Mikasa, graduated from the army staff college in December 1941 and then served for one year in China.

cendant of the feudal aristocracy, Matsudaira Tsuneo, father-in-law of Prince Chichibu and former Ambassador to London and Washington, served as Minister of the Imperial Household from 1936 until the end of the war. But the man who exerted the greatest influence on the emperor during the war was a member of the new aristocracy, Marquis Kido Kōichi, grandson of the Meiji leader Kido Kōin. Educated with Japan's other

aristocrats, he was a lifelong friend of Prince Konoe and enjoyed
the support of Prince Saionji. Kido started his career as a civil
servant, and was connected by marriage with the military. (His
wife was the daughter of General Kodama Gentarō, and his
daughter married the son of General Abe Nobuyuki.) He was
secretary to Lord Keeper Makino at the time of the 26 February
rebellion, and gained the confidence of the emperor by advising
him to resist the demands of the rebels. Later he was Minister of
Education and Minister of Welfare in the first Konoe cabinet,
and Home Minister in the Hiranuma cabinet. In June 1940 the
fifty-one-year-old Kido was appointed Lord Keeper of the Privy
Seal, a position which he held until the end of the war. Kido's
intelligence, connections, and background made him an ideal
adviser to the emperor. Since there were no more *genrō*, it was
his task to recommend new prime ministers, and this he did in
consultation with the former prime ministers (*jūshin*, or senior
statesmen).[91]

When Konoe resigned in October 1941, the emperor agreed
with Kido that only Tōjō could restrain the military if there was
going to be peace, or lead the country if there was war; as the
emperor told Kido: 'You cannot get a tiger's cub, unless you
enter the tiger's den' (*koketsu ni irazunba koji o ezu*).[92] When
Hirohito appointed Tōjō as Prime Minister, he did not instruct
him to pursue friendly relations with England and the US, as he
had done with his predecessors, but only requested him to
strengthen co-operation between the army and the navy. However, after the ceremony was over Kido told Tōjō that the
government was not bound by the 6 September decision to go to
war, and should try to reopen negotiations with the US. The
negotiations were resumed, but the impasse remained.[93]

The imperial conferences that decided on war against the US
and Britain were essentially formal meetings, at which decisions previously reached at the Liaison Conference were
approved and sanctioned in the presence of the emperor.
Although the emperor was not obliged to concur with those
decisions and could in fact overrule them, custom and conviction worked in the opposite direction. Custom required that
the emperor concur with the collective recommendation of his
top advisers, while his personal conviction seems to have been
that Japan had no other option but war. There is no evidence

that Hirohito, or anyone else in the palace during those crucial days, believed otherwise.

With the immense prestige that he enjoyed, it is probable that had Hirohito expressed a clear objection to the war, he could have averted it, or at least delayed it for some time. But such action would have required that the emperor have better strategic judgement than all his military and political advisers, which was not the case. By approving and sanctioning the resolutions of the imperial conferences, he followed the constitutional example of his father and grandfather, who had scrupulously avoided arbitrary rule. Hirohito was neither the bloodthirsty tyrant that David Bergamini has described, nor the reckless reactionary depicted by Inoue Kiyoshi.[94] Rather, he appears as a worried monarch, acting on mistaken advice, for a cause that he believed at the time to be right and noble.

Until the last moment, the emperor was apprehensive about the outcome of the war. On 3 September 1941 he discussed the matter with the Army Chief of Staff General Sugiyama. When Sugiyama said that military operations would be over in three months, the emperor replied angrily that when the war with China had broken out, Sugiyama, who was then Army Minister, had promised that it would be over in a month. Sugiyama explained that China was a vast country that could not easily be conquered. But the emperor persisted: 'If the interior of China is immense, is not the Pacific Ocean even bigger? How can you be sure that the war will end in three months?'

When the moment of decision arrived, the emperor did not allow any personal reservations that he might have had to influence his public behaviour. Three days after the conversation with Sugiyama, he attended the imperial conference which decided that war with the US and Britain would break out if negotiations did not bear positive results by 10 October. During the conference the emperor did not voice any objection, but only expressed regret that people had to fight instead of living in peace and harmony. This he did by quoting a short poem that his grandfather the Meiji emperor had composed when the cabinet decided on war with Russia in 1904:

> If all the seas are brothers, as I deem them to be,
> Why do the waves and winds so rage?

(Yomo no umi mina harakara to omou yōni,
nado adanami no tachisawaguramu?)

By identifying himself with Emperor Meiji at the start of the
Russo-Japanese War, Hirohito seemed to imply that the outcome of the Pacific War might be the same. He was to quote his
grandfather again in August 1945, when he called on his people
to 'endure what is difficult to endure' and accept defeat.[95]

According to his 1946 monologue, the emperor decided to
support the army's demand for an attack on the US and Britain
out of fear that if he declined to do so a coup d'état would
occur, as a result of which he would be deposed or killed. In
such a case, a fanatic government would seize power and drag
the nation into a 'stupid war' that no one would be able to
stop. Hirohito thus did not deny that he had supported the
war, but he justified his decision on the grounds that it was
the only way of ensuring his moderating influence on the course
of the war and on its ultimate termination.[96] As this claim was
made when the emperor was facing the possibility of being
persecuted as a war criminal, his statement can be regarded
as the basis of his future defence. Yet, even this monologue
shows that the pre-war and wartime emperor was not a robot
or 'portable shrine', as historians would later describe him.
He emerges clearly as a monarch deeply involved in the
decision-making process. He is informed of what is going on,
asks questions, expresses his opinion, advises, warns, and
exhorts. But he hardly ever commands. As a conscientious
constitutional monarch following the examples of his father
and grandfather, and as a scion of a dynasty that for centuries
had reigned but not ruled, Hirohito finally abides by the decisions of the civilian and military authorities which he himself
has appointed.

The emperor approved all the war plans and followed their
implementation with great interest. He was elated by the initial
victories and praised the successful commanders. After the
attack on Pearl Harbor, he dispatched a letter of congratulation
to Admiral Yamamoto Isoroku, in the same manner that the
Meiji emperor had praised Admiral Tōgō after the naval battle
of Tsushima in 1905. On the occasion of the fall of Singapore,
the emperor proclaimed an amnesty for prisoners who volunteered for military service. In March 1942 he told Kido, with

seeming delight, that the war was progressing favourably.[97] In his capacity as Supreme Commander (*daigensui*), the emperor often appeared in public in uniform, riding his white horse. He reviewed troops, attended ceremonies, and bid farewell to departing soldiers and sailors. By these actions he bestowed on the war the legitimacy and the aura which the military desired, and helped to make it a 'holy war' (*seisen*). From March 1943 the weekly cabinet meetings were held at the imperial palace and not at the prime minister's office. This was a return to the custom of the early Meiji era, and was designed to enhance the image of the cabinet as the emperor's government, although the emperor himself did not take part in the meetings.[98]

When the first setbacks occurred, the emperor's mood changed. After hearing about the naval débâcle at Midway, he expressed sorrow over the losses and warned the navy to be more careful in the future. But although his concern was growing, he did not change the tone of his public utterances. Opening the Diet in December 1942, the emperor said: 'Now the war situation is grave. All of us ought to be of one mind, strengthen the national power and destroy the inordinate ambition of the enemy.' A year later, when he opened the Diet session in December 1943, he declared: 'The war situation is most serious. The nation should throw its total strength, with a united will, to smash the enemy's ambitions.' In December 1944 the emperor addressed the Diet in his military uniform, and his message was the same: 'Our officers and men, fighting in defiance of death, are crushing the formidable enemy everywhere. . . . We rely on the loyalty and valour of all our subjects.'[99]

The emperor's inviolable position as a sacrosanct monarch helped the military to marshal the nation behind the war effort. But that position also granted considerable immunity to the emperor from government constraints. Only the emperor could prevail on Tōjō to resign in the middle of the war, and only he could rule in favour of a humiliating surrender. As with the bureaucracy, the imperial institution helped prevent the rise of a dictatorship in Japan during the war because of the very circumstances which had previously obstructed the development of a true democracy.

Tōjō's Downfall

There may be times in the life of a man when he has
to close his eyes and jump from the veranda of the
Kiyomizu Temple.
Prime Minister Tōjō Hideki, October 1941

I. THE GROWING OPPOSITION

Like the prime ministers before him, Tōjō could stay in office
only as long as he kept together the different power groups and
achieved the goals for which he had been selected. But his
ability to maintain consensus and implement policies was
limited. In addition to the limits posed by internal competition,
there was the almost impossible goal of winning the war or
preventing the enemy from approaching Japan. To cope with
the dangers and inspire the people to greater efforts Tōjō
needed more powers, but the failures of his government on the
front made it more difficult to get these powers. As long as the
troops were victorious, he could exact obedience and compliance, but when the setbacks started, his position became
increasingly vulnerable. Tōjō's power base lay in the army, but
he had never been the army's unquestioned leader, and he
needed the support of the other generals in order to function as
their representative. Any attempt on his part to raise himself
above the others ran the risk of antagonizing his peers, and any
failure on the battle front or the home front enabled his rivals to
demand his dismissal. Since there was no charisma in his
personality or position, there was no stigma in opposing him.

One of Tōjō's rivals in the army was General Terauchi
Hisaichi, who was six years his senior. Terauchi came from a
distinguished family. His father, Count Terauchi Masataka,
had been Prime Minister at the end of World War I, and he
himself had served as Army Minister in the Hirota cabinet and,
later, as Commander of the Expeditionary Army in North
China. In November 1941 Tōjō nominated him for Com-

mander of the Southern Front, in an attempt to keep him a long way from Tokyo. When the war broke out a month later, the general was in one of the most important commanding positions in the army, and he stayed in that post until the end of the war. Tōjō recognized Terauchi's abilities and avoided a confrontation with him. In June 1943, Terauchi was raised, together with Chief of Staff Sugiyama and Commander of the Expeditionary Army in China Hata, to the rank of Field Marshal, a rank that Tōjō himself never attained.[1]

Another rival was Brigadier-General Ishiwara Kanji. Ishiwara and Tōjō came from the same north-east region of Japan and both had distinguished themselves in Manchuria, but there was a marked difference between them. Ishiwara, four years Tōjō's junior, was a brilliant strategist, a popular figure with the troops, and a political activist who cultivated contacts with right-wing elements. He was also a religious mystic and an ardent believer in the approaching Armageddon between East and West, about which he had written a book. Although he had fought the Chinese, by the late 1930s Ishiwara preached an alliance with China, and in 1939 he sponsored the establishment of an East Asia League Association (*Tōa remmei kyōkai*).[2]

When Tōjō became Army Minister, Ishiwara made the unprecedented move of criticizing him in public. In a speech at Kyoto University in early 1941, he described him as an enemy of the people who should be arrested and executed. Tōjō reacted by dismissing Ishiwara from active service, but no further steps were taken against him. In December 1942, Tōjō invited Ishiwara to his office and tried to persuade him to change his views, but Ishiwara refused, telling Tōjō bluntly that he was incompetent and should resign. No punitive action was taken against Ishiwara, and he remained free throughout the war. Newspapermen used to meet him, although they could not publish his views. In March 1943, long before the massive air raids on Japan, Ishiwara admitted to an *Ashahi* correspondent that he was pessimistic about the outcome of the war and that Tokyo would soon go up in flames.[3]

There was opposition to Tōjō in the general staff of the army, where the rivalry with the Army Ministry over war supplies was always simmering. Thus, when the ministry refused to provide the army with the 620,000 tons of shipping that the army demanded for its campaign on Guadalcanal, Major-General Tanaka Shin'ichi of the general staff was not afraid to go to Tōjō in December 1942 and call him 'fool' (*bakamono*) to his face.[4]

The fiercest opposition was in the navy, where many officers resented the fact that the Army Minister was also the Prime Minister. The competition between the army and the navy, which had always plagued the armed forces, was exacerbated after the outbreak of the war. Each branch made its own strategic and tactical planning, amassed its own resources, and ruled its own occupied territories with hardly any consultation with the other branch. As shortages of war materials and aeroplanes developed, the competition between the services became acrimonious. In April 1942 Colonel Suzuki Teiichi, President of the Planning Board, complained to Prince Higashikuni that even civilians connected with the armed forces were forced to take sides in the inter-service rivalry. Suzuki warned that the friction was assuming ominous proportions and might engulf the whole nation. On 10 February 1944 the emperor found it necessary to reprimand Army Chief of Staff Sugiyama and Navy Chief of Staff Nagano for failing to reconcile their differences at a very grave moment.[5]

Navy Minister Admiral Shimada Shigetarō, who collaborated with Tōjō, was ridiculed by his navy subordinates as 'the tea servant of Tōjō'. Shimmyō Takeo, who covered the Navy Ministry for the *Mainichi*, reveals that Shimada was so afraid of being attacked that he was escorted, day and night, by an armed guard. According to the memoirs of General Satō Kenryō, a routine newspaper photograph in which Shimada appeared standing *behind* Tōjō aroused indignation in the navy, because it was interpreted as a sign of subordination. By the spring of 1944, pamphlets against Shimada were circulating in the navy.[6]

Among politicians the fiercest critic of Tōjō was the right-wing agitator Nakano Seigō, leader of the *Tōhōkai*. Being a rightist and a fervent supporter of the war, he was not afraid of being branded a defeatist. Nakano deplored Tōjō's 'dictatorship', as well as the fact that the Prime Minister failed to emulate Hitler and Mussolini. He did not regard these two accusations as being contradictory, because, according to Nakano, the Nazi and fascist leaders expressed the wishes of the masses, whereas Tōjō was an autocratic bureaucrat.

Nakano ran for the Diet in April 1942 and was elected together with six of his colleagues. Although the *Tōhōkai* was officially dissolved together with the other political groups in the Diet, it continued to exist as a 'thought organization' under the name *Tōhō dōshikai* (Association of Those Who Support the Idea of the East). Nakano was a gifted orator, who appeared often in rallies to support the war. Sometimes he used these occasions as opportunities to criticize Tōjō. In October 1942, in a public symposium with Commerce and Industry Minister Kishi Nobusuke, Nakano attacked the economic policies of the government, and his remarks received great applause. In November he spoke at his Alma Mater, Waseda University, where his son Yasuo was a member of the students' council. In that speech, Nakano praised the concept of liberty and urged the students to fight the bureaucratic tyranny of government, as the great Saigō had done seventy years earlier. He also praised Hitler who, in his words, 'embodied the free will of the German people'. The students cheered him and the police did not interfere. The following month, addressing a rally at the Hibiya Hall, Nakano, while praising Japan's part in the war, reminded his audience that victory depended on good leadership, which was difficult to find in Japan. He was not interrupted, but after that address he was not invited to make any more public speeches. Ten days after the speech at Hibiya Hall, the 1943 New Year edition of the *Asahi* went on sale. Page two carried an article by Nakano, together with his picture. The article, entitled 'An Opinion about Wartime Prime Ministers', discussed the virtues needed by wartime prime ministers and hinted that Tōjō lacked them. No steps were taken against the writer or the editor.[7]

Nakano did not limit himself to speeches and articles. He and his associate Diet member Mitamura Takeo appealed to the *jūshin* and to Princes Higashikuni and Takamatsu to help topple Tōjō. According to the diary of Prince Higashikuni, Nakano visited him on 25 June 1943 to complain about the autocracy of the government, and urged him to do his best to change it. Mitamura attacked IRAPA on the Diet floor and accused it of suppressing debate and encouraging docile flattery. In June both Nakano and Mitamura left IRAPA, declaring themselves independents, and sent a circular letter to their supporters, in which they accused the government of trying to set up a new shogunate in Japan. Two months later, members of their group distributed punning leaflets in the Ginza which said: 'American planes should be destroyed, British planes should be destroyed.' But the characters for 'British planes', *eiki*, were those of Tōjō's given name, Hideki. So one could also read the last phrase as 'Hideki should be destroyed' (*Hideki otosubeshi*).[8]

Other right-wing groups were also dissatisfied with Tōjō. The 1942 report of the Police Bureau listed several such groups that necessitated special surveillance: the *Sekiseikai* (Sincerity Association), a youth organization led by Reserve Colonel Hashimoto Kingorō, who had been elected to the Diet in 1942; the *Kinnō makoto musubikai* (Association of Those Bound by Imperial Loyalism and Sincerity), led by Amano Tatsuo, who had been involved in the terrorist *Shimpeitai* (Heavenly Soldiers) affair of 1933; and the *Dai Nippon kōdōkai* (Association for the Imperial Way of Great Japan), of Akao Bin, who had been elected to the Diet that year. In June 1943 Akao gave a speech in the Diet in which he attacked the government for suppressing patriotic organizations and encouraging opportunists and flatterers. Akao then followed the examples of Nakano and Mitamura in leaving the IRAPA. The right-wing activist Ōkawa Shūmei, famous for his involvement in the 15 May Affair of 1932, advocated a new cabinet headed by Prince Higashikuni with Ishiwara Kanji as Army Minister. There were even rumours that rightists were planning to assassinate the Prime Minister.[9]

Although Tōjō was worried by the subversive activities of the extreme rightists, it was a long time before he clamped down on them. Mitamura was arrested on 6 September 1943, and on 21 October 101 members of right-wing organizations, including Nakano and Amano, were also arrested. In December members of Hashimoto's *Sekiseikai* were arrested, but Hashimoto and Akao, who were Diet members, remained free. Since Nakano and Mitamura were also Diet members, the question of their immunity soon arose. On 25 October, when the police asked to extend their arrest, the examining judge, Kobayashi Kenji, refused to do so, on the grounds that an extraordinary Diet session had been called for the following day. The police protested, but the judge was immovable in his conviction that the constitutional right of a Diet member to participate in a session could not be violated. Article 53 of the constitution stated clearly: 'The members of both Houses shall, during the session, be free from arrest, unless with the consent of the House, except in cases of flagrant delicts, or of offences connected with a state of internal commotion or with a foreign trouble.' The next morning both Nakano and Mitamura were released.

When Nakano left the police station, he was detained again by the Military Police, who questioned him for several hours. He was finally released in the afternoon and went straight to the Diet. On his way home that night he was escorted by two military policemen, who entered his house and installed themselves on the ground floor. At midnight, after Nakano had retired to his room, the policemen heard a strange noise. When they entered the room, they found him dead in his armchair, his abdomen slashed by a sword. A cryptic poem by his side said:

> Decision in a moment
> Words cannot be stopped
> Three days of selfish joy
> An absurd allegation
> No one should be implicated.[10]

The reason for Nakano's suicide remains a mystery. Certainly Tōjō could not have kept him in gaol for long. Mitamura, who was released together with Nakano, was not arrested again. The Japanese historian Kojima Noboru lists four possible explanations for Nakano's death: (1) The military threatened to send his son, who was then serving in the army, to a dangerous front. (2) The police discovered Nakano's connections with high-ranking persons and threatened to implicate them. (3) The police found out that Nakano had been receiving secret donations from Chief of Staff Sugiyama and the German Embassy and threatened to expose this. (4) Nakano was a communist agent and he preferred to die when the police discovered it.[11]

The fourth allegation, absurd as it may sound, was made by several people, including some who had known him. Kojima mentions a former Diet member, Ogawa Heikichi, who before his death in 1942 had compiled a file in which he tried to prove that Nakano was a secret agent of the Comintern. His 'evidence' was that Nakano opposed the Siberian Intervention of 1918–22, that he had never attacked the Soviet Union, and that he had amassed a large fortune. Indeed, before being arrested Nakano gave his son 80,000 yen to be deposited with friends. Yatsugi Kazuo, formerly one of the directors of IRAPA, heard a similar theory from a prosecution officer. Tōjō himself might have believed in the truth of such an allegation. When the correspondent Takamiya Tahei asked him about Nakano a few days after the suicide, Tōjō replied: 'He was a traitor', and refused to elaborate.[12] However, there is no evidence to support the charge that Nakano was a communist agent, driven to suicide by police discovery. It seems more likely that he was driven to despair by police harassment, and by his own failure to topple Tōjō. Accordingly, he decided to defy Tōjō by an ultimate act of protest, in the tradition of the *samurai*. By doing so, he might also have hoped to protect other persons, such as Princes Higashikuni and Takamatsu, with whom he had maintained secret connections.

The government was apprehensive about the impact which Nakano's *seppuku* might have on the public and asked the family to limit the funeral to immediate relatives and friends. But the family defied the request and the funeral, which took place at the Aoyama Cemetery on 31 October, was attended by 20,000 people. This huge gathering thus became an anti-Tōjō demonstration. The master of ceremonies was Nakano's friend Ogata Taketora, the chief editor of the *Asahi*, and the procession was led by Amano Tatsuo's son, Masakatsu, who rode Nakano's favourite horse.[13]

2. SENIOR STATESMEN VERSUS TŌJŌ

The *jūshin*, or former prime ministers, had exercised since 1940 the role of recommending a new prime minister when that post became vacant, but otherwise they had little influence on the government. Nevertheless, the fact that the emperor depended on them to advise him on the most important political nomination provided them with a high status and instilled in them a sense of responsibility.

Tōjō maintained correct relations with the *jūshin*, though they did not interest him very much. Once a month he would lunch with them and brief them on developments. But, as former Prime Minister Wakatsuki later admitted, he did not tell them more than they had already read in the newspapers. According to Tōjō's friend General Satō Kenryō, the Prime Minister had little sympathy for the senior statesmen, whom he regarded as 'a bunch of old gentlemen'.[14]

There were seven *jūshin* in 1944: Baron Wakatsuki Reijirō, Admiral Okada Keisuke, Hirota Kōki, Prince Konoe Fumimaro, Baron Hiranuma Kiichirō, General Abe Nobuyuki, and Admiral Yonai Mitsumasa (General Hayashi had died in 1943). Most of them were quite old: Wakatsuki was 78, Hiranuma 77, Okada 76, Abe 69, Hirota 66, Yonai 61; only Konoe was a relatively young 50. Four of them were civilians; of the three military men, two (Okada and Yonai) were admirals; and only one (Abe) was a general. No wonder General Abe was the closest *jūshin* to Tōjō and the only one who also held another senior position, that of President of IRAPA.

Konoe, despite his youth, was the most respected among the *jūshin*, because of his status as a scion of the old aristocracy. Having been Tōjō's predecessor in office, he also felt responsible for the behaviour of the Prime Minister whom he had helped to select. Like all the others, Konoe was at first enthusiastic about the victories, but he remained pessimistic about the outcome of the war, which he feared Japan could not win. His main concern was that a major setback or a defeat would cause an internal upheaval that would enable hidden communists in the army, the IRAA, and the universities to stir up a revolution in Japan. Some senior officials like Hata Shigenori of the Special Higher Police shared his fear.[15] In Konoe's opinion, it was better to end the war without victory than to risk a revolution which would sweep away the imperial institution. Konoe tried to convince Prince Higashikuni, in the hope that his warning would be conveyed to the emperor. On 1 May 1942 he told the prince that one should not be deceived by the external complacency of the people, which would last only as long as the armies were victorious. Once defeats occurred, the festering resentment against the government would explode and reach revolutionary proportions. Konoe met Higashikuni on 16 December to try again to persuade him of the validity of his theory.

Prince Konoe believed that only the *Kōdōha* generals, who had been purged in 1936 and were therefore in no way responsible for the war, could save Japan. On 6 January 1943 he met two of these reserve generals, Mazaki Jinzaburō and Obata Binshirō, at the house of the former Ambassador to Britain, Yoshida Shigeru. Among those also present was Ikeda Seihin, the former director of the Mitsui concern, who had once supported the *Kōdōha*. They all agreed that Tōjō should resign and be replaced by a reserve general, preferably General Ugaki. On the basis of that meeting, Konoe reported to Lord Keeper Kido that there was opposition to Tōjō 'among political leaders and businessmen'. On 27 January Konoe told Higashikuni that the opposition to Tōjō 'among political, financial, and industrial circles' was very strong.[16]

That year another *jūshin*, Okada Keisuke, also became convinced that Tōjō should go. Okada had been Prime Minister at the time of the 26 February 1936 rebellion, and had escaped death only because the rebels mistook his brother-in-law for him and shot him on sight. This event, as Okada's biographer claims, had made Okada determined to devote the rest of his miraculously granted life to the cause of his country, even at the risk of death. As a retired admiral, he continued to get information from the navy, and shared the navy's resentment against Tōjō. In addition, there were several relatives who supplied him with up-to-date news about the war: his eldest son, Commander Okada Sadatomu, was Chief of the Operation Section of naval headquarters; Lieutenant-Colonel Sejima Ryūzō, son-in-law of his murdered brother-in-law, was a member of the Operation Section of the army's general staff; and his son-in-law and former secretary Sakomizu Hisatsune was a senior official of the Planning Board.[17]

On 8 August 1943, Okada sent Sakomizu to persuade Lord Keeper Kido that Tōjō should be replaced. Kido remained uncommitted, but he did promise to report to the emperor any serious signs of opposition to the government. When Sakomizu asked what would constitute a serious sign, Kido replied that a unanimous rebuke by the *jūshin* might do. After consulting Konoe and Hiranuma, Okada then invited the Prime Minister to meet the *jūshin* at the Peers' Club, hoping to achieve a confrontation between the senior statesmen and Tōjō that could lead to such a rebuke. But Tōjō did not come alone. When he arrived on 30 August he was accompanied by Navy Minister Shimada, Foreign Minister Shigemitsu, and Finance Minister Kaya. The *jūshin* questioned him about the military situation, but instead of admitting his failures, Tōjō asked them pointedly whether they doubted the outcome of the war. Far from rebuking the Prime Minister, the senior statesmen found themselves being lectured by him.[18] The desired confrontation did not materialize.

Tōjō hoped that the impressive state ceremonies, scheduled for October and November of that year, would bolster his position and silence the critics. On 21 October he reviewed a huge parade of mobilized students at the Meiji Shrine gardens; on 5 November the Great East Asia Conference opened in Tokyo with a great fanfare. The participants included Wang Ching-wei of China, Chang Chung-hui of Manchoukuo, Ba Maw of Burma, José Laurel of the Philippines, Wan Waithyakon of Thailand, and Subhas Chandra Bose, head of the Provisional Government of Free India. The conference issued a proclamation in support of Japan's war aims.

Later that month President Roosevelt, Prime Minister Churchill, and Generalissimo Chiang Kai-shek met in Cairo and vowed to wage war with Japan until her unconditional surrender. Thus the war of proclamations and counter-proclamations was being waged with fierce intensity by both sides. The Japanese government dismissed the Cairo declaration as a propaganda device, but it was more difficult to dismiss the military defeats in the Pacific. In February 1943, the Japanese were defeated on Guadalcanal. In April, Admiral Yamamoto Isoroku was killed in his aeroplane. In May, the garrison on Attu Island was wiped out by Americans. In November, the garrisons on Makin and Tarawa Islands shared the same fate. In February 1944 US forces occupied Kwajalein in the Marshall Islands, and bombarded Truk in the Caroline Islands. The 'impregnable perimeter' in the Pacific was collapsing. The Americans were approaching the Mariana Islands, from which their long-range bombers could reach Japan.

Reacting to the increasingly dangerous situation, Tōjō decided to enhance his powers. On 21 February 1944 he dismissed the Chief of Staff of the Army, Field Marshal Sugiyama, and appointed himself to the post. At the same time, Navy Minister Shimada dismissed the Chief of Staff of the Navy, Fleet Admiral Nagano, and assumed that post himself. Tōjō was now Prime Minister, Army Minister, Munitions Minister, and Army Chief of Staff. He also reshuffled the cabinet: Finance Minister Kaya Okinori was replaced by Ishiwata Sōtarō; Commerce and Agriculture Minister Yamazaki Tatsunosuke was replaced by Uchida Nobuya; and Transportation and Communication Minister Hatta Yoshiaki was replaced by Gotō Keita.

In a statement to the press, Tōjō justified his move, saying: 'At a time when the US and Britain are pressing hard on our inner lines in the South Pacific, we have carried out a great reshuffle, to permit closer co-ordination of administration and command.' At the closing session of the 84th Diet on 22 March, Tōjō declared: 'The war situation was never more serious than it is now. There is no longer a distinction between the front and the rear. If the one hundred million people of Japan are determined to make the same efforts as our officers and men on the fronts, we shall certainly win the war.' His new position was explained as a necessary move to cope with the current emergency. To his secretary, Colonel Akamatsu Sadao, Tōjō justified his move by citing the example of the French Commander-in-Chief General Joffre, who assumed the position of a divisional commander when the Germans were approaching Paris in World War I, and thus was able to stop the enemy.[19]

Such explanations did not convince the critics, who regarded Tōjō's move as an attempt to gain absolute power. The dismissed Field Marshal Sugiyama sent a memorandum to the emperor, in which he warned that if the Prime Minister was also Army Minister and Chief of Staff, Japan was on her way to a new shogunate.[20] Even Diet members, who had kept quiet until then, were not afraid to add their voices in protest. On 25 March, at a farewell party to members of the 84th session of the Diet, held at the Prime Minister's official residence, the Speaker of the House of Representatives Okada Tadahiko called on Tōjō to assume responsibility for the situation and resign. Ōki Misao, the Chief Secretary of the House of Representatives, who was there, recorded in his diary that when the speech was over many Diet members applauded. The Prime Minister was pale and did not respond.[21]

Tōjō had no intention of resigning, whatever the old gentlemen of the *jūshin* or the Diet thought. When Admiral Okada realized that, he changed his strategy. He would now use his influence in the navy to bring about the resignation of Admiral Shimada, in the hope that the man who would replace him would be less servile to Tōjō. This would impair the relations between the army and the navy and thus force Tōjō to resign. Okada would have preferred Admiral Yonai to be the new Navy Minister, but if this was not possible he would accept Admiral Suetsugu. However, both were on the reserve list, and unless recalled to active service were not eligible for the ministry post.

On 2 June Okada met the two reserve admirals at the home of his friend Fujiyama Aiichirō, the President of the Chamber of Commerce. They agreed to work together to persuade Shimada to resign. On 16 June Okada met the Navy Minister, who was fifteen years his junior, himself. He explained to Shimada that it was improper for one man to hold the posts of Minister and of Chief of Staff, and urged him to resign the post of Navy Minister. He also requested that Shimada recall Admirals Yonai and Suetsugu to active service, so that one of them could replace him as Navy Minister. Shimada replied that he would discuss the matter with Tōjō. On the following day, Okada was suddenly summoned by Tōjō. The Prime Minister rebuked the old Admiral for trying to weaken the cabinet at such a grave moment in history. Okada replied that if the situation was grave, then the Navy Minister, who had lost the support of his subordinates, should resign. Tōjō disagreed and the meeting ended with no changes.[22]

On 6 June, American and British forces began landing in Normandy and the second front in Europe was opened. On 15 June, American forces landed on Saipan in the Mariana Islands, which was nicknamed 'the doorway to Tokyo' (*Tōkyō no genkan*). The government had tried desperately to prevent the Americans from establishing a beach-head on the island and dispatched Vice-Admiral Nagumo, who had commanded the task forces in Pearl Harbor and Midway. But the 30,000 Japanese defenders were outnumbered and out-gunned by the 70,000 American invaders, who were supported by enormous sea and air power. As the Japanese forces on the island were retreating, a controversy erupted in Japan as to who was responsible for the débâcle. The navy blamed the army for refusing to lend its aeroplanes for the defence of the island, and naval officers blamed Shimada, whose servility to the army had left the navy without adequate means. On 2 July Okada told Prince Konoe that opposition to Shimada in the ranks was so intense that unless the Navy Minister resigned, a new 26 February Incident might occur. On the following day, Admiral Suetsugu remarked to Konoe that an effort should be made to recapture Saipan. When Konoe said that the cabinet had already written off the island, Suetsugu replied that in that case the whole cabinet should resign.[23] Dissatisfaction with Tōjō was also spreading in other quarters. On 4 July leading members of IRAPA, after a meeting with representatives of the navy, agreed that the cabinet should assume responsibility and resign.[24] Three days later, on 7 July 1944, Saipan fell to the enemy. After three weeks of desperate resistance, the last defenders of the island made a suicidal charge against the Americans and were annihilated. Vice-Admiral Nagumo committed suicide. The doorway to Tokyo was open.

3. DISSATISFACTION IN THE COURT

Tōjō's feeble attempt to establish himself as the wartime leader of Japan posed a threat to the status of the emperor. When Tōjō assumed the position of Chief of Staff, some of the imperial princes, who had already been suspicious of the Prime Minister and his motives, started voicing their concern. Prince Chichibu, ailing in Gotemba, was the first to express his dismay. According to his friend Lieutenant-Colonel Tanemura Sataka, the prince feared that Tōjō might become a modern *Shogūn* or even try to usurp the throne. Chichibu also had a personal grudge against Tōjō, who had blocked his promotion to the rank of major-general for five years on the grounds that the prince was in actual retirement.[25]

In late February 1944 Prince Chichibu wrote a letter to the head of the Personnel Section of the Army Ministry, Colonel Okada Jūichi, in which he expressed his anxiety about Tōjō's new powers. On 21 April he sent his aide-de-camp Major Shizuma Katsuyuki to Vice-Chief of Staff General Ushiroku

Jun, with the following questions: Why had the army violated the rule that the functions of chief of staff and minister should be separated? Was it possible for one man to fulfil the responsibilities of these two posts? If there was a disagreement between the cabinet and the general staff, which opinion would Tōjō recommend to the emperor? If the war reached a point at which it would be necessary to decide whether to stop or continue, would Tōjō react in his capacity as Prime Minister or as Chief of Staff? Ushiroku replied that Tōjō had no intention of changing the rules and that his appointment as Chief of Staff was merely an emergency measure. The answer did not satisfy the prince, and in mid-May he dispatched his aide to the general again, repeating the two last questions. After consulting Tōjō, General Ushiroku went to visit the prince in Gotemba to assure him in person that nothing would be done to undermine the emperor's position as Supreme Commander.[26]

Hirohito's second brother, Prince Takamatsu, a navy captain attached to the naval headquarters in Tokyo, shared the navy's displeasure with Tōjō. In September 1943 he confided to Kido that the navy resented the fact that the Prime Minister was also Army Minister. In February 1944 the prince asked Kido's support for the navy's demand for more aeroplanes to stop the Americans in the Pacific. But the army, waging a separate war in China and Burma, refused to reduce its own quota.[27]

Since Prince Chichibu was ill and away from the capital, Prince Takamatsu was the second man in importance in the court and the obvious candidate for the post of regent if the emperor resigned. When Prince Konoe decided to appeal to the emperor to remove Tōjō, he contacted his son-in-law Hosokawa Morisada who was Prince Takamatsu's secretary. According to Hosokawa's memoirs, he met Takamatsu in November 1943 and again in February 1944, in an attempt to convince him that Tōjō should be dismissed. On 13 June Konoe himself met Takamatsu and warned him that unless the government were changed, Japan would face the danger of state socialism.[28] However, Prince Takamatsu's influence on the emperor was limited, and as a junior officer he lacked the authority of the military chiefs. Hirohito was often upset when his brother interfered with affairs of state and sometimes even scolded him for doing so. Prince Konoe reports that when Takamatsu urged the emperor to replace Shimada in July 1943, Hirohito retorted that he would not listen to the 'prattling of an irresponsible prince'. Prince Kaya revealed to Konoe that because of frequent quarrels with his brother, 'His Majesty is suffering from a nervous breakdown and often gets excited.'[29]

Takamatsu's views were shared by Prince Higashikuni, uncle of both the emperor and the empress and father-in-law of their eldest daughter. As an army General and Commander of Japan's Home Defence, his opinion carried more weight, but his influence on the emperor was also limited. According to Higashikuni's diary, three weeks after Pearl Harbor he recommended that Japan should end the war and come to terms with the Allies, but his suggestion was not heeded. When he reported to the emperor on the damages caused by the Doolittle air raid in April 1942, he was reprimanded by General Sugiyama, because only the Chief of Staff had the right to make military reports to the emperor. Higashikuni did not make further reports, but he continued to see the emperor in his capacity as an imperial prince.[30] Higashikuni maintained more contacts with political and government figures who were dissatisifed with the official policy than any other prince of the blood. Thus in 1942 Foreign Minister Shigemitsu and the chief editor of the *Asahi*, Ogata, tried to persuade him that Japan should make peace with Chiang Kai-shek. In 1943 Marquis Sanjōnishi, the brother-in-law of the emperor, urged him to replace Tōjō. During the first three months of 1944, three different people, the counsellor in Japan's Berlin embassy Ushiba Nobuhiko, the industrialist Ishihara Kōichirō, and Professor Hiraizumi of Tokyo Imperial University, confided to him separately that Japan was losing the war. Higashikuni did not hesitate to tell the emperor his opinions, and after the fall of Guadalcanal he told Hirohito that the impending débâcle would teach the army a lesson just as the 1939 defeat in Nomonhan had done.[31]

Higashikuni's position and his easy access to the emperor made him attractive to Tōjō's critics as well as to his supporters. On 11 April 1944 Prince Konoe asked him to help remove Tōjō. On 20 June Tōjō's secretary, Colonel Akamatsu, told him that the Prime Minister was ready to resign if a suitable successor could be found. On 23 June Tōjō himself visited the prince to assure him that he had no particular interest in remaining in office. Higashikuni replied that before Tōjō resigned, he should find a way to end the war that he had started.[32]

Major-General Prince Kaya, cousin of the empress and a nephew of Higashikuni, also had reservations about Tōjō. On 10 December 1942 he told his uncle that the general staff of the army blamed Tōjō for failing to provide the ships that were needed for the defence of Guadalcanal. In July 1944 Prince Kaya became alarmed about the war situation and told his uncle that unless Japan sought peace, she would face disaster. He suggested that the three imperial princes who held senior ranks in the army, Higashikuni, Asaka, and Kaya, appeal together to the emperor to dismiss Tōjō and appoint Prince Fushimi as the over-all commander of the imperial forces. Prince Kaya had a special reason to be concerned. The 43rd Division, which he had commanded until April 1944, had been dispatched to defend Saipan, where it now faced annihilation.[33] Sixty-nine-year-old Prince Fushimi, a Fleet Admiral and the senior Imperial Prince in the navy, did not take part in these machinations, because Navy Minister Shimada was his protégé. in June 1944, when Okada asked the prince to arrange for him to be received by the emperor, Fushimi declined to do so, but he did promise to help arrange the recall of Admiral Yonai to active service.[34]

The man who enjoyed the greatest influence on the emperor was Lord Keeper of the Privy Seal Marquis Kido and by January 1944 he too began to fear that the war was lost. According to his diary, Kido came to the conclusion that Japan should try to make peace through the mediation of the Soviet Union before it was too late. But he knew that the army would oppose such an idea and shunned an open confrontation. So in June Kido rejected Konoe's suggestion that the emperor dismiss Tōjō, telling Konoe that only if the war reached a point at which it would be necessary to 'stop it' would the emperor ask the Prime Minister to resign and appoint an imperial prince to take over his post.[35]

Konoe, however, was convinced that such a moment had already arrived. He was supported by reports from General Sakai Kōji of the army's general staff and Rear-Admiral Takagi Sōkichi of the navy's general staff, which said that if Japan did not stop the war very soon, she would be lost. On 1 February 1944 Konoe confided to his son-in-law Hosokawa that the country was facing a 'disastrous defeat'. On 2 July he wrote to Kido that in order to avoid an imminent defeat, the emperor should appoint Prince Takamatsu as Prime Minister and make peace with the Allies. He warned that continuing the war would mean destruction and revolution. Kido agreed that the situation was grave, but did not think it warranted the summary dismissal of Tōjō. The best solution was for the Prime Minister to resign of his own will, as his predecessors had done in the face of major failures.[36]

While the people around the throne were deliberating on how to influence the emperor's actions, the emperor himself began to have doubts about the war. According to Kido's diary, after the defeat of Guadalcanal in 1943 Hirohito remarked: 'Strangely, the war is lasting too long.' Later he supported Foreign Minister Shigemitsu's idea that a special envoy be dispatched to Moscow to negotiate a peace, but he did not insist on it when the army objected. Following the Allied landing in France in June 1944, the emperor, according to his 1946 monologue, wanted Japan to work out a Soviet–German reconciliation, probably in the hope that the Soviet Union would then reciprocate by bringing about a Japan–American reconciliation, but Hitler showed no interest in this plan.[37] When the fall of Saipan became imminent, the emperor made an unusual move by summoning the Board of Field Marshals and Fleet Admirals (*gensui-in*), a prestigious body with little power that had rarely been convened. The meeting, which took place in the presence of the emperor on 25 June, was attended by former Army Chief of Staff Field Marshal Sugiyama, former Navy Chief of Staff Fleet Admiral Nagano, and the imperial princes Fleet Admiral Fushimi and Field Marshal Nashimoto. Tōjō and Shimada attended ex officio. The Board recommended the setting-up of a new line of defence in the Pacific and the unification of the air forces of the army and navy.[38] The former recommendation was already being implemented, but the latter was never carried out.

The emperor wished to bring the war to an end, but did not know how to do so, and was afraid to clash with the army. On 8 July Kido revealed to Konoe: 'It would be good if the emperor ordered the troops to return home and would assume responsibility for everything, in order to avoid internal turmoil.' But the government objected to a unilateral surrender. Theoretically, the emperor could overrule the government by dismissing it and appointing a new one, but no emperor had done so before in modern times. Amazing as it may seem, Hirohito's hesitation and uncertainty at that crucial moment produced suggestions about his removal. Strangely enough, both the hawks and the doves started considering the possibility of changing the man on the throne or transferring him from Japan. On 8 July Konoe confided to Kido: 'It seems to me that the army is planning to transfer the emperor to Manchuria or even replace him with another imperial prince who opposes his peace plans.'[39] Later that day, Konoe met with Higashikuni and both agreed that in order to facilitate the peace process, 'the present emperor should abdicate, the Crown Prince should succeed him and Prince Takamatsu should be appointed regent'.[40] A new cabinet, headed by Higashikuni, would terminate the war and make peace. Three days later, Prince Higashikuni told Prince Takamatsu that the emperor's resignation would be a wise move, because it would be received favourably by the Allies and thus serve the cause of peace. But no emperor in modern Japan had ever abdicated, and Hirohito did not think that he should assume responsibility for the war and resign. Quite the contrary; he believed that it was his duty to stay on the throne and guide his nation out of the predicament. He was ready to change the cabinet, but Tōjō also thought that it was *his* responsibility as Prime Minister to stay in office until the war was brought to a statisfactory end. Tōjō might have concluded that both he and the emperor were in the same boat and that as long as the emperor remained in formal command, he too could retain his position.

On 12 July Tōjō presented to the emperor a plan for the strengthening of the government so that it could cope with the new situation. He asked the emperor to issue a proclamation on the occasion of the fall of Saipan, that would encourage the people and call for national unity. But Hirohito refused to issue a statement that would link his name with the débâcle, and he remarked that a mere reshuffle of the cabinet would not solve the problem. This rebuff did not convince Tōjō that the emperor had lost confidence in him. After the audience, he told Kido that at such a crucial moment in history it was dangerous to change the leadership and therefore he had decided to stay in office. When Kido reported Tōjō's message to the emperor, Hirohito expressed concern that the Prime Minister might assume still greater powers, which would jeopardize the throne. On the following day Tōjō came again to speak to the emperor, this time in his capacity as Chief of Staff. The atmosphere at the meeting was tense, Hirohito mentioned the mounting opposition to Shimada in the navy and requested that the Navy Minister be changed.[41] The trap was starting to close on Tōjō.

There were also other ways of removing a prime minister from office. Between 1921 and 1936 three Japanese prime ministers had fallen victim to assassins, and a fourth, Admiral Okada, had barely escaped death. The wartime government of Japan had clamped down on the extreme rightists, but there were always hot-headed young officers and right-wing civilians who might be ready to 'destroy the traitors around the throne'. In the summer of 1944 a strange plot to assassinate the Prime Minister was conceived. The leader of the plot was Major Tsunoda Tomoshige of the general staff, who had returned from China a few months earlier. He came from a well-to-do family of Nagano Prefecture, and his uncle was Diet member Kosaka Takeo. Tsunoda's civilian accomplices were Ushijima Tatsukuma and Asahara Kenzō who belonged to Ishiwara Kanji's East Asia League, and he himself was acquainted with the emperor's youngest brother Prince Mikasa, under whom he had served in China. In July 1944, Prince Mikasa showed Prince Higashikuni a pamphlet that he had received from Tsunoda, which called for the resignation of Tōjō, the establishment of a cabinet under Higashikuni, and immediate peace talks with the Allies through Moscow. The plot was uncovered in August 1944, after Tōjō's resignation, when Prince Mikasa notified the Military Police about it. After the ringleaders were arrested in early September, it was discovered that they were supporters of Reserve General Ishiwara Kanji, and had planned to kill the Prime Minister with a bomb loaded with potassium cyanide. Tsunoda was convicted and sentenced to two years in prison, while the others were acquitted. General Ishiwara was not even arrested. It was a strange coincidence that at exactly the same time that Major Tsunoda and his friends were plotting to assassinate Tōjō, a group of German officers, led by Colonel Klaus von Stauffenberg, were plotting to kill Hitler. Had these two attempts succeeded, the wartime leaders of Germany and Japan might have died on the same day. But the bomb which went off in Germany on 20 July failed to kill Hitler, and on the following day General Tōjō, unaware of the plot on his own life, sent a telegram to the German Führer congratulating him on his narrow escape from death.[42]

4. TŌJŌ'S RESIGNATION

Tōjō was determined to stay in office. He planned to placate his opponents by dismissing the unpopular Shimada, giving up his controversial post of Chief of Staff, and inviting some of his critics, like Admiral Yonai, to join the cabinet. But these changes required the consent of the persons involved, for in Japan even in time of war people could not be shifted in and out of the cabinet by diktat. Accordingly, on 14 July Tōjō resigned the post of Army Chief of Staff, which he had held for five months. On his request, Admiral Shimada resigned his post as Navy Minister, remaining the navy's Chief of Staff. General Umezu Yoshijirō, Commander of the Kwantung Army since 1939, was appointed as the new Chief of Staff of the army, and Field Marshal Sugiyama was made Inspector-General of Military Education. Admiral Nomura Naokuni, Commander of the Kure naval base, was appointed Navy Minister.

These changes in the supreme command were to be followed by changes in the cabinet. Tōjō invited Admiral Yonai to join his cabinet as a State Minister, and, since the number of State Ministers was limited by law, he asked State Minister Kishi Nobusuke, his trusted deputy in the Munitions Ministry, to resign his cabinet post to make room for Yonai. To Tōjō's surprise, both men turned down his request. Admiral Yonai replied that he would join the cabinet only in the capacity of Navy Minister; Kishi, after consulting Okada, refused to quit. The cabinet-reshuffle plan was thus thwarted in a way most humiliating to Tōjō.[43]

While Tōjō was wrangling with Yonai and Kishi, Lord Keeper Kido moved in to throw his weight against the Prime Minister. On 17 July Kido told Konoe that if the *jūshin* agreed that the Prime Minister should resign, he would support that decision and report it to the emperor. Konoe acted swiftly and that evening all seven *jūshin* met at the house of Baron Hiranuma. Yonai told them about the pressure exerted on him to join the cabinet, but he made it clear that unless he was offered the post of Navy Minister he would not do so, even if the emperor himself ordered him to. The other participants too, with the exception of General Abe, criticized the government. Since it was an informal meeting, no resolution was adopted, but following the meeting Okada could report to Kido that the *jūshin* wanted Tōjō to resign. Kido then went to the emperor and informed him that the senior statesmen were dissatisfied with the cabinet. When Kido left, Princes Higashikuni and Asaka were received in audience and recommended that Tōjō be dismissed. The emperor agreed. In his 1946 monologue, the emperor stated that although Tōjō was an honest and hard-working person, he could not continue in office because of the growing resentment against him that had been caused by the fall of Saipan, the concentration of powers in his hands, and his excessive use of the Military Police.[44]

Confronted by defiance in his own cabinet and mistrust in the court, Tōjō acted as his predecessors had done in similar circumstances: he resigned. Had he been a dictator, he would have used force against his opponents or would have accused them of treason. But Tōjō was only a Prime Minister, an Army Minister, and a Munitions Minister. His power was limited and he could not break the rules. On the morning of 18 July he handed his resignation, and the resignation of his cabinet, to the emperor.[45] His term in office had lasted two years and nine months.

In the afternoon, Kido convened the *jūshin* in order to recommend a successor. Nine people attended that meeting at the imperial palace: the seven *jūshin*, Kido, and the President of the Privy Council, Baron Hara Yoshimichi. Their enemy was gone, but it was difficult to find a successor. The task of the man who would succeed Tōjō was an almost impossible one. He had to achieve victory on the battlefield, but he was also expected to end the war and make peace. He had to impose a united policy on all branches of government, a task which Tōjō had failed to perform, but he had to give up most of the special powers which

Tōjō had accumulated. In other words, with less power he would be expected to accomplish more.

Since none of the *jūshin* wanted that office for himself or his friends, an interesting dispute ensued, in which each participant gingerly tried to remove himself from consideration for the post. General Abe, the only army man among the *jūshin*, suggested that the new prime minister be a navy man, preferably Admiral Yonai. Yonai, however, said that the candidate should be a civilian. But the civilian Baron Wakatsuki was quick to suggest that a military man, preferably General Ugaki, would be the obvious choice. Hirota, who carried no aristocratic title, proposed that an imperial prince be nominated to the post. Baron Hara, who was not a former prime minister, suggested that all the former prime ministers collectively form a cabinet. The civilian Prince Konoe agreed with Baron Wakatsuki that only an army general could control the military. Kido supported that view and gradually all the others agreed that the new prime minister should be, as before, a general, though not necessarily on the active list.

Who was the general who could fulfil all these expectations? Yonai suggested Field Marshal Terauchi, the commander of the Southern Front, who was stationed in Manila. The others accepted the proposal, but were not sure whether Terauchi could leave his post. Kido therefore asked that two alternative names be selected. Yonai proposed Reserve General Koiso Kunaiki, the Governor-General of Korea, and Marshal Hata Shun'roku, Commander of the Expeditionary Army in China. The proposals were unanimously accepted and the conference decided to recommend Field Marshal Terauchi, General Koiso, and Marshal Hata, in that order.[46] When Kido conveyed the decision to the emperor that evening, Hirohito summoned Tōjō to ask his opinion. Tōjō said that Terauchi's presence in the south was essential for the conduct of the war and his transfer to Tokyo might hurt the morale of the troops. Thus, in his last act in office, Tōjō succeeded in preventing his rival from becoming prime minister. The emperor then decided to nominate Koiso and asked that he be summoned to Tokyo.

When Konoe heard about the decision, he thought that a Koiso cabinet might fail to attract the support of the navy. Therefore on the following day he suggested to Kido that the emperor invest General Koiso and Admiral Yonai together with the task of forming a cabinet. Kido agreed and sent his secretary to secure the consent of the *jūshin*. Yonai accepted the task, but, again only on the condition that he be appointed Navy Minister. Kido and the senior statesmen agreed. Kido then went again to the emperor to modify his previous recommendation and suggest a Koiso–Yonai cabinet, on the model of the Okuma–Itagaki cabinet of 1898. Later that day, the emperor summoned General Koiso, who had just arrived from Korea, and Admiral Yonai. The two men, who were the same age (65), were received together in audience and were asked to form the new cabinet. It was customary on such occasions for the emperor to provide broad guidelines to the new cabinet, and the two guidelines that Hirohito gave to Koiso and Yonai were: observe the constitution, and do not provoke the Soviet Union. This laconic injunction could mean less arbitrary rule at home and a more prudent conduct of the war, but Konoe thought that it was intended as a rebuke to the *Kōdōha*, which had once advocated a suspension of the constitution and war with Russia.[47]

Koiso was a reserve general and therefore ineligible for the post of Army Minister. So the Big Three of the army, current Army Minister Tōjō, Chief of Staff Umezu, and Inspector-General of Military Education Sugiyama, met to select the minister. Tōjō wanted to retain that post, so that he could remain a powerful member in the new cabinet. But Koiso and the other army chiefs would not agree to this, and Tōjō's last attempt to cling to the reins of power failed. It was decided that Field Marshal Sugiyama would be Army Minister, a position he had already held in the Hayashi and first Konoe cabinets. Field Marshal Hata would succeed Sugiyama as Inspector-General of Military Education, a position he had held during the first Konoe cabinet. Since Hata could not be relieved of his post until November, General Noda Kengo would fill in for him until then. As for the navy, Admiral Nomura, who had only recently been appointed Navy Minister, agreed to step down in favour of Admiral Yonai, who was then reinstated on the active list. Navy Chief of Staff Admiral Shimada, who had been associated with Tōjō for a long time, had to resign. He was replaced by Admiral Oikawa Koshirō, who had already served in that post in the second Konoe cabinet.[48] The supreme command was thus again reshuffled, only a few days after Tōjō had carried out his own changes. Field Marshal Sugiyama was therefore Inspector-General of Military Education for only three days, and Admiral Nomura Navy Minister for four days.

All this time the Japanese public knew nothing about what was happening, either in the Pacific or at home. Only on 19 July, twelve days after the event, did the newspapers report the fall of Saipan. The short statement was followed by an announcement by Prime Minister Tōjō, which said in part:

Saipan Island has finally fallen into enemy hands. I deeply regret the anxiety that this event has caused to His Majesty. . . . Our empire has entered the most difficult state in its entire history. But these developments have also provided us with the opportunity to smash the enemy and win the war. The time for decisive battle has arrived.[49]

There was no hint in the announcement that Tōjō was no longer the Prime Minister.

It was only later in that day that the surprised nation heard on the radio of the resignation of the cabinet and the nomination of General Koiso and Admiral Yonai as the architects of a new cabinet. The government tried to play down the significance of the change. The *Nippon Times*, explaining the development to its foreign readers, wrote in its editorial of 22 July:

Whereas a change of cabinets in other countries may mean a change of governmental authority, a change of cabinets in Japan means only a shift in administrative detail. . . . The significance of the present cabinet change cannot be interpreted in terms of the experience of other nations.[50]

The overthrow of Tōjō, the first and almost only orderly change of government among the major belligerent nations in World War II, was achieved smoothly, with no violence, no arrests, and no clashes. Unlike in a dictatorship, in which a deposed leader is often killed or arrested, Tōjō retired into the respectable role of a senior statesman. No one slandered him or blamed him for Japan's misfortunes. Two weeks after their resignation, the emperor gave a farewell luncheon for Tōjō and his ministers at the palace, and praised their 'meritorious services' to the nation. In October 1944 Tōjō went on an official tour of Manchuria and was received by the Manchu emperor. He stayed in Tokyo until the end of the war, offering advice when asked, but otherwise refraining from interference in politics.[51]

The Last Year of the War

The people are disgusted with the military and with
the government, and they do not care any more
about the outcome of the war.

Reserve General Ishiwara Kanji, September 1944

I. GOVERNMENT AND POLITICS UNDER KOISO

Koiso Kuniaki had been away for two years and had little
political experience and no first-hand knowledge of the war.
The son of an ex-*samurai* from Yamagata Prefecture, he had
distinguished himself as a military administrator. During the
plot of 1931 known as the 'March Incident', he was chief of the
Military Affairs Bureau and supported the plotters, but the plot
did not materialize and his career was not hurt. In 1932 he was
selected by Army Minister Araki as his deputy and held that
position for six months. He retired from active service in 1938
and in the following year was appointed Minister for Colonial
Affairs in the Hiranuma cabinet. When Admiral Yonai formed
his cabinet in January 1940, Koiso was again Minister for
Colonial Affairs. In May 1942, when General Minami Jirō
completed his term as Governor-General of Korea, Koiso was
appointed his successor.

General Koiso had no public stature to rely upon. Unlike
Tōjō, he had not arrived at the premiership from an important
cabinet post, and being on the reserve list he could not function
as an army leader. Yet dissatisfaction with Tōjō was so strong
that anyone who had not been associated with the outgoing
cabinet would have been welcomed.

Yonai and Koiso together selected the new ministers, but
once the cabinet was formed Yonai limited himself to the
position of Navy Minister and was thus equal to the new Army
Minister General Sugiyama Hajime, the Chief of Staff at the
time of Pearl Harbor. Two key ministers of the Tōjō cabinet
were retained: Finance Minister Ishiwata Sōtarō and Foreign

Minister Shigemitsu Mamoru. Shigemitsu was also appointed Minister of Great East Asia Affairs, thus actually abolishing the separation of the two ministries, which had prompted the resignation of Tōgō in 1942. The most unusual cabinet appointment was that of Ogata Taketora, vice-president of the *Asahi* newspaper, to the post of State Minister and President of the Information Bureau. Ogata was an outsider, with no previous government experience, and his inclusion was a clear overture to the intellectuals and the media.

As before, the cabinet was a coalition of military leaders, bureaucrats, and politicians. It included three generals (Prime Minister Koiso, Army Minister Sugiyama, and Education Minister Ninomiya), two admirals (Navy Minister Yonai and State Minister Kobayashi), five bureaucrats (Foreign Minister Shigemitsu, Home Minister Ōdachi, Finance Minister Ishiwata, Justice Minister Matsuzaka, and Welfare Minister Hirose), three Diet politicians (Agriculture and Commerce Minister Shimada, Transportation and Communication Minister Maeda, both previously from the *Seiyūkai*; and State Minister Machida, formerly of the *Minseitō*), one aristocrat (State Minister Count Kodama Hideo), one businessman (Munitions Minister Fujihara), and one newspaperman (State Minister Ogata). Most of the ministers were over sixty, the oldest being Machida (81) and the youngest Ōdachi (52). There was nothing particularly impressive about the new cabinet, except the fact that it was new. Since Koiso and some of his top advisers had come from Korea, the cabinet was sometimes dubbed 'the Korean Cabinet'. More often it was nicknamed 'the charcoal-bus cabinet' (*mokutan-basu naikaku*), after the charcoal-powered buses of that time.[1]

Because Koiso could not serve as Army Minister, his main problem was how to control the armed forces. On 4 August 1944 the Imperial Headquarters and Cabinet Liaison Conference, which had become, under Tōjō's premiership, a mere rubber stamp of the military, was abolished and replaced by a Supreme Council for the Direction of the War (*saikō sensō shidō kaigi*). This was a more prestigious and better-defined body, which functioned as a small war cabinet. It was composed of six members: the Prime Minister, the Foreign Minister, the two service ministers, and the two chiefs of staff. Others, like the vice-chiefs of staff and heads of the military and naval affairs bureaux, attended as observers. The Supreme Council met twice a week at the imperial palace and, like its predecessor, became an Imperial Conference (*gozen kaigi*) whenever the emperor attended it. On the whole, it was not much different from the Liaison Conference, and the influence of the Prime Minister over it remained limited.[2]

Unable to control the military, Koiso tried to bolster popular support for his cabinet. In September 1944, he revived the institution of parliamentary vice-ministers (*seimu jikan*), which had been suspended by Konoe in 1940. Twenty-four Diet members were appointed as parliamentary vice-ministers, two for each ministry. Nineteen of them were members of the House of Representatives, and five were members of the House of Peers. The delicate balance between the now defunct political parties was still maintained; of the nineteen parliamentary vice-ministers from the House of Representatives, nine had formerly belonged to the *Minseitō*, eight to the *Seiyūkai*, and two to other parties.

In October of that year, thirteen 'distinguished persons' from outside the government were appointed 'cabinet advisers' (*naikaku komon*). The purpose of these appointments was to demonstrate that the new cabinet was more attuned to the wishes of the people. The editorial of the *Nippon Times* of 2 November echoed this policy: 'The Koiso Cabinet now draws its strength from a far wider and deeper source than any preceding cabinet and . . . is supported by a still fuller representation of the people than ever before.' Yet in reality these were only window-dressing appointments. Neither the parliamentary vice-ministers nor the cabinet advisers had any power to influence the ministries to which they were attached.[3]

Koiso also tried to strengthen his grip on the semi-official mass associations. As Prime Minister, he was ex-officio President of the IRAA, but real power in that organization was wielded by Vice-President Gotō Fumio, a veteran bureaucrat who had been appointed to that post by Tōjō in April 1943. In August 1944, Koiso made Gotō resign, so that he could replace him with his own trusted friend, Ogata Taketora, the new President of the Information Bureau.

In September Koiso recalled another friend, General Tatekawa Yoshitsugu, from his post as Ambassador to Moscow, in order to appoint him President of the Young Men's Corps. The post in Moscow went to a professional diplomat, Satō Naotake. Tatekawa appointed Diet member Colonel Hashimoto Kingorō, leader of the right-wing group *Sekiseikai*, as Director-General of the Corps. The three had already been linked in the March Incident of 1931, when Koiso and Tatekawa were known to have supported Hashimoto's group the *Sakurakai*. The rank and file of the Corps did not like these appointments, which were sharply criticized in the local branches. Bothered by such an independent attitude, Koiso decided to dissolve it and reorganize on a new basis. But even his own appointees, Tatekawa and Hashimoto, were opposed to this far-reaching plan. In January 1945 General Tatekawa resigned and Colonel Hashimoto publicly declared his opposition to the dissolution plan. The Prime Minister preserved and appointed Ogata Taketora as President of the Young Men's Corps. Resentment against Ogata in the Corps was so strong that there was even an attempt on his life, but Koiso and Ogata were not deterred. Despite the support of the army, the Corps could not confront the cabinet, and it was finally dissolved on 30 May 1945.

Tōjō's favourite, Reserve General Abe Nobuyuki, President of IRAPA since its establishment in 1942, also had to resign. Abe, one of the *jūshin* who had selected Koiso, was appointed in July 1944 to succeed Koiso as Governor-General of Korea. State Minister retired Admiral Kobayashi Seizō, who had served as Governor-General of Taiwan until 1940, was appointed as the new President of IRAPA, with Ogata Taketora as his deputy. The concentration of political posts in the hands of Ogata ensured Koiso's control over them.[4]

The new cabinet allowed more freedom of expression than its predecessor. On 8 September 1944 two Diet members, Andō Masazumi and Matsumura Kenzō, attacked the oppressive regulations against speech and publication. In his Diet speech, which the press were not allowed to report, Andō said:

The recent measures against the press, whatever their purpose, have resulted in covering the people's eyes and ears and in shutting their mouths. . . . Newspapers have become dull and the magazines have lost their lively character. Sincere patriotism can no longer be expressed in public speeches or lectures. This policy has damaged morale and weakened the people's willingness to fight.

The measures against which Andō was speaking remained in force, but his speech showed that at least in the Diet one could now voice 'sincere patriotism', even if it conflicted with the official view. This was also evident when Katsura Eiichi attacked the IRAA in the Diet on 2 February 1945.[5]

Koiso's public attitude towards the war was uncompromising. Addressing an Osaka rally on 30 October, he declared: 'If there are any who think to save the Japanese people by a compromise, they are insulting our nation and endangering its existence.' But in private he was trying to arrange some sort of disengagement through the mediation of a third power. According to his memoirs, he planned to send Kuhara Fusanosuke, Matsuoka Yōsuke, or Hirota Kōki, three distinguished statesmen who had met Stalin before, to ask the Soviet leader to mediate. But the Soviet Union remained cool to the idea, and the Japanese military were loath to sue for peace from a position of weakness. The army and navy insisted on first smashing the enemy in a 'decisive battle' (*kessen*), and only after that would a political solution be sought. This planned scenario was similar to that adopted by Japan at the time of the Russo-Japanese War, when after the naval victory at Tsushima she had asked the US to mediate.[6]

The change of cabinets had no impact on the front. The American offensive in the Pacific, like the American advance in Europe, was progressing and gaining momentum. In September, the islands of Guam and Tinian in the Marianas fell, and their garrisons were wiped out. In October, the bulk of the Imperial Navy was destroyed in the Gulf of Leyte in the Philippines, and in December the island of Leyte itself was lost. From November American planes, taking off from airfields in the Mariana islands, were bombing Tokyo and other Japanese cities. The Pacific War had suddenly, shockingly, penetrated into the very heartland of Japan.

Lacking the appropriate aircraft and carriers, the navy embarked on a desperate project of suicide attacks against enemy vessels. Bomb-laden aeroplanes and man-guided torpedoes were now the only weapons that the navy could feverishly throw into the battle. The Special Attack Corps (*tokkōtai*), nicknamed 'Divine Wind' (*kamikaze*, also pronounced *shimpū*), was created in September 1944. In October, the first suicide sorties against American ships in the Philippines were carried out. The heroic accomplishments of the kamikaze were widely reported in Japan. But although thousands of pilots lost their lives in these suicide attacks in the last year of the war, they had little impact on the progress of the Americans. The Divine Wind which had saved Japan from the Mongols in the thirteenth century was no longer blowing.[7]

The government's inability either to stop the enemy or work out a negotiated peace caused deep disenchantment in the imperial palace. On 26 September, four imperial princes with the ranks of General and Field Marshal, Higashikuni, Asaka, Kaya, and Nashimoto, met the emperor's brother, Major Prince Mikasa, and asked him to persuade Hirohito to dismiss the Army Minister. Lord Keeper Kido did not approve of their action and told the princes not to interfere with military appointments. But as the situation grew worse, Kido too became concerned. On 4 January 1945 he told the emperor openly that he was depressed by the navy's débâcle in the 'decisive battle' of Leyte. On 30 January the senior statesmen met and anxiously asked Kido to made sure that the emperor was fully informed about the serious military situation.[8]

It was probably this appeal that made the emperor decide to summon each senior statesman individually and hear his views about the war. This was an unprecedented move, because the only advice the *jūshin* were customarily expected to give concerned the selection of prime ministers, and even that advice was never presented directly, but through the Lord Keeper. Now the emperor wished to listen to the senior statesmen's suggestions on how to terminate the war. Of the eight former prime ministers of that time, only six were summoned, as Yonai was Navy Minister and already in close touch with the emperor, and Abe was in Korea. The senior statesmen were dissatisfied with the situation, but they had no clear plan on how to end the war, and the advice they gave was not co-ordinated. Baron Hiranuma, who was received on 5 February, recommended stepping up the attacks against the enemy and increasing food production. Hirota, who was received on 9

February, favoured Soviet mediation, but only after Japan had inflicted heavy blows on the enemy. Prince Konoe, who was received on the 14th, was the only one who presented a comprehensive and detailed recommendation. In a long memorial to the throne, he outlined his pet theory that there were hidden communists in the army and the bureaucracy who were waiting for a national disaster in order to carry out a revolution. His conclusion was that only a prompt termination of hostilities could save Japan from that danger. The senior statesmen who followed Konoe repeated the prevalent views of that time. Wakatsuki said that it was vital to prevent the enemy from setting foot on Japanese soil. Okada shared Hirota's opinion that Japan should inflict a heavy blow on the enemy and then start negotiating for peace. Tōjō, the newest of the *jūshin*, was received on 26 February and voiced the army's view, that Japan should continue to fight with full determination, in order to deter the Russians from entering the war and to persuade the Americans to negotiate an honourable peace.[9] There were no immediate results from the meetings with the senior statesmen, but they helped to impress on the emperor the urgent need for peace.

Meanwhile, the military and the government were frantically preparing for the impending American invasion, which would trigger the 'decisive battle for the homeland' (*hondo kessen*). At that gigantic battle, the enemy was to be cut off from his supply lines and destroyed by suicide attacks and guerrilla tactics, in which the whole population would take part. To conduct such an immense operation, vast administrative reforms were needed. Koiso wanted the cabinet and the Imperial Headquarters to merge into one solid body, which would both control the population and command the troops, and in which he would play the dominant role as Prime Minister and Army Minister. But the army leaders refused to share their prerogative of command with civilians, and objected to the reinstatement of Koiso on the active list, so that he could be Army Minister. The Army Chief of Staff General Umezu suggested instead that the army and the navy be merged into one fighting service, in order to make better use of the limited resources. But Navy Minister Yonai objected to this plan, fearing that it would mean the end of the navy. Consequently, no military reforms were carried out until the end of the war, and the only change that both services agreed upon was to allow the Prime Minister to attend the meetings at the Imperial Headquarters. By joining this body in March 1945, Koiso could get a better over-all picture of the war situation, although he could not achieve greater control over the military.[10]

It was easier to change the civilian organizations. On 30 March the IRAPA was dissolved and replaced by the Great Japan Political Association (GJPA, *Dai Nihon seijikai*) which was to serve as a political party on the totalitarian model. The president of the new party, seventy-one-year-old General Minami Jirō, stressed the independent character of the new body. Speaking at a press conference, he said:

We will not place ourselves under the thumb of the government. We may be depended upon to act with determination in forcing upon the cabinet the wishes of the people. The same thing may be said of our attitude towards the military. To co-operate with the military will not mean our doing its bidding. . . . From time to time it will be necessary for us to advise the military or cause it to reflect.[11]

Despite these high-sounding promises, the GJPA did not develop into a genuinely independent party but remained, like its predecessors, subservient to the government.

The creation of the new party changed the political composition of the Diet, in which until then only one political organization had existed, the IRAPA. Of the 466 members of the House of Representatives, only 376 joined the GJPA. The others declared themselves independents or set up new parliamentary groups. Hashimoto Kingorō, whose Young Men's Corps had just been dissolved, formed a new group, the *Gokoku dōshikai* (Patriotic Society for Defending the Country) which attracted thirty-one Diet members. Twenty others formed the *Yokusō giin dōshikai* (Young Men's Corps Diet Members' Association), which tried to preserve the name of the defunct organization.[12]

These political developments were overshadowed by unremitting enemy attacks on all fronts. On 3 March Manila fell to the Americans after bitter fighting. On the 16th, the strategic island of Io (Iwo Jima) in the Bonins was lost, after a fierce battle in which almost 20,000 Japanese soldiers were killed. The air raids on Japan also intensified. On the night of 9–10 March, as the authorities were preparing to celebrate Army Day (*rikugun kinenbi*), 130 American bombers raided Tokyo in the worst air attack the capital had ever known. Most of the city was on fire; the centre was razed, and nearly 80,000 people lost their lives. The emperor, whose first grandchild was born that very night, was greatly affected by the extent of the destruction. On 18 March he went out personally to inspect the worst-hit areas. Accompanied by Marquis Kido and Grand Chamberlain Reserve Admiral Fujita Hisanori, he walked through the ruins and saw with his own eyes the devastation that the war was causing Japan. This first-hand experience no doubt contributed to his growing realization that the war had to be stopped as quickly as possible.[13]

The enemy with whom a negotiated peace seemed easiest to arrange was China, because on this front the Japanese still had a military advantage. Koiso contemplated a process of peace which would start in China and then, with the aid of the Chinese mediation, spread to the other fronts. In mid-March a secret agent of Chiang Kai-shek, Miao Pin, arrived in Tokyo and proposed a peace plan, based on total Japanese withdrawal from China. Koiso supported the plan, as did State Minister Ogata who had helped to arrange Miao's mission, and Prince Higashikuni who had met with the envoy for a long talk. But the plan was vetoed by the military, as well as by Foreign Minister Shigemitsu, who objected to the 'sell-out' of Japan's puppet regime in Nanking.[14]

Unable to impose his view on the military or to initiate peace negotiations with China, Koiso realized that he could not continue as Prime Minister. His position was further weakened by the military and diplomatic setbacks. On 1 April the Americans landed on Okinawa, not yet part of the 'homeland' (*hondo*), but already a Japanese prefecture. On 5 April the Soviet Union made the ominous announcement that it would not renew its neutrality pact with Japan when it expired in April 1946. On that very day Koiso tendered his resignation to the emperor, after only eight and a half months in office.[15]

There was nothing unusual about Koiso's resignation. By stepping down from office when he could neither carry out his policies nor gain the support of his peers and the court, he acted as his predecessors had done before him. The only difference was that his resignation took effect in the midst of all-out war, and on the eve of an enemy invasion. The fact that he could resign without causing any rift or disruption in the government, and without being punished or vilified, demonstrates again the remarkable stability of the political system of Japan even in time of war.

2. SUZUKI AND THE END OF THE WAR

A few hours after Koiso tendered his resignation, the *jūshin* were summoned to the palace to select a successor. All the six senior statesmen who had been received in audience in February were present, as well as Lord Keeper Kido and the seventy-eight-year-old President of the Privy Council Admiral Baron Suzuki Kantarō. Kido opened the conference by describing the difficult situation confronting Japan, and emphasizing that the people were disappointed not only with the government but also with the military. He did not talk about policy, but advised the participants to select a person who could regain the trust of the nation. It the discussion that followed, both Tōjō and Okada suggested that the man selected must be someone who could bring the war to an end.

Where could such a person be found? Admiral Suzuki claimed that at a grave time, when people were losing confidence in the military, only a civilian prime minister could restore the public trust. He therefore proposed that Prince Konoe, the youngest and most prestigious of the *jūshin*, be nominated to that post. Konoe declined the nomination, arguing that in time of war the country should be led by a military man. Suzuki disagreed and pointed out that during the First Sino-Japanese War Japan was led by a civilian prime minister, Prince Itō Hirobumi. He emphasized that it was better to have a civilian directing the war than to have a military man meddling in politics. History had proved, he said, that whenever the military tried to run the state, the state was doomed: 'This has occurred at the fall of Rome, at the collapse of the Kaiser, and at the downfall of the Romanovs.' The others were not convinced. After long deliberation Baron Hiranuma proposed that the next prime minister should combine the attributes of a military leader with those of a civilian statesman. He pointed out that the only man who fulfilled these conditions was Baron Suzuki, who had distinguished himself as a naval commander and then achieved fame as a palace statesman. Kido and Okada, who had earlier agreed that Suzuki was the best choice, supported Hiranuma's proposal.

But Suzuki was a naval officer and his nomination could be regarded, with good reason, as an expression of no confidence in the army which had provided the previous wartime prime ministers. Tōjō, the only army officer among the assembled *jūshin*, therefore proposed the candidacy of Field Marshal Hata Shun'roku, warning that the army might not co-operate with a man whom it did not trust. This open threat infuriated Marquis Kido, who replied that the question was not if the army would co-operate with the cabinet, but rather if the people would endure the army for much longer. Kido's blunt words silenced Tōjō. In the confrontation between the Reserve General and the emperor's official, the latter proved to be stronger. Suzuki was unanimously approved as the recommended candidate, and that evening the emperor summoned Suzuki and requested that he form a new cabinet.[16]

It would have been easy for the army to prevent Suzuki from forming a cabinet by simply refusing to nominate an Army Minister. But such a refusal could have caused a political crisis which nobody wanted. It also happened that Suzuki's candidate for the post of Army Minister, General Anami Korechika, had been a personal friend of Suzuki since the late 1920s, when both had served at the imperial palace, Suzuki as Grand Chamberlain and Anami as a military aide-de-camp. Consequently, the army leaders reluctantly accepted Anami's view that Suzuki could be trusted, but they insisted on three conditions before agreeing to co-operate with him: (1) that the cabinet carry on the war vigorously, (2) that the cabinet continue preparations for the final battle, and (3) that the cabinet work out a better formula for co-operation between the army and the navy. Suzuki agreed to these terms, and Anami was designated Army Minister. Admiral Yonai remained Navy Minister. The army and navy also agreed that the new Prime Minister, like his predecessor, should attend the meetings of the Imperial Headquarters.[17]

The cabinet that Baron Suzuki presented to the emperor on 7 April included, for the first time since the outbreak of the war, more officers from the navy than from the army. It had four admirals (Prime Minister Suzuki, Navy Minister Yonai, Munitions Minister Toyoda, and State Minister Sakonji), as compared to only two generals (Army Minister Anami and State Minister Yasui). In addition, Chief Cabinet Secretary Sakomizu Hisatsune was the son-in-law of Admiral Okada, and Okada helped Suzuki in selecting the cabinet members. Three of the new cabinet members had played important roles during the 26 February Incident of 1936. Baron Suzuki himself, who was then Grand Chamberlain, had been shot by the rebels as one of the 'villains around the throne', and left bleeding when his wife had pleaded with the rebels to let her give him the *coup de grâce*. General Yasui Tōji had been the Chief of Staff of the Martial Law Headquarters that suppressed the rebellion, and Sakomizu had rescued his father-in-law Prime Minister Okada after the rebels had thought that he was dead.

Like previous prime ministers, Suzuki invited leaders from both former major parties to join his cabinet. He appointed Diet member Okada Tadahiko, formerly of the *Seiyūkai*, as Welfare Minister; and Diet member Sakurai Hyōgorō, formerly of the *Minseitō*, as State Minister. The intellectuals and the media were represented by Dr Shimomura Hiroshi, a writer, former vice-editor of the *Asahi* newspaper and later president of the broadcasting service (NHK), who replaced Ogata Taketora as State Minister and president of the Information Bureau.

Suzuki's choice for the post of Foreign Minister was Tōgō Shigenori, who had left the Tōjō cabinet in 1942 in protest over the establishment of the Great East Asia Ministry. Tōgō had an intimate knowledge of the Soviet Union (where he had been Ambassador at the time of the outbreak of World War II in Europe) and had maintained an independent position *vis-à-vis* the army. Suzuki summoned Tōgō from Karuizawa, where he and his German wife had found refuge from the bombs, and offered him the post of Foreign Minister. Tōgō first wanted to know Suzuki's views about the prospects of the war. When the Prime Minister told him that the war might drag on for a few more years, Tōgō declined the offer, claiming that in his view it should end in less than a year. So when Suzuki presented his cabinet to the emperor on 7 April he himself was also holding the portfolio of Foreign Minister. Only after Admiral Okada, Chief Cabinet Secretary Sakomizu, and other influential people promised Tōgō that he would have a free hand in conducting foreign affairs, did he agree to join the cabinet; and on 9 April he was appointed Foreign Minister and Minister of Great East Asia affairs.[18]

The seventy-eight-year-old Suzuki was not exactly the inspiring figure who could lead the nation into heroic battle against the approaching enemy. Advanced in age, half deaf, and often drowsy, he resembled the old prewar prime ministers more than wartime leaders like Tōjō or Koiso. But Suzuki's age was also an advantage, because he could appear as a grand-fatherly figure, above personal ambitions. The newspapers compared him with Georges Clemenceau, who at the age of seventy-six had assumed the post of premier of France and led his country to victory in World War I.[19]

Suzuki's advantage over Koiso was his close relationship with the emperor. When he retired from the navy in 1929, Suzuki had been appointed Grand Chamberlain. In 1936, after recuperating from his wounds, he joined the Privy Council and in August 1944 he succeeded Baron Hara Yoshimichi as President of the Council. Suzuki's wife, Taka, had been Hirohito's nurse. The trust and affection which the emperor held for Suzuki was to prove of great value in the following months.

Suzuki's public attitude to the war was not an optimistic one. In a radio address to the nation upon assuming office, he declared:

The current war . . . has entered a serious stage in which no optimism whatsoever is permissible. It is truly a matter of intense shame for us that despite the continuous noble sacrifices on the front and the courageous efforts at home, the enemy has seized a corner of our homeland. It must be said that if the situation continues to develop in this manner, the existence of our empire will be in danger.

But he assured his listeners that if the people did their utmost and were determined to fight until death, the enemy would ultimately be destroyed.[20]

One week after Suzuki's inauguration, President Roosevelt died. Hitler immediately expressed his joy over the demise of 'the greatest war criminal of history', but Suzuki's reaction was surprisingly mild. Talking to a *Dōmei* correspondent, he expressed his 'profound sympathy' to the American people over the loss of their 'effective' leader.[21]

Suzuki's personality and views were disliked by those who still believed in a military victory. General Tōjō admitted to newspaperman Takamiya Tahei privately in April 1945: 'This is the end. This is our Badoglio Cabinet.' Colonel Inaba Masao of the General Staff revealed after the war that many army officers had regarded the Suzuki cabinet as a coalition of naval officers and senior statesmen, determined to follow in the steps of the Italian Badoglio and surrender. But despite these gloomy feelings, the army made no attempt to overthrow the cabinet or undermine its position.[22]

The massive American air raids on Tokyo and other Japanese cities continued throughout the spring and summer of 1945, but the evacuation of children and old people from the big cities to the countryside was slow and only partially effective. By the end of July, 188,310 people had died in air raids, a quarter of a million had been wounded, and about nine million were homeless. The newspapers, concealing the number of casualties, reported that the population was reacting stoically to the air raids, but a secret document adopted by the Imperial Conference on 8 June admitted that a decline in public morale had indeed occurred.[23]

The intensive bombing of the capital posed a grave danger to the emperor and his family. As early as July 1944, the army had proposed that the emperor move to a safe place outside the capital, but Hirohito refused, claiming that such a step would be a blow to the people's morale. In April 1945 the pupils of the Gakushūin School, including twelve-year-old Crown Prince Akihito, were evacuated to Shizuoka Prefecture. Beneath the imperial palace, an elaborate air-raid shelter was constructed, in which the emperor, his family, and the palace officials stayed during the raids, and in which the most important Imperial Conferences took place. In the case of an American invasion, the emperor, the government, and the Imperial Headquarters were to be transferred to an underground post near Matsushiro, Nagano Prefecture, where 30,000 workers were completing Japan's largest tunnel.[24]

Although the American pilots had orders not to destroy the imperial palace, it was impossible to prevent stray bombs or fires from reaching the palace. The first bombs fell in its grounds during the raid of 25 February, but caused little damage. On 13 April more bombs fell and one of the palace wings caught fire—but this was quickly extinguished. However, on 25 May when incendiary bombs were falling in the vicinity a strong wind carried the flames across the moat and many of the palace buildings caught fire. Despite the strenuous efforts of the firemen, half the buildings were burnt down before the flames were finally put out. In normal times such a disgrace would have brought down the cabinet, but as the times were far from normal, only Army Minister Anami and Imperial Household Minister Matsudaira Tsuneo tendered their resignations. The emperor refused to accept Anami's resignation, but Matsudaira's was accepted. The former diplomat and father-in-law of the emperor's brother Prince Chichibu was replaced by Ishiwata Sōtarō, the former Finance Minister.[25]

As Suzuki had promised, preparations for the 'final battle' were continued and intensified. On the day that the new cabinet was formed, Imperial Headquarters announced the establishment of three independent army commands (*sōgun shireibu*): The north and east of Japan, down to Suzuka Pass in Mie Prefecture, were entrusted to the First Army, under the command of Field Marshal Sugiyama, with headquarters in Tokyo. The south and west were the domain of the Second Army, under the command of Field Marshal Hata, with headquarters in Hiroshima. A separate air command was set up under General Kawabe Masakazu. Civilian administration was also decentralized: the country was divided into eight regional headquarters (*chihō sōkanbu*), each under a governor-general, which could act independently in time of emergency. The regional capitals were located in Sapporo, Sendai, Tokyo, Nagoya, Osaka, Hiroshima, Takamatsu, and Fukuoka.[26]

Able-bodied adults of both sexes were to be organized in a militia to assist the military in fighting the invaders. The new organization, called the People's Volunteer Fighting Corps (*Kokumin giyūtai*) was set up on 13 April and started training the population in guerrilla tactics. The 87th extraordinary session of the Diet, which convened on 12 June, passed a law obliging all males between the ages of fifteen and sixty, and all females between the ages of seventeen and forty, to join the corps. However, the Fighting Corps was not a branch of the army; it remained under the control of local governors and its

Commander-in-Chief was the Prime Minister. It was also to replace all other organizations. On 13 June the IRAA, the Great Japan Women's Association, the Great Japan Industrial Patriotic Association, and similar organizations, were all dissolved and their members incorporated into the *Kokumin giyūtai*. The IRAA, set up five years earlier amid great expectations, thus passed away without a stir.[27]

Deploying the whole population in the approaching battle for the homeland required powers which the wartime government of Japan did not possess. The simplest way to acquire such powers was by declaring martial law, because that would enable the authorities to waive legal procedures. Article 31 of the constitution allowed the emperor to proclaim martial law in times of war or national emergency. This had been done five times in the past: during the First Sino-Japanese War in the city of Hiroshima and the port of Ujima; during the Russo-Japanese War in the ports of Nagasaki and Hakodate; during the Hibiya riots of 1905 in Tokyo; during the Great Kantō Earthquake in Tokyo and Yokohama; and during the 26 February Incident in Tokyo.[28]

None of the above-mentioned cases was as serious as the situation that confronted Japan in the summer of 1945. Nevertheless martial law was not declared, and the government preferred to embark on the more cumbersome procedure of passing laws through the Diet. One reason for that was that none of the leading élites wanted the others to gain more power. The civilians and the navy were opposed to the strengthening of the army, and the army refused to delegate any of its powers to civilians or to the navy. The authorities could only hope that the legislative procedure would yield the same results as a declaration of martial law.

Consequently, on 12 June the Diet passed a Wartime Emergency Measure Bill (*senji kinkyū sochi-hō*) which authorized the government to take all necessary measures to ensure military production, supply of foodstuffs, transport, payment of taxes, and care for the victims of air raids. The original draft required the government to 'report' on the use of these powers to a special Diet committee. But the House of Peers amended the bill, requiring the government to 'consult' the Diet committee, rather than merely 'report' to it.[29] Thus, even under the most extreme circumstances, the Diet was eager to retain the last vestiges of its power.

Commenting on the new law, the editorial of the *Nippon Times* on 14 June said:

The simplest short-cut to the exercise of emergency powers, and one which would be free from all questions as to constitutionality, would have been to invoke Article 31 of the constitution. . . . Indeed the invocation of this article of the constitution had been urged in certain quarters including some sections of the Diet itself. But the government chose instead to ask for emergency powers through a legislative authorization from the Diet, which can only mean that the government sought to associate the people in partnership with it in the assumption of emergency powers, rather than to impose the exercise of these powers from above.

On 25 June, when the new law was proclaimed, the newspaper returned to the subject in its editorial:

All these provisions regulating the conduct of the government in the execution of the Emergency Measure Law make it clear that even under the unusual conditions of wartime, the government of Japan scrupulously avoids becoming a dictatorship.[30]

The vast preparations for the final battle were not accompanied by mass arrests of potential trouble-makers, although some people suspected of anti-war opinions were detained. On 15 April a number of Prince Konoe's advisers were arrested on charges of spreading 'defeatist rumours'. This was a futile attempt by the army to suppress the 'peace group' of which Konoe was the leading figure. Among those arrested were former Ambassador to Britain Yoshida Shigeru (the future Prime Minister), former Attorney-General Ueda Shun'kichi, and the disgraced commentators Baba Tsunego and Iwabuchi Tatsuo. Yoshida was questioned about Konoe's memorial to the throne, which he had helped to formulate and which had called for an immediate peace; but after a month and a half in prison he was released. None of the leaders of the peace movement were arrested. The lot of all prisoners in the last year of the war was one of great suffering, and hundreds died of malnutrition and sickness. During the air raids, the warders would sometimes unlock the doors of the cells of ordinary prisoners, but political prisoners were not granted that privilege and many of them perished in their cells.[31]

Despite his public insistence that Japan should fight until the end, Suzuki was making secret efforts to bring the war to a speedy end. His initial step was taken on 22 June when the emperor, addressing the Supreme Council for the Direction of the War, called on its members 'to give immediate and detailed thought to the ways of ending the war, notwithstanding hitherto accepted concepts'.[32] Although this was only an 'advice' and did not rule out the preparations being made for the 'final battle for the home islands', it nevertheless signalled the new government line of trying to end the war speedily before it would be too late. Yet it was Prime Minister Suzuki himself who, blindly trusting the much-expected mediation by the Soviet Union, made the careless public remark that Japan would 'ignore' (*mokusatsu*) the Potsdam Declaration issued on 26 July by the Presidents of China and the US, and the Prime Minister of Britain in which Japan was called upon to surrender unconditionally or face destruction. This remark provided President Truman with the needed pretext for dropping the first atomic bomb on Japan.

Following the atomic bombings and the Russian invasion, both the military and the civilian leaders were ready to end the war, that is surrender, according to the terms of the Potsdam Declaration as they interpreted it. The dispute was whether to ask for clarifications and make the Japanese interpretations a condition for surrender, or to surrender first and then try to make the best of it. The army leaders claimed that Japan still possessed a strong fighting power, which could be used to obtain assurances that, when she surrendered, her integrity would be preserved, the imperial institution maintained, and that she would be allowed to disarm by herself and try her own war criminals. The civilians were afraid that any stalling would invite further and unprecedented destruction, and demanded prompt surrender upon the 'understanding' that the imperial institution would be preserved. At the Supreme Council which met on 9 August to decide the issue, the views were evenly divided, with the Army Minister and the two chiefs of staff demanding the former course of action, and the Prime Minister, Foreign Minister, and Navy Minister demanding the latter.[33]

Under normal conditions such a deadlock would lead to further consultations or, if they proved futile, bring about the resignation of the cabinet. But the perilous circumstances which prevailed during the second week of August 1945 did not allow for normal procedures. It was necessary to break the deadlock quickly, and only the emperor had the power to do so.

Hirohito had occasionally expressed his opinions at meetings with senior officials and on the investiture of new prime ministers, but his views were formulated in general terms and were of an exhortative nature. At no time had the emperor been called upon to decide between conflicting views, and his advisers had always been careful not to involve him in controversial issues. However, in the summer of 1945 the feeling at the palace that the emperor should use his prestige in favour of ending the war was growing. Lord Keeper Kido, who until then had been anxious to preserve the detached position of the emperor, saw no other way out. On 8 June he submitted a memorial to the throne, in which he recommended a 'courageous imperial decision' (*goyūdan*) to save Japan from total destruction. He advised that the emperor issue an order to the armed forces to cease fire, and to the Foreign Ministry to start immediate peace negotiations.[34] Such a dramatic step was not taken, but when the Imperial Conference reached its stalemate, recourse to an imperial decision became inevitable.

Prime Minister Suzuki knew Hirohito's views about the war. According to Abe Genki, who was then Home Minister, there existed a deep understanding (*ishin denshin*) between the two men, so that Suzuki could be sure that when he turned to the emperor for a decision, the reply would be in favour of peace.[35] Consequently when the Imperial Conference met on the night of 9 August, and after both sides had stated their opposing views, the Prime Minister rose and declared that the government should seek advice from the emperor. Hirohito, who had probably been warned in advance that this would happen, expressed himself clearly in favour of the Prime Minister's view. The chiefs of staff and the Army Minister, who had oppposed that policy until that moment, bowed to the 'sacred decision' (*seidan*) and accepted it.

Five days later, on the night of 14 August, the same body found itself deadlocked again. The Americans had given a

vague response to Japan's offer to surrender on the understanding that the emperor's status would not be hurt. It stated
that the authority of the emperor and the government of Japan
would be subject to the Supreme Commander of the Allied
Powers and that the ultimate form of government would be
decided by the freely expressed will of the people. The Army
Minister and the two chiefs of staff found that response unsatis-
factory and demanded further clarifications, while the other
three members favoured immediate surrender on those terms.
Once again Suzuki had to turn to the emperor for a decision to
break the stalemate, and once again Hirohito supported the
Prime Minister's view.[36]

The readiness of the military leaders to abide by the
emperor's decision shows that their loyalty to the state and its
constitutional authorities was stronger than their fanaticism
about the war. Unconditional surrender meant for them utter
humiliation and retribution at the hands of the enemy, but
defiance of the imperial decision was unthinkable. It was better
to surrender as a united nation than to continue fighting as a
divided one.

On 15 August the emperor, in yet another unprecedented
move decided on by the cabinet, addressed the nation on the
radio. In his recorded speech, Hirohito praised the ideals for
which Japan had gone to war, hailed the courage of the fallen
soldiers and sailors, but blamed no one for the tragedy that had
befallen the nation. He explained that he had decided to accept
the terms of the Allied declaration because of the changing
world circumstances (that is, the defeat of Germany and the
entry of Russia into the war) and the deployment of a new and
cruel bomb by the enemy, which endangered not only the
existence of Japan but the existence of all mankind. Repeating
his grandfather's admonition at the time of the Triple Intervention, Hirohito called on his people 'to endure what is difficult to
endure, and to suffer what is difficult to suffer' (*taegataki o tae,
shinobigataki o shinobi*).[37]

There were some sporadic disturbances before and after the
imperial speech. On the night of the 14th a group of middle-
ranking officers killed the Commander of the Imperial Guards
Division, forged orders, and deployed a contingent of that
division to seal off the palace. But their attempts to destroy the

disc on which the emperor's speech was recorded before it was broadcast failed, and by the morning of 15 August the rebellion had been suppressed and the ringleaders committed suicide. A few other fanatics attacked the residences of the Prime Minister and the Lord Keeper, but both were then at the palace and were not hurt. During the following days, some naval airmen dropped leaflets on Tokyo demanding continuation of the war, and some groups tried to seize public installations in Tokyo. But these were all small-scale outbursts and they were quickly suppressed. There was no serious attempt to overthrow the government, and no senior officer did anything to jeopardize the decision to surrender.[38]

Following their leaders, the rank and file of the armed forces accepted the 'sacred decision' obediently. By August 1945 the imperial army had 5.4 million men in uniform, of which 2.1 million were stationed in Japan. The navy had 1.8 million men, including about 2,000 kamikaze pilots resolved to die for Japan. There were about a quarter of a million officers in the army, and about a third of that in the navy.[39] These men had been educated for years to prefer death to surrender, and their comrades had done so time after time at the front. Now they were told to lay down their arms and meekly surrender, and they obeyed. The huge war machine, heading full-steam towards the final battle, was halted on the spot without overturning. The image of the fanatical and insubordinate Japanese officer, manipulating his superiors towards national disaster, turned out at the last moment to be a gross exaggeration.

Those who could not bear the shame took the path of honour as prescribed by the warrior tradition. Army Minister Anami (whose son had been killed in action), Field Marshal Sugiyama, the founder of the kamikaze corps Vice-Admiral Ōnishi Takijirō, and others, committed suicide. But the great majority of the military leaders preferred to stay alive, despite the humiliating prospects.[40]

On the afternoon of 15 August Prime Minister Suzuki submitted his resignation, assuming responsibility for Japan's surrender and for having troubled the emperor with controversial issues. Suzuki had also realized that a man with greater prestige than his would be needed to implement the surrender. This time the *jūshin* were not summoned. Kido might have been afraid that the senior statesmen, among whom there were now two generals (Tōjō and Koiso), might not be co-operative. Consulting only the President of the Privy Council, Baron Hiranuma, he recommended the emperor's uncle, General Prince Higashikuni. The prince's name had already been mentioned many times in the past, but Kido had until then opposed the candidacy on the grounds that an imperial prince should not be involved in politics. This time, however, it was urgently necessary to use the prestige of the imperial family to give legitimacy to the surrender process. Higashikuni accepted the nomination and received the emperor's mandate to form a cabinet. His chief adviser was Prince Konoe, who joined the cabinet as a State Minister. It was the first time in modern Japanese history that an imperial prince had become a Prime Minister.[41]

The Higashikuni cabinet was composed in a way that would please the Americans. Admiral Yonai, who had favoured peace, remained Navy Minister; General Shimomura Sadamu, Commander of the North China Expeditionary Army, who had not been involved in hostilities with the Americans, became Army Minister; Shigemitsu Mamoru, who had served as Ambassador to Great Britain before the war, replaced Foreign Minister Tōgō; the journalist Ogata Taketora was again State Minister and president of the Information Bureau, and this time he was also Chief Cabinet Secretary. The other State Ministers were Prince Konoe and the former *Kōdōha* general Obata Binshirō. Two ministries, those of Great East Asia Affairs and Munitions, were abolished.[42]

The new cabinet issued several imperial edicts to the armed forces, ordering them to lay down their arms. The edicts were carried to the fronts by members of the imperial family. Major-General Prince Kan'in Haruhito, son of the former Chief of Staff Field Marshal Prince Kan'in Kotohito (who had died in May 1945), was dispatched to Saigon and Singapore. Higashikuni's brother General Prince Asaka Yasuhiko was sent to Peking and Nanking. Hirohito's cousin Colonel Prince Takeda Tsuneyoshi went to Manchuria. When a group of disgruntled naval airmen threatened to prevent the landing of General Douglas McArthur at the Atsugi airfield near Tokyo, the emperor's brother Navy Captain Prince Takamatsu was sent to pacify them.[43]

Japan was once again preparing for the Americans, but this time they were awaited as the accepted conquerors rather than as the hostile invaders. The country was in ruins and the people impoverished and in a state of shock, but the political framework had not fallen apart as many had feared it would.

The Wartime Press

It is best to inform the people of the news that does
not cause disturbance.
President of the Information Bureau Amō Eiji,
May 1943

I. REPORTING THE WAR

On the eve of the Pacific War Japan possessed one of the most
sophisticated mass media networks in the world. Books, magazines, and newspapers were printed by the million, distributed
to every corner of the country, and read by an inquisitive and
literate public. The national broadcasting service (NHK)
reached about half the population with programmes of information, education, and entertainment. Newsreels, speeches,
exhibitions, and posters carried the official message to all strata
of society. The most highly developed medium was the press,
which reached a daily circulation of about nineteen million
copies, an average of more than one newspaper per household.
The press was divided into the large national newspapers,
which appeared seven days a week twice daily, and the smaller
or local newspapers. The national newspapers had a total
circulation of about seven million copies a day and catered for
all classes. The largest one was the *Asahi shimbun*, which had a
daily circulation of two and a half million copies. Next in
prestige and circulation were the *Mainichi shimbun* of Osaka and
its sister newspaper the *Nichi nichi shimbun* of Tokyo, which
together sold nearly two and a half million copies a day. The
third in rank was the *Yomiuri shimbun* which had a daily circulation of more than one million copies. Four other newspapers,
the *Hōchi shimbun*, *Kokumin shimbun*, *Miyako shimbun*, and *Chūgai
shōgyō shimpō*, had a combined circulation of about one million.
Production of newspapers was highly developed. The
national newspapers employed hundreds of reporters, in Japan
and overseas, who transmitted their reports by telegraph and

telephone. The large national newspapers issued regional editions and were printed simultaneously in different parts of the country. Some newspapers even operated their own aeroplanes for instant coverage and long-distance deliveries. Extra editions (*gōgai*) were printed whenever something important happened, and were sold, or, as in Osaka, distributed freely in the streets. But most readers received their newspapers through home delivery, and subscription fees ranged around 1 yen (23 US cents) per month.[1]

In 1940, the government started encouraging the newspapers to amalgamate in order to facilitate control and save newsprint. In September 1940 the Tokyo and Osaka branches of the *Asahi shimbun* were combined; in January 1943, the Tokyo *Nichi nichi* and the Osaka *Mainichi* merged into the *Mainichi shumbun*; in 1942, the *Yomiuri* and *Hōchi* became the *Yomiuri-Hōchi*, the *Miyako* and *Kokumin* became the *Tōkyō shimbun*, and the economic newspapers *Chūgai shōgyō shimpō*, *Nikkan kōgyō*, and *Keizai jiji* were amalgamated into the *Nippon sangyō keizai*. The Osaka economic newspapers were combined to create the *Sangyō keizai*.

In October 1942 the government decided to reduce further the number of local newspapers by limiting each prefecture to one local newspaper only. This forced the provincial dailies to amalgamate in order not to disappear. As a result, the total number of newspapers dropped from 848 before the war to 54 in 1943. These local amalgamations did not affect the circulation of the national newspapers; indeed, their readership increased as people switched from local newspapers to the national ones which gave more comprehensive coverage of the war. Thus, the circulation of the *Asahi*, *Mainichi*, and *Yomiuri-Hōchi* rose slightly during the war, while the circulation of local newspapers dropped by one half, from about 12 million before the war to about 6 million in 1944. Competition among newspapers, which had been fierce before the war, was curbed in December 1941 when the government ordered the national newspapers to set up a joint distribution company. The company divided the profits according to the newspapers' share of total circulation at that time.[2]

Unlike totalitarian countries, there were no government or party newspapers in Japan, and all the major newspapers were private non-partisan enterprises. There had always been intricate links between the press and the political and economic élites of Japan, but the prewar newspapers felt free to attack individual politicians and expose cases of corruption. On basic issues such as foreign relations, the prewar newspapers tended to support the official attitudes, and thus helped to create a public consensus in favour of government policy. The outbreak of war with China, and later with the US and Britain, accelerated this process by which the press, and public opinion, united behind the nation-in-arms against the hostile West.

The wartime government expected the newspapers to demonstrate loyalty by exercising their own self-control, but it did not fully trust them. Since the Meiji Restoration there had been laws which empowered the authorities to censor newspapers or to close them down. Among these were the Newspaper Ordinance (*shimbunshi jōrei*) of 1875, the Publication Law (*shuppanhō*) of 1893, the Newspaper Laws (*shimbunshihō*) of 1885 and 1909, the Military Secrets Protection Law (*gunki hogohō*) of 1899, and the Peace Preservation Law (*chian ijihō*) of 1925.

Following the outbreak of the China War, controls over the press were tightened. In 1937 all items concerning national economy and foreign relations were designated as state secrets that could not be published without the prior consent of the authorities. The Newspaper and Publication Control Ordinance (*shimbunshi-tō keisei seigenrei*) of January 1941 authorized the government to issue guidelines to newspapers and to punish them if they failed to abide by them. In March 1941 the National Security Law (*kokubō hoanhō*) imposed severe penalties for the revelation of any information which could help Japan's enemies. On 19 December, eleven days after the outbreak of the Pacific War, the Diet passed the Press, Publication, Assembly, and Association Special Control Law (*genron, shuppan, shūkai, kessha-tō rinji torishimarihō*) which banned all unauthorized publications, assemblies or organizations.[3]

Censorship of newspapers was handled by several government departments. Items related to military affairs had to be cleared in advance with the press sections of the army or the navy, while those having to do with international affairs required the approval of the Foreign Ministry or the Ministry of Great East Asia. The rest fell under the jurisdiction of the

Censorship Department (*Ken'etsu-ka*) of the Home Ministry's Police Bureau (*naimushō keihokyoku*), which supervised newspapers, magazines, books, films, records, and even toys. But this department, which was staffed by only twelve people, could not read all the diverse materials published in Japan, and had to rely on the self-discipline of publishers as well as on the vigilance of other government agencies. In 1943, for instance, about 90,000 newspaper items were submitted for prior clearance to the various censorship agencies. Of these, about 12,000 items, or 13 per cent, were banned. The collaboration of newspapers with the censorship authorities was usually smooth and there was seldom a need to admonish or punish a newspaper. Consequently no major newspaper was shut down during the war and no editor of a major daily newspaper was arrested or prosecuted.

Barring unwanted news was one side of the coin; disseminating 'positive' information and commentaries was the other side of it. In January 1936 the semi-official news agency *Dōmei* was established by the amalgamation of two private agencies. In September 1937, following the outbreak of war with China, the government set up the Cabinet Information Office (*naikaku jōhōbu*), which in December was elevated into the Cabinet Information Bureau (*naikaku jōhōkyoku*). The Bureau was headed by a president (*sōsai*) responsible directly to the Prime Minister; its staff of about 600 men included military officers on active duty and officials from the Home and Foreign Ministries. The Bureau was responsible for public information, guidance of the media, and overseas propaganda. It instructed editors on what should be printed, how the news should be presented, and who could interpret it. But the Information Bureau dealt only with civilian matters. War bulletins were the domain of the Press Department of Imperial Headquarters (*dai hon'ei hōdōbu*), which was made up of the press sections of the army and the navy. The Department deployed its own war correspondents and occasionally drafted civilian reporters for on-the-spot coverage of military operations.[4]

As in other sectors, the government preferred not to deal with each newspaper directly, but to control all of them through an umbrella organization. In May 1941 the Japan Newspaper League (*Nihon shimbun remmei*) was established under official auspices. It was led by the major newspapers and its main function was to allocate newsprint. Membership was not obligatory, but every newspaper interested in the uninterrupted supply of newsprint found it advisable to join the league. In February 1942 the league was reorganized into the Japan Newspapers' Association (*Nihon shimbunkai*), in which the Information Bureau had greater influence. Throughout the war, this Association controlled the newspapers' editing, management, sales, newsprint allocation, and the accreditation of newspapermen.[5]

Commentators had always played an important role in the Japanese press. Each newspaper could boast of some distinguished intellectuals or retired military men on its staff, who would comment on anything that happened. In February 1941 the Information Bureau distributed among the editors a black list of writers whose articles they were advised not to print any more. After the outbreak of the Pacific War, the official spokesmen themselves became the most popular commentators. These were the chief of the army press section, Major-General Yahagi Nakao, who had spent nine years with the forces in China; the chief of the navy press section Captain Hiraide Hideo, who had been naval attaché at Rome for four years and had returned to Japan as an admirer of Mussolini; and the vice-president of the Information Bureau Okumura Hideo. These three men addressed press conferences, spoke on the radio, and wrote their own commentaries in newspapers. Other outstanding commentators included Tokutomi Sohō, who had already distinguished himself in the Meiji period and now, nearing the age of eighty, wrote fiery articles in support of the war in the *Mainichi*; Retired Admiral Nakamura Ryōzō of the *Yomiuri*; and Itō Masanori of the *Chūgai shōgyō*.[6]

As long as the Japanese forces were victorious, there was little need to distort the news, and the war bulletins were usually correct. But when the setbacks began, the reliability of the official statements gradually declined. As in most other countries at war, public morale was considered more important than the truth. This was clearly illustrated in the official report on the battle of Midway in June 1942, which proved to be the turning-point of the war. In that battle, Japan lost four carriers, one cruiser, 322 planes, and 3,500 men, as against only one carrier, one destroyer, 150 planes, and 307 men lost by the US. Nevertheless, Imperial Headquarters described the battle as a naval victory and claimed that Japan had lost only one carrier as against two carriers lost by the US. The announcement, which was issued a whole week after the event, included a long refutation of 'enemy propaganda' that the battle had been a defeat for Japan. This report raised some suspicion among the more sceptical readers, but most people were ready to believe the official version. The disasters on Guadalcanal were also reported as military successes, until in February 1943 the public suddenly learned that Japanese forces on the island had completed a 'sideward advance' (*tenshin*). The death of Admiral Yamamoto Isoroku, shot down over the Pacific in April 1943, was only announced five weeks afterwards. The death of his successor Admiral Koga Mineichi, which occurred in March 1944, was not reported until May of that year.

The first major defeat admitted by the government was the fall of the island of Attu in May 1943, where the entire Japanese garrison, numbering about 2,000 soldiers, died in what has been called since then a 'heroic fighting to the end' (*gyokusai*, literally: breaking of the jewel). After Attu, the tone of the war reports became grimmer. On 1 June 1943 the editorial of the *Mainichi* said: 'At the beginning of the war, when the victories were spectacular, there was a tendency to be optimistic about the outcome. . . . Now there is not a single Japanese who takes such an easy view. The desperate struggle on Guadalcanal, the gallant death of Admiral Yamamoto, and the heroic stand of the 2,000 soldiers at Attu have clearly shown us the grimness of the war.'[7]

Reports about the war in Europe tended to be more objective than those about the war in the Pacific. Although the German announcements were given full display and credit, the newspapers also printed the Russian version, since Russia was not an enemy country. From time to time a correspondent stationed in Moscow or Kuibishev would have his report printed. The Japanese public knew about the Russian offensives in East Europe and about American advances in the West. The Allied bombings of Berlin, including the destruction of the Japanese embassy there in January 1944, were reported by eyewitnesses. On 13 August 1944 the *Yomiuri-Hōchi* admitted that 'Japan's ally Germany, fighting desperately on both the east and the west . . . faces innumerable difficulties. This accounts for the recent pessimistic view concerning her future.'[8]

The kamikaze attacks, launched in the autumn of 1944, were widely reported and hailed by the newspapers. Describing the first such sortie, the *Mainichi* wrote on 1 November 1944: 'All of us should learn from the serene spirit of these youths. If the same spirit that imbued them characterized our other actions, there would be no obstacle that we could not surmount.' Any public suggestion of surrender or of a negotiated peace was taboo. The war was to be fought until the end. The *Mainichi*'s editorial of 2 November 1944 expressed this mood when it said: 'This is a war of survival . . . a war in which the vanquished will be exterminated . . . a war which we cannot afford to lose.' Even the surrender of Germany in May 1945 did not alter the tone. On 10 May 1945 the *Tōkyō shimbun* commented: 'We deeply regret that our ally Germany had to meet such a fate. . . . Though we all want victory and peace, conclusion of the war by surrender is unthinkable for us. Fortunately, we have never lost a war.'[9] The official view, as expressed by the newspapers, was that in case of an American invasion the whole population would fight until death in defence of the homeland. Such an unwavering spirit, it was believed, would deter the invaders or, if they dared to come to Japan, would inflict fatal blows upon them.

2. PROPAGANDA AND CRITICISM

The collaboration of the press with the wartime authorities was the result of coercion as well as conviction. The excitement created by the initial victories swept over the whole nation, including editors and writers who, like most of their compatriots, believed in the justice of Japan's cause and in her ultimate victory. These men were not fanatics or bigots. The editors of the daily newspapers were intelligent and sophisticated men, versed in international affairs, with a Western-type education and often with a liberal background. They believed that in time of war it was their responsibility to 'guide public opinion' in a way that would help achieve victory, and they thought the press was an important weapon in the 'ideological war' (*shisōsen*). As Hōjō Seiichi of the *Nichi nichi* wrote in

December 1942: 'In time of war journalists are the front-line fighters in the ideological war, and newspapers are the ideological bullets.'[10]

The leading personality of the *Asahi* was Ogata Taketora, a colourful figure who, like the Meiji liberals, combined liberalism and nationalism. He was born in 1888 in Fukuoka Prefecture, graduated from Waseda University in 1911 and then joined the Osaka *Asahi*. From 1920 until 1922 he studied in the US and Europe, where he came to admire the Western liberal press. At the same time he was a close friend of the ultranationalist leaders Tōyama Mitsuru and Nakano Seigō, his two compatriots from Fukuoka Prefecture. Tōyama, for a long time the grand old man of the nationalistic societies, had served at Ogata's wedding as the go-between, a role traditionally entrusted to an elder family friend. Nakano was Ogata's senior at Waseda and they remained close until the former's suicide in 1943. In 1936 Ogata became chief editor of the Tokyo *Asahi* and in that capacity he confronted the young rebel officers who ransacked the newspaper's offices in February 1936 in protest against *Asahi*'s liberal views. In 1940 he was appointed chief editor of the amalgamated *Asahi*; and became its vice-president in 1943. Ogata supported the war, but he also wished to preserve the image of the *Asahi* as an independent newspaper.[11]

The chief editor of the Tokyo *Nichi nichi* from 1941, and of the enlarged *Mainichi* from 1943, was Takata Motosaburō. A graduate of the English Literature Department of Tokyo Imperial University, he spent many years in the West, first as a correspondent and later as chief of the *Mainichi*'s bureaux in New York and London. The director of the *Mainichi* was Takaishi Shingorō, who had studied in England and served for many years as a correspondent in Western capitals. In 1937 he toured the US on a semi-official mission to win public support for Japan following the outbreak of war in China.[12]

The leading personality of the *Yomiuri* was its president Shōriki Matsutarō. Unlike his colleagues, Shōriki had come from a government background. Born in 1885 in Toyama Prefecture, he graduated from the Law Department of Tokyo Imperial University and joined the Metropolitan Police, where he became a senior officer in the Special Higher Police (*tokkō*), in charge of suppressing left-wing organizations. When the anarchist Namba Daisuke made an attempt on the life of Crown Prince Hirohito in 1924, Shōriki assumed responsibility and resigned from the police. On the recommendation of his patron, Home Minister Gotō Shimpei, he was then offered the presidency of the *Yomiuri*, a once-famous newspaper which had fallen into decline. Shōriki's successful management turned the *Yomiuri* into a national newspaper, and its daily circulation rose within fifteen years from 40,000 to about one million, making it the third-largest newspaper in Japan. The *Yomiuri* was the most nationalistic of the three major newspapers, encouraging the jingoistic and anti-Western feelings of its readers. Shōriki was not a liberal, but when he wanted to criticize the government, his background as a former police officer and later as a member of the House of Peers made it possible for him to do so without fearing that his patriotism might be questioned.

All the editors were jealous guardians of their newspapers' limited autonomies and objected to attempts by the government to interfere. In 1941 when the government, on the initiative of the army, tried to amalgamate all newspapers into one, Shōriki led a staunch opposition. The plan was eventually dropped and the regimentation of the press was never carried to such an extreme.[13]

When the Pacific War broke out, the newspapers rivalled each other in praising the brilliant achievements of the armed forces and in calling for national unity. On 10 December 1941 all major newspapers sponsored a rally in Tokyo on the theme of 'Crushing the US and Britain'. The main speakers were Ogata Taketora, Shōriki Matsutarō, and Tokutomi Sohō. They hailed the military and condemned the wickedness of the US and Britain. The editorial of the *Nichi nichi* on 17 December declared: 'The War of Great East Asia is not a war of destruction. There has never been a more constructive war than this. Every bullet fired from the guns of the Japanese forces carries the destruction of the old order and helps to bring a new and better one.'

In January 1942 the government designated the eighth day of each month as Imperial Rescript Proclamation Day (*taishō hōtaibi*), and from that time, all newspapers carried the imperial proclamation of war on their front pages on the eighth day of each month. On these days Ogata, according to his biographers, used to come to his office in a national uniform (*kokumin fuku*) and conduct a thanksgiving prayer towards the imperial palace.[14] In this way the newspapers used their prestige and credibility for the purpose of whipping up support for the war, and by doing so became propaganda tools of the wartime regime.

The populist spirit of the press was suppressed, but it did not die. Stifled beneath layers of censorship, propaganda, and war hysteria, it often expressed itself in criticism of mismanagement and incompetence, without questioning the basic tenets of the war or the regime. Such criticism was sometimes welcomed by the authorities, as they too were interested in increasing production and efficiency. In 1942, for instance, the *Nichi nichi*'s editorials called on the government to improve the supply of foodstuffs (3 March), complained about the inefficiency of local government (4 March), urged a revision of the price system (18 April), criticized the method of food distribution (3 August), and denounced rudeness in public places (7 August). During the same year, the *Asahi* complained about the poor condition of the anti-air raid facilities (1 June), and expressed misgivings about the structure of the national budget (26 December). In the following year, the *Asahi* called on the government to protect small-scale industries (2 March), criticized the official pricing of rice (17 April), urged the authorities to guarantee the people a minimum standard of living (12 May), exposed the government's failure to disperse population and industry (5 July), and warned against the domination of industry by appointed officials (2 November). The *Yomiuri* was critical of food distribution (31 January 1942), complained about public grievances which went unheeded (9 November 1942), and objected to excessive restrictions on private travel (10 April 1944). An example of this kind of critical editorial is the one carried by the *Mainichi* on 22 March 1944. Under the title 'Healthy Amusement in Wartime' it said in part: 'The greater the burden of war, the more important the question of sound amusement. . . . No matter how sublime the aims of the authorities, if all we get are illustrated sermons and dry lectures dressed up as drama, this may be sound, but it certainly is no amusement.'[15] The newspaper's charges were not based on abstract principles of the people's rights, but on pragmatic considerations about how victory might be achieved. Criticism could be accepted if it was directed towards increasing the effectiveness of the war effort, but not if it questioned or opposed the necessity for war.

Unable to express open opposition to the regime, the newspapers sometimes resorted to innuendo. If they wanted to indicate support for democratic procedures, they could praise the government for its supposed deference to the Diet. Thus in March 1942 the *Hōchi* (the president of which was Diet member Miki Bukichi) congratulated Tōjō who, according to the newspapers, unlike his predecessors showed great respect for parliamentary procedures. The *Nippon sangyō* complimented Tōjō for repudiating dictatorship and for regarding himself as a servant of the emperor. Following the election of April 1942, the *Nichi nichi* carried a report which said that even the enemy countries were surprised that 'unlike totalitarian states' Japan clung to constitutional government.[16]

The press could not question the legality of the general election, and it aided the government by joining in the call to elect the recommended candidates. But the newspapers reminded the government of its promise not to interfere in the election and not to discriminate against any candidates. On 30 January 1942, the *Nichi nichi* wrote: 'The government must be fully aware that official interference with the election will not promote national unity. . . . We believe that the government wants only men of high calibre, worthy of representing the people and capable of leading the nation, to be elected.' When it became evident that eighty-five unrecommended candidates had been elected to the House of Representatives, the *Chūgai shōgyō* called on the government to treat with equal respect all the new Diet members, whether they had been recommended or not. The *Asahi* appealed to the members of the newly formed Imperial Rule Assistance Political Association not to forget their duty to express the wishes of the people. The *Nichi nichi* reminded the government that even those who did not join IRAPA might have views worth listening to. A call for strengthening the power of the Diet was included in the *Mainichi*'s editorial on 15 June 1943, which said: 'It is about time that parliamentary affairs be left in the hands of the Diet members. . . . It should be made clear that the Diet represents the people. . . . The public wants the Diet to merit more confidence and increase its prestige.'[17]

The newspaper editors resented the official policy of silencing free discussion and suppressing unpleasant news for the sake of national morale, because they believed they were more competent than the bureaucrats in gauging the reactions of the people to the news. They claimed that the public was mature enough to absorb bad news when it occurred, and that accurate reporting and more discussion would serve to enhance the credibility of the press. When the government introduced a bill for stricter restrictions on speech in February 1943, the *Asahi* dared to write: 'The phraseology of national interests has been stretched to great length to justify a ban on the discussion of any matter which might disturb public peace. It has become more and more difficult for us to understand the reason behind such legislation.' A year and a half later, on 12 September 1944 the *Mainichi* wrote: 'The people wish to know the truth about the war situation at home and overseas, even if the truth is not pleasant. Concealing the facts will only weaken our fighting spirit.'[18]

Unlike totalitarian states, in which the party is above open criticism, the Imperial Rule Assistance Association did not enjoy an unassailable position in wartime Japan. Its nature as a quasi-political organization was never clearly understood, and its dependence on the bureaucracy did not endear it to the people. So the newspapers could criticize it within certain limits. One month after Pearl Harbor, the *Asahi* warned: 'The IRAA has accomplished very little . . . since the Tōjō cabinet was established. . . . Yet there are people who still advocate investing this organization with political powers. In time of war, our country does not need parallel lines of authority. Creating a rival organ of government will only cause internal strife.' In February 1942 the *Nichi nichi* revealed that many people were critical of the IRAA and favoured its outright dissolution.[19]

There was no personality cult around Tōjō in wartime Japan, although his pictures appeared in the newspapers and his speeches were reported and praised. Open opposition to Tōjō was not allowed, but on certain occasions newspapers published articles which included small criticisms of him. The January 1943 issue of the economic magazine *Tōyō keizai shimpō*, which appeared in December 1942, carried an article by its editor Ishibashi Tanzan (the post-war Prime Minister of Japan), criticizing the interference of the Military Police in political affairs. Tōjō wanted to punish the magazine, but Ishibashi's connections with such influential figures as Count Makino Nobuaki saved him and his magazine from reprisal. Shortly afterwards the 1943 New Year edition of the *Asahi* appeared with Nakano Seigō's article 'Senji saishō-ron' (An Opinion About Wartime Prime Ministers). The subtitle was: 'Loyalty should be absolutely strong.' The article, which carried Nakano's picture, described wartime leaders of the twentieth century, such as Clemenceau, Lenin, and Katsura. Then, referring to Tōjō but not mentioning him by name, it concluded: 'In the difficult times that we face now, the Prime Minister should be a strong man, one who possesses the qualities of loyalty, integrity, and magnanimity, and who is always ready to re-examine himself.' On the face of it there was nothing unusual in these words, and the article, solicited by Nakano's friend Ogata Taketora, was cleared by the censor for publication. But those who knew Nakano and his views could read between the lines a rebuke to Tōjō, who presumably did not possess the above-mentioned qualities and did not tend to re-examine himself. This veiled criticism did not escape Tōjō, who ordered the confiscation of the *Asahi*'s issue of that day. But by the time the order was given, most copies had already been delivered or sold.[20]

The following year, Tōjō was again upset by a newspaper. On 23 February 1944 the *Mainichi* printed a front-page article under the headline 'Will It be Victory or Will It Be Defeat?' The article's second paragraph was headed: 'Bamboo Spears Are Not Enough; We Need More Aeroplanes.' The unsigned article was written by the newspaper's naval correspondent, Shimmyō Takeo. By that time, most of the navy's aeroplanes had been destroyed and the navy was demanding more aircraft to stop the American advance in the Pacific, but the army refused to give up its share of aeroplanes, which it needed in China. Instead, the army was training the population in bamboo-spear fighting, as part of the general preparations for an American invasion. Shimmyō's article, which reflected the navy's resentment against Tōjō and the army, was written after he had met Commander Tominaga Kengo of the navy's press section. That evening's edition of the *Mainichi* carried a front-page article, written by Shimmyō's assistant Shimizu Takeo, under the banner: 'No More Retreat Should Be Allowed. The Whole Nation Is Poised To Hit The Enemy.'

Tōjō was angered by these two articles and wanted to close down the *Mainichi*. But Murata Gorō, vice-president of the Information Bureau, cautioned him that closure of a national newspaper would harm public morale. Instead, the chief of the army's press section summoned *Mainichi*'s chief editor, Takata Motosaburō, and told him that Shimmyō should be dismissed, But Takata refused to do so and took the responsibility upon himself. Takata's deputy, head of the editorial department Yoshioka Bun'roku, resigned, and the issue of that day was banned, but again the ban came too late to be effective. The only way for the army to remove Shimmyō from the *Mainichi* was to draft him. And indeed, eight days later, the thirty-seven-year-old reporter received a special summons to enter barracks as a private. But the navy did not let its man down. In June, Shimmyō was transferred to the navy and sent to the Philippines as a war correspondent. In July, after the resignation of the Tōjō cabinet, vice-editor Yoshioka was back at his post.[21]

The case of Shimmyō demonstrates that although it was difficult to publish anything critical about Tōjō or his policies, even Tōjō himself could not punish a newspaper or its writer, as long as they remained within their legal limits or enjoyed the support of some other élite. The government had the authority to close newspapers and gaol editors for various kinds of misbehaviour, but it shrank from doing so because punishing a national daily was counter-productive. It was better to exploit the newspaper's credibility with the public and mould a favourable image of the government than to risk an open rift with the press. As usual the government preferred compromise to confrontation. This need for consensus and for a façade of national harmony provided the newspapers with a measure of power which they did their best to utilize.

In the last year of the war, as the military situation deteriorated, it became more and more difficult to suppress criticism. Tōjō's successors in office lacked his powers and stature and therefore had greater need of the co-operation of the press in building up their public images as wartime leaders. The formal restrictions on the press were not lifted, but their application became less severe. Koiso's policy of currying favour with the press was evident when, on assuming office in July 1944, he appointed Ogata Taketora, vice-president of the *Asahi*, as State Minister in charge of the Information Bureau, and later as vice-president of the IRAA. The appointment of a leading newspaper figure as the watchdog of the press was unprecedented. It might ensure the further submissiveness of the press at a time when the government badly needed its support, but it could also give the press more say in the highest organs of government. The president of the *Yomiuri*, Shōriki Matsutarō, was appointed adviser (*komon*) to the new cabinet.

Despite the fact that its former vice-president had become a cabinet minister, the *Asahi* criticized the composition of the Koiso cabinet in terms hitherto unprecedented. Its editorial of 23 July 1944 said: 'The Japanese people have been looking forward with great expectations to the new cabinet. But whether General Koiso and Admiral Yonai have fulfilled these expectations remains a question. . . . We think that the new cabinet should have included more experienced statesmen and more capable men.' As for the freedom of expression, the editorial commented: 'For some time past, the people have not been able to express their patriotism, for fear that this would incur the wrath of the authorities.'[22] That such things could be written in the largest national newspaper and published without reprisal was a sign that the new cabinet was going to allow greater freedom of the press than its predecessor had ever dared.

Speaking before the Diet on 8 September 1944, Ogata declared that a 'vigorous' press was essential for maintaining the fighting spirit of the people, and he promised to review the restrictions on newspapers.[23] But nothing came of this promise. The government was ready to allow a little more criticism, but it refused to revamp the framework which enabled it to control the press. In February 1945 the Japan Newspaper Association was dissolved and replaced by a looser Japan Newspaper Public Corporation (*Nihon shimbun kōsha*). When Suzuki became Prime Minister, Ogata was replaced by Shimomura Hiroshi, a former vice-president of the *Asahi* and, from 1936, president of the broadcasting service (NHK), who was also a well-known poet.

The dilemma of how much bad news should be disclosed was compounded in the last year of the war, when the issues at hand were no longer military setbacks on far-away fronts, but devastating air raids on the home islands which could not be concealed. The authorities feared that if the full extent of the air raids were revealed, many Japanese, including soldiers, might think that the war was lost. So the fact of the raids was acknowledged, but no casualty figures were reported. Following the devastating 10 March 1945 air raid on Tokyo, in which nearly 80,000 people perished and a quarter of a million houses were destroyed, the government banned the circulation of metropolitan newspapers outside the big cities, so that people in other places could not learn what had happened. But the millions of refugees who streamed from the bombed cities spread the story in the countryside. Four days after the great air raid on Tokyo, the *Yomiuri-Hōchi* wrote: 'The value of information lies in its accuracy. . . . Why have the authorities forgotten this simple truth, and why are their reports so vague? . . . A striking example are the air raids. . . . No doubt the enemy is better informed on them than we are.' An 11 April 1945, the same newspaper wrote: 'Propaganda cannot accomplish everything. . . . You can make a success of eighty per cent appear as a hundred per cent success . . . or a hundred per cent failure look like an eighty per cent one. But you cannot make a total failure appear as a success. . . . Nevertheless, such mistaken ideas are still adhered to.'[24] Indeed, a public opinion poll conducted by the Dōmei news agency at that time revealed that the vast majority of the population was dissatisfied at the lack of reliable information.[25]

Among the buildings destroyed by the air raids were also the offices and printing houses of the daily newspapers, but the newspapers recovered quickly and used makeshift offices and substitute press to resume production. Throughout the war there was only one day (27 May 1945), when the Tokyo dailies, unable to appear separately, issued a joint newspaper, *Kyōdō shimbun*.[26]

When the Suzuki cabinet dissolved the IRAA and replaced it with the People's Volunteer Fighting Corps (*Kokumin giyūtai*) in

May 1945, the *Asahi* welcomed the move. On 18 May 1945 it wrote: 'Ever since the IRAA was established, we urged it to adopt reasonable objectives. Unfortunately, it did not heed our advice and became a huge body with no clear functions. Under such circumstances its dissolution became inevitable.' The newspaper called on the new organization to avoid the mistakes of its predecessor and keep out of politics. The *Mainichi* advised the leaders of the Fighting Corps not to entertain any political ambitions.[27]

On 28 July, two days after the Potsdam Declaration was issued, the newspapers were allowed to print it in an abridged form on their front pages. But the passages that were quoted made it clear that the Allies demanded only the surrender of the armed forces and had no wish to destroy the Japanese nation or deprive it of statehood. They also included the statement that the occupation of Japan would be terminated when a peaceful and responsible government, based on the free will of the people, was set up. On the same day the newspapers reported the government's decision to disregard the Potsdam Declaration because it offered nothing new.[28]

The first atom bomb, dropped on the morning of 6 August, destroyed the whole city of Hiroshima. After two days had passed, a short announcement, carried on the front pages of the newspapers of 8 August, said that a 'new-type bomb' deployed by the Americans had caused 'considerable damage' to Hiroshima. The announcement was printed alongside the Imperial Declaration of War, which appeared routinely on the eighth of each month. There was no mention of the number of people killed, but the readers could understand from the front-page display of the item that it was exceptionally high. The *Asahi*'s headline said: 'A cruel new bomb ignoring basic human principles.' The newspaper also reported that the Pope had lodged a protest with the US over the use of the new bomb. On 10 August the English-language *Nippon Times* carried an editorial on Hiroshima, which said: 'How can a human being with any claim to a sense of moral responsibility let loose an instrument of destruction which can at one stroke annihilate an appalling segment of mankind? This is not war, this is not even murder, this is pure nihilism. This is a crime against God and humanity which strikes at the very basis of moral existence.' On that day the newspapers also announced in banner headlines that the Soviet Union had declared war on Japan.[29]

On 9 August the first stories from Hiroshima appeared in the press, together with instructions about how one should defend oneself against the new bomb. If this type of air raid was expected, the readers were told, one had to find immediate shelter and expose as little of oneself as possible. The word 'atomic bomb' (*genshi bakudan*) was first mentioned on 11 August, when the newspapers quoted President Truman's speech which warned that more of these bombs would be dropped if Japan refused to surrender. On 12 August the *Yomiuri-Hōchi*'s correspondent, who had returned from Hiroshima, wrote that what he had seen was utterly beyond description. On that day the dropping of the second atomic bomb on Nagasaki on 9 August was first reported.[30]

The Imperial Proclamation of surrender, broadcast by the emperor at noon on 15 August, was published by the newspapers that same afternoon, under huge banners. The editorials praised the 'sacred decision' as a wise and courageous step made by the emperor himself. The *Mainichi*'s editorial carried the headline: 'Let us not forget the past, but let us look at the future.' That day the full text of the Potsdam Declaration was made public, together with details about the way Japan had communicated her acceptance of it.[31]

The *Yomiuri-Hōchi*, for a long time the most militant of the large newspapers, wrote in its editorial of 16 August: 'No Japanese ever imagined that the War of Great East Asia would end in this way. . . . We have been defeated. But we should lose like men. . . . The nation should turn over a new leaf and free itself from the bonds of the past. . . . This will not be easy. The great task cannot be carried out by discredited leaders and old-fashioned politicians. Only a government that enjoys the support of the people can face up to the new challenge.'[32] The same newspapers which four years earlier had stirred public opinion into war were now leading it towards the new ideals of peace and democracy.

Most of the editors and writers who had shaped the character of the newspapers before the Pacific War were still there when the war ended. Their durability, in spite of all the upheavals of those years, attested to the stability of Japanese society and the

Japanese state. Their enthusiasm for democracy could be opportunism, an attempt to placate the new rulers, but the new tone could also reflect a sincere desire on the part of the press to return to its traditional role as the guardian of the public good. It was thus a genuine harbinger of the peaceful and constructive attitudes towards the democratic reforms that would prevail in the coming years.

Scholars, Writers, and the War

> There is something worse than war and that is
> peace. . . . From the peace of slaves let us go to war!
> Writer and Critic Kamei Katsuichirō,
> December 1941

I. THE PEN AS A BAYONET

Intellectuals always enjoyed high prestige in modern Japan, although their participation in affairs of state was usually marginal. The esteem in which they were held derived from the Confucian tradition which equated wisdom with morality, as well as from the important role they had played in introducing Western culture in modern times. Nevertheless, politicians and bureaucrats tended to suspect the allegedly bookish and impractical scholars, while the intellectuals themselves often preferred to remain sequestered in their ivory towers.

The scholars' influence was strongest in the realm of values and tastes, and their power was exercised through the printed word. No visitor to prewar Japan could fail to notice the numerous news-stands and bookshops, where young and old crowded to buy or just to browse. The book-publishing industry was enormous and it continued to prosper during the first years of the war. In 1942 alone 15,200 new titles were published, not including official publications. Of these 1,907 were novels and plays; 863 were poetry books; 2,609 were books about law and politics; 526 were about philosophy; 2,269 dealt with economic and social problems; 1,137 with travel, and 459 were about military affairs. The popular publishing house Iwanami Shoten, whose series of low-priced and high-quality paperbacks had started in the 1920s, continued to publish books throughout the war, notwithstanding the air raids and the growing shortage of paper.

Magazines had flourished in the prewar years. At the time of Pearl Harbor there were 2,739 different magazines in Japan, with a total circulation of 6.5 million. Most of them were popular monthlies which catered to the masses, like *King*, *Hinode*, *Gendai*, *Kōdan kurabu*, or the women's magazines *Shufu no tomo*, *Fujin kurabu*, and *Fujin no tomo*. There were also special magazines for adolescents and children, and more serious magazines for specialists in all kinds of subjects. Two hundred and ninety-seven magazines were devoted to philosophy and religion, 345 to literature and poetry, 258 to economics, 216 to social studies, 104 to art, 63 to history, 212 to medicine, 290 to engineering, and 19 to science. The most prestigious were the 'general magazines' (*sōgō zasshi*), which aimed at the best-educated stratum of Japanese society. Appearing around the middle of the month, they carried hundreds of pages of essays, commentaries, reviews, and symposia, together with short stories, poems, plays, and literary articles. Their contributors were journalists, scholars, men of letters, as well as budding authors. The oldest and most famous of these magazines was *Chūō kōron*, established in 1887. Others like *Kaizō*, *Bungei shunjū*, and *Nihon hyōron* were products of the Taishō era. Some of them like *Bungei*, *Bungaku*, and *Bungakukai*, were mainly literary magazines.[1]

In the 1930s, as the war clouds thickened and the demands for a national-defence state increased, intellectuals began to involve themselves more in the justification and propagation of the official goals. The nonconformist intellectuals of the 1920s gave way to the conformist writers of the 1930s and early 1940s, who generally supported the international claims of their country. Marxism was no obstacle to this trend. Many left-wing intellectuals, having been disillusioned with Moscow, espoused the cause of Japan as the world's underdog. Their self-image as society's vanguard helped to propel them to the position of the new nationalist standard-bearers.

In November 1936 when Gotō Ryūnosuke, Prince Konoe's close friend, organized the *Shōwa kenkyū-kai* (Shōwa Research Society), to advise the prince on long-range political and economic planning, he invited distinguished scholars, such as the philosopher Miki Kiyoshi, the political scientist Rōyama Masamichi, the sinologist Ozaki Hotsumi, and the economist Hosokawa Karoku, to join it. There was no pressure on these or other scholars to join the group, and those who did so presumably believed that they were helping their country in a time of peril. Miki, Rōyama, Hosokawa, and Ozaki, all of them former Marxists, favoured a controlled economy that would curb capitalism at home, and a militant foreign policy that would expel Western imperialism from East Asia. Miki justified the war in China by claiming that Japan was not fighting the Chinese people but rather the reactionary regime of Chiang Kai-shek. In the late 1930s the *Shōwa kenkyūkai*, inspired by Western fascist models, formulated Konoe's plan for a New Political Order (*shintaisei*), by which Japan was to be transformed into a semi-totalitarian state. These designs were opposed by conservative elements in the bureaucracy and in the business world, which accused the Shōwa Research Society of being leftist. The society was dissolved in 1940, after some of its members were arrested on charges of communism. It was finally discredited in October 1941, when one of its leading members, Ozaki Hotsumi, was discovered to be a member of the Sorge spy ring.[2]

The crusade to liberate Asia from Western exploitation had a strong appeal to intellectuals. Four philosophers from Kyoto Imperial University, Kōsaka Masaaki, Suzuki Shigetaka, Kōyama Iwao, and Nishitani Keiji, appearing in the *Chūō kōron* of January and April 1942, justified the Pacific War as a legitimate response by Asia to Western imperialism.[3] The famous Japanese philosopher Nishida Kitarō, who was seventy-one when war broke out, wrote a draft for the Great East Asia Declaration, which was issued by the governments of Japan and its client states in December 1943. Part of his draft, entitled 'The Basic Principles of a New World Order' (*sekai shin-chitsujo no genri*), said:

The Great East Asia War is a sacred war, because it is the culmination of the historical progress of Asia. For a long time, the Anglo-Saxon imperialists have oppressed the peoples of East Asia and exploited their resources. The task of the liberated peoples now is to win the war and establish the Great East Asia Co-Prosperity Sphere, in co-operation with the Germans, Italians, and other peoples in Europe, who are engaged in a heroic struggle to create a new order in Europe. . . . Japan will win this war because her people are determined to sacrifice their lives for it. . . . Japan's victory will save Asia and will offer a new hope for mankind.[4]

Nishida died in June 1945, two months before Japan's defeat.

Mushanokōji Saneatsu, a novelist, playwright, and critic known for his romantic and humanist views, as well as for his attempts to set up 'ideal villages' on a Tolstoyan model, wrote articles in the wartime *Bungei shunjū* and other journals in which he denounced Western imperialism. Kawai Kazuo, a former assistant professor of history at the University of California, Los Angeles, was editor of the *Nippon Times*, a semi-official newspaper which constantly attacked the US and Britain. Professor Kinoshita Hanji, an expert on French political thought (and postwar critic of Japanese fascism), defended Tōjō's extraordinary powers in an article he wrote for the *Chūō kōron*.[5] Scholars served as advisers to government agencies and as members of various research institutes. Fujisawa Chikao of Kyushu Imperial University, formerly a senior official of the League of Nations, became chief of the IRAA's Research Department, and in that capacity directed propaganda at foreign countries and at American and British prisoners of war. Historians were assiduously writing new textbooks, in which Japan was depicted as the eternal champion of East Asia, and Hideyoshi as the pioneer of the Co-Prosperity Sphere. Kagawa Toyohiko, writer, Christian preacher, trade-union organizer, and social worker, famous for his humanitarian work in the slums of Kobe, supported the war enthusiastically, and his radio speeches were beamed overseas. He even toured occupied China and in 1945 was appointed a member of the National Board of Health.[6]

For the more nationalistic intellectuals, the war was the fulfilment of a dream. The eighty-year-old Tokutomi Sohō, who constantly heaped abuse on the US and Britain, was awarded the Cultural Medal of 1943. Yasuoka Masaatsu, Kanokogi Kazunobu, Hiraizumi Tōru, and other right-wing scholars produced a stream of nationalistic literature. Ōkawa Shūmei, who had been sentenced to five years in prison for his part in the 15 May 1932 incident and paroled shortly afterwards, was engaged in whipping up support for the war.[7]

In December 1942, one year after Pearl Harbor, the Great Japan Patriotic Writers Association (*Dai Nihon genron hōkokukai*) was established to serve as a 'mass organization' of journalists, essayists, and commentators dedicated to helping their country win the war. Membership was not obligatory, but members were more likely to stay in work than non-members. Many intellectuals were flattered that after years of alienation they had been asked to play an important role in national life and at a time of a national crisis it certainly felt good to belong.

Tokutomi Sohō was president of the new organization, and the board of directors included distinguished figures such as the philosophers Kōsaka Masaaki and Kōyama Iwao of Kyoto Imperial University, Ono Seiichirō of Tokyo Imperial University, Sugimori Kojirō of Waseda University, and the feminist leader Ichikawa Fusae. At the inaugural ceremony, the eighty-two-year-old journalist Miyake Setsurei led three shouts of *banzai* for the emperor. When the first convention of the association was held in March 1943, Tōjō sent a congratulatory message, which read: 'Thought should become a bullet, and the pen should be a bayonet to win the War of Great East Asia.'[8]

The intellectuals' support of the Pacific War contrasted with the critical attitude adopted by a group of writers and scholars towards the Russo-Japanese War some forty years earlier, when Kōtoku Shūsui, Yosano Akiko, and others expressed their pacifist views. There were several reasons for this difference. At the beginning of the century, intellectuals were few and their education was Western. The war was fought because of an immediate threat, and there was as yet no precedent of a military victory over a Western power. Moreover, the war was not an ideological one: in 1904 Japan did not champion the cause of the oppressed peoples, and Asia was the spoil to be won rather than an area to be freed. However, by the 1940s there were more intellectuals and they had all received a nationalistic education, in which the 1905 victory over Russia was already depicted as the shining example of Japan's spiritual superiority. The Pacific War had been preceded by a decade of growing militarization, resentment against the West, and gradual suppression of speech and writing. Asia was no longer a backward continent from which Japan wished to dissociate herself, but the oppressed brother waiting to be liberated. During both wars the intellectuals regarded themselves as teachers of the masses, with a mission to lead the people in time of confusion. This principle of the social responsibility of the scholar, deriving from both Confucianism and Marxism, was shared during the war by many intellectuals, nationalists, liberals, and socialists alike.

As Donald Keene and Japanese historians have pointed out, most men of letters greeted the Pacific War with great enthusiasm. Dazai Osamu, nihilist writer and former communist, described his feelings on the morning of Pearl Harbor: 'My whole personality suddenly changed. I felt invisible rays piercing through my body, and holy spirits wafting around me. . . . A new Japan was born on that morning.' The novelist Nagayo Yoshirō wrote: 'Never in my life have I experienced such a wonderful, such a happy, such an auspicious day. The heavy clouds hanging over our heads . . . suddenly dispersed.' Takamura Kōtarō, who belonged to the humanist literary group Shirakabaha, sang the glories of the war and was awarded the Art Academy Prize of 1943. One of his poems, called 'On the Day of Pearl Harbor', published in *Chūō Kōron*, said in part:

> When I heard the declaration of war
> My body started trembling . . .
> I knew the emperor was in danger,
> This made me even more resolved . . .
> I shall sacrifice my life
> To defend His Majesty.[9]

The literary critic Nakajima Kenzō, director of the Japan Poets, Essayists, and Novelists (PEN) Club, later described that morning: 'I felt that what was bound to happen had finally happened' (*tōtō kuru mono ga kita*). Horiguchi Daigaku, in his poem 'The Joy of Fighting and Dying', published in the 1942 collection *Daitōa sensō aikoku shi-ka-shū* (Patriotic Poems and Songs of the Great East Asia War), proclaimed:

> A man born in this land
> Has the great privilege
> Of fighting for His Majesty
> And dying for His Majesty.
> The joy of fighting for the emperor
> And dying for him in battle
> Is something a foreigner cannot understand,
> A joy that only we can experience.[10]

All the literary magazines vied with each other in exuberant expressions of joy.

Literature was considered to be an important instrument for arousing the fighting spirit of the people. In May 1942 the Information Bureau sponsored the establishment of the Japan Literary Patriotic Association (*Nihon bungaku hōkoku-kai*). Membership was not obligatory, but most of Japan's 3,100 novelists, playwrights, critics, and poets chose to join in, either out of patriotism or out of fear that non-membership would damage their publication prospects. Among those who joined were the great novelists Tanizaki Jun'ichirō and Shiga Naoya. The association was divided into eight sections, each headed by a noted writer in that field: novels (Tokuda Shūsei), drama (Mushanokōji Saneatsu), poetry (Takamura Kōtarō), tanka (Sasaki Nobutsuna), haiku (Takahama Kiyoshi), history of Japanese literature (Hashimoto Shin'kichi), history of Western literature (Chino Shōshō), and literary criticism (Takashima Beihō). Tokutomi Sohō was president of this organization too. The board of directors included the poet Satō Haruo, the playwright Yamamoto Yūzō, and the ethnologist Yanagita Kunio. The inauguration ceremony, held on 18 June, was attended by Prime Minister Tōjō Hideki, Education Minister Hashida Kunihiko, and the President of the Information Bureau, Tani Masayuki. The chairman was the novelist and playwright Kikuchi Kan, founder and editor of *Bungei shunjū*. The first convention of the association, held in April 1943, concentrated on the task of strengthening the people's resolve 'to smash the US and Britain', and among the speakers were the novelists Hino Ashihei and Kume Masao. The newspapers' headlines reporting the convention announced: 'The Pen Fighters Charge To Win The Ideological War.'

The Literary Patriotic Association's first step was to sponsor the collection and publication of patriotic poems. The thirteenth-century *Ogura hyakunin isshu* (Ogura Collection by One Hundred Poets), which had been used for hundreds of years in playing the New Year card game, was replaced by the new *Aikoku hyakunin isshu* (Patriotic Poems by One Hundred Poets), which went on sale in late 1942. The previous poems about love and nature, that seemed out of tune with the martial atmosphere of the times, were replaced by 'heroic poems' from the *Man'yōshū* and from Edo-era nationalists such as Hirata Atsutane. In 1943 the association published a collection of

3,398 war poems (*Daitōa sensō kashū*) and a collection of short stories about the war.[11]

After the outbreak of the China War, the army started sending writers to the front, so that the public would be impressed by their recorded first-hand experiences. The result was a crop of patriotic war novels, like Hino Ashihei's *Mugi to heitai* (Barley and Soldiers, 1938). After the outbreak of the Pacific War this practice was expanded. Hino, who had started as a 'proletarian writer', went to Bataan in 1942 and to Imphal in 1944, and his novel *Rikugun* (Army) was serialized in the *Asahi* from May 1943 to April 1944. Niwa Fumio took part in the naval battle of Tulagi, where he was wounded, and his 1942 novel *Kaisen* (Naval Battle) became a best seller. The novelist Yoshikawa Eiji was commissioned to write the history of the naval battles.

The war was the most popular topic of literary works during the years 1942–5. It fired the imagination of writers and readers alike and produced a stream of novels, short stories, and poetry glorifying the victorious army and navy. Writers such as Hayashi Fusao, Ozaki Shirō, Hibino Shirō, Toyoda Saburō, Kitamura Komatsu, Tsuruta Tomoya, Abe Tomoji, Funayama Kaoru, Ueda Hiroshi, Takeda Rintarō, Kimura Sōjū, and Kon Hidemi wrote books in praise of the war and the Co-Prosperity Sphere.[12]

Literature also played a central role in developing the new East Asian awareness. Men of letters were rediscovering their Asian roots and Chinese themes became very fashionable. Takeda Taijun wrote a popular biography of the ancient Chinese historian Ssu-ma Ch'ien (*Shi-ba sen*, 1943). Nakajima Atsushi wrote a novel about the ancient Chinese General Li Ling (*Ri Ryō*, 1943), who was captured by the Huns and rose to eminence in their army. In 1943 the *Chūō Kōron* serialized the last, and unfinished, novel by Shimazaki Tōson, *Tōhō no mon* (Gate of the East), which denounced the cultural aggression of the West in East Asia. Writers of the romantic school (*rōman-ha*) such as Yokomitsu Riichi, Kobayashi Hideo, and Kamei Katsuichirō were inspired by the Japanese conquests and sang the glories of the new Asia. Postwar scholars have found that wartime writers used more Chinese characters than they had done before the war, in order to convey a more masculine, serious and 'Chinese' impression.[13]

Intellectuals went to the occupied territories to promote Japanese culture and enlist the support of the local intelligentsia. In December 1942 the *Nichi nichi* carried a symposium with a group of Japanese writers in Manila, among whom were Miki Kiyoshi, Hino Ashihei, Ueda Hiroshi, Ishizaka Yōjirō, and others. On that occasion, Miki advocated teaching the Filipinos the Japanese language, so that they would be able to appreciate Japanese culture, and Ueda wanted to convince the Filipinos that the Japanese possessed superior cultural qualities. Miki's impressions of the Philippines was published in the *Kaizō* in 1943.[14]

In November 1942, the first Great East Asia Literary Conference (*Daitōa bungaku taikai*) was convened in Tokyo. It was attended by fifty-seven representatives from Japan and twenty-six from Korea, Manchoukuo, Taiwan, Mongolia, and Nanking China. Among the leading Japanese delegates were the poet Noguchi Yonejirō and the novelist Kume Maseo. The chairman was Dr Shimomura Hiroshi, president of NHK, who also wrote under the pen-name of Shimomura Kainan. At the second conference, held in Tokyo in August 1943, the speakers included the novelist Yokomitsu Riichi and the critic Kobayashi Hideo. At the closing ceremony Hino Ashihei read an oath, in which all participants pledged to expel American and British influences from Asia and work together to construct a new East Asia culture. The third and last of these conferences was held in Nanking in November 1944, and was attended by 100 delegates, about half of them from Japan.[15]

When the war situation worsened, writers tried to do something more than just writing. In January 1943, the *haiku* section of the Literary Patriotic Association started sending poets to the fronts and to factories, to introduce the hard-pressed soldiers and workers to the joys of poetry. In December 1943, a Writers' Labour Corps was established in Tokyo. It was composed of 522 novelists, poets, and playwrights above the age of fifty, who volunteered to work in munitions factories. The Commander of the Corps was the poet Ozaki Kihachi. In May 1945 Kawabata Yasunari, who was then attached to a kamikaze base, was reported to be collecting books for the kamikaze pilots, presumably to enable them to enjoy literature while waiting to embark on their suicide missions. In June 1945, as Japan was preparing for the American invasion, a Volunteer Corps of writers was formed in Kamakura, with Satomi Ton as Commander and Osaragi Jirō as his lieutenant. The mood of the times was expressed by the poet Kurahara Shinjirō, who described the feelings of a young soldier stationed at an observation post to watch for approaching American bombers. Part of his poem said:

> . . . I have been standing here since the morning
> At this observation post,
> It is already four in the afternoon,
> But no enemy planes have been sighted.
> Any moment these villains may invade
> The sacred skies of Japan.
> Oh, let them come . . .[16]

Artists, composers, and actors were as enthusiastic as their literary colleagues. In January 1943 the Japan Patriotic Arts Association was established with the support of such leading painters as Yokoyama Taikan and Wada Sanzō. Artists went to the fronts to paint the glories of the imperial forces and to decorate military and naval installations, donating their talents for the war effort. The chief court musician, Ōno Tadatomo, composed music for a martial song in praise of the naval officers who died in the submarine attack on Pearl Harbor. In July 1943, a Roving Musical Patriotic Volunteer Corps was established to propagate 'national music' throughout the country. The famous *kabuki* player Ichimura Uzaemon called on his colleagues to leave the stage and to entertain, instead, the workers at the factories. Modern ballet dancers, such as Ishii Baku and Eguchi Takaya, created dances that depicted aerial battles. Even the all-girl Takarazuka revue troupe presented martial shows in honour of the brave soldiers, as it had already been doing in the late 1930s.[17]

As in the realm of politics, the patriotic mood generated by an all-out war, on top of the repressive measures of the government, created a remarkable consensus in the fields of thought, literature, and the arts. In a country like Japan, where the group values of loyalty and harmony were still considered very important, there was less need of coercion in order to line up the intellectuals, the writers, and the artists behind the nation in arms than there was in other countries.

2. SUPPRESSING THE OPPOSITION

Intellectuals who opposed the regime were silenced or suppressed. Arrests of communist writers had already started after the promulgation of the Peace Preservation Law (*Chian iji-hō*) of 1925, and continued throughout the 1930s; socialist and liberal professors were dismissed from the universities and some of them were prosecuted. In the aftermath of the 1931 Manchurian Incident, when a nationalistic wave swept the nation, many of the arrested intellectuals recanted. This ideological conversion (*tenkō*) became widespread after 1933, when the two communist leaders Sano Manabu and Nabeyama Sadachika repudiated their former allegiance to Moscow and expressed loyalty to the emperor. Their sentences of life imprisonment were then commuted to fifteen years by a court of appeal, and in 1943 they were released and sent to help the army in Peking. The communist writer Hayashi Fusao, after a short period in gaol in the early 1930s, embraced nationalism and was released to become one of its main exponents. Of the 500 authors who belonged to the leftist literary associations NAPF (Japan Proletarian Artists Federation) and KOPF (Federation of Proletarian Cultural Organizations), 95 per cent were reported to have 'recanted'. It is impossible to determine how many of these conversions were genuine and how many were a convenient disguise (*gisō tenkō*), especially since conversion did not demand a fundamental change of principles. As in the cases of Miki Kiyoshi and Ozaki Hotsumi, one could support Japan's war aims and still advocate social and international justice.[18]

Only a small hard core of communist intellectuals refused to recant and stayed in gaol until the end of the war. They included Miyamoto Kenji, Shiga Yoshio, Kasuga Shōjirō, Konno Yojirō, and Hakamada Satomi. Unlike the situation in the Soviet Union, which they adored, or in Nazi Germany, which they hated, in Japan ideological opponents of the state were not killed and most of them were released after the surrender. Nevertheless, life in prison was harsh. Tozaka Jun, a socialist philospher who had been arrested in 1941, died in prison in August 1945. The liberal economist Kawai Eijirō, an outspoken opponent of militarism and fascism, who was dismissed from Tokyo Imperial University in 1939, was detained several times for interrogation and in October 1941 was found guilty of violating the Peace Preservation Law and fined 300 yen. But the interrogation and the trial had taken their toll, and he died in early 1944, a broken man at the age of fifty-three.[19]

After the outbreak of the Pacific War, more scholars and writers were arrested, among them Yamada Katsujirō of Kyoto Imperial University (the younger brother of Rōyama Masamichi) and Kido Mantarō of Hōsei University. But not all of them remained in gaol. Miyamoto Yuriko, wife of the communist leader Miyamoto Kenji, who was detained after Pearl Harbor, was released a few months later for health reasons and then joined the Literary Patriotic Association. The Marxist economist Kawakami Hajime, who had translated *Das Kapital* into Japanese, was arrested in 1933, sentenced to five years in prison, and released in 1937. The communist writer Takami Jun, arrested in 1933 and released in 1934, was sent to Burma and China as a war correspondent, and in November 1944 he participated in the Great East Asia Literary Conference in Nanking. The historian Tsuda Sōkichi of Waseda University, who was prosecuted in 1940 for having 'slandered' the divine origins of the imperial family in his books on ancient history, was sentenced in 1942 to three months in prison while his publisher Iwanami Shigeo was sentenced to two months. But both appealed to the Supreme Court and were acquitted in 1944.[20]

Official policy towards ideological dissenters was erratic. The navy, for instance, employed scholars that the army had branded as leftists. Some left-wing intellectuals, like the historian Hani Gorō, remained free through most of the war, but were arrested in the spring of 1945. The former Marxist philosopher Miki Kiyoshi was arrested in March 1945, when a fugitive communist was found hiding in his house. He died in prison in September of that year, six weeks *after* the end of the war.[21]

Censorship, already strict in the late 1930s, became more severe after the outbreak of the Pacific War. The police had the power to ban or withdraw any book which, in their judgement, was harmful to public security. As a result, books of Marxist or pacifist leanings, or those including favourable opinions of the US and Britain, were withdrawn from the stacks. Often parts of books or magazines were cut out with scissors or blotted out with ink. But unlike Nazi Germany, there was no deliberate destruction of books. Banned books remained in private hands and were available to those who knew how to get them. The diary of Professor Yabe Sadaji of Tokyo Imperial University reveals that during the war he read books by such proscribed authors as Edgar Snow, Pearl S. Buck, and Chiang Kai-shek.[22]

The 'general magazines', the last bastion of liberal writing, were curbed. In May 1941 their editors were ordered to submit in advance the contents of each issue to the censor. At the same time, the Information Bureau provided the magazines with a black list of liberal writers whose articles could not be published. The list included the names of famous journalists such as Baba Tsunego, Kiyosawa Kiyoshi, and Yanaihara Tadao. However, some former Marxists who supported the war, such as Miki Kiyoshi, were not included in the list. When Hatanaka Shigeo, the editor of *Chūō kōron*, wanted to know how the dismissed writers would earn their living, he was told that they would have to change their occupation as other citizens had already done.

The army showed great zeal in 'guiding' the monthly magazines. Beginning in January 1942, representatives of the army's press section used to meet, on the sixth of each month, with the editors of *Chūō kōron, Kaizō, Bungei shunjū, Nihon hyōron, Kōron,* and *Gendai*. At these 'Sixth Day Meetings' (*muika-kai*), which were informal gatherings held at a Tokyo restaurant, the editorial policy of the magazines for the following month was decided. The army's wishes were expressed in the form of requests, but according to one of the editors these requests were almost as binding as commands.[23] Consequently, after the outbreak of the Pacific War the magazines lost their independent character and became to a large degree mouthpieces for the regime. The *Chūō kōron* issues of 1942 had the following topics as their central themes:

January: 'Our Fatherland Requires'
February: 'Progress of the Great East Asia War'
March: 'Basic Principles of Great East Asia'

April: 'The Elections: Theory and Practice'
May: 'The Economic Structure of Great East Asia'
June: 'New Politics and New Policies'
July: 'The Rationing System and Wartime Life'
August: 'Building a New Culture'
September: 'Advances in Wartime Agriculture'
October: 'Moral Power and the Progress of History'
November: 'Towards an Invincible Wartime Industry'
December: 'The First Anniversary of the Great East Asia War'

Anti-liberal views, previously characteristic of right-wing magazines, were now appearing in the serious ones as well. The April 1942 issue of *Chūō kōron* carried an article which praised the government-controlled election and described it as the first phase of a new restoration. In September, Suzuki Masabumi, formerly of the *Asahi* and later vice-president of the Printers' Association, wrote in *Chūō kōron*: 'The old concept of freedom of the press cannot be accepted at this time of super-emergency. Similarly, old-fashioned journalists are now out of place. . . . Newspapers should no longer be regarded as private enterprises. They are valuable assets of the state, responsible for shaping public opinion and propagating national enlightenment.' No wonder that Kiyosawa Kiyoshi, writing in his diary on 14 December 1943, remarked that the *Chūō kōron* had deteriorated to a level at which it was praising everything Japanese and denouncing anything Western.[24]

But even at that level, the serious magazines retained some of their critical spirit. The Kyoto philosophers who justified the war in the pages of *Chūō kōron* did so in moralistic rather than chauvinistic terms. They advocated the granting of independence to the conquered peoples of Asia and attacked nationalistic narrow-mindedness. In the January 1942 issue of the magazine, one of these philosophers, Suzuki Shigetaka, criticized the teaching of history in the schools as being too Japan-oriented, with insufficient attention devoted to other cultures. He warned that if pupils studied only Japanese history, without knowing what had happened in other parts of the world, they would not be able to understand the history of their own country. Suzuki expressed his dismay that the subject of

Japanese history was allotted eighty-five points in the entrance examinations to senior high schools, whereas foreign languages, mathematics, and physics were allotted a total of only seventy points. Hayashi Kentarō, an expert on German history at Tokyo Imperial University, attacked that argument in the December 1942 issue of *Chūō kōron*, claiming that old historical concepts were no longer valid, and that Japanese history should be taught on its own merits and not through categories derived from foreign nations.[25]

The army–navy rivalry also affected the magazines. The army was hostile to the Kyoto philosophers and suspicious of the *Chūō kōron*. The navy, on the other hand, was sympathetic towards them, perhaps because the head of the navy's research department, Rear-Admiral Takagi Sōkichi, was an admirer of the philosopher Nishida Kitarō. The editor of *Chūō kōron* during the war, Hatanaka Shigeo, revealed afterwards that in addition to the meeting with army representatives, he and the editors of *Kaizō* and *Bungei shunjū* used to meet secretly with representatives of the navy under the guise of a Pacific Research Society (*Taiheiyō kenkyūkai*) in order to obtain a more balanced view of the war.[26]

The stories and plays which appeared in the magazines were carefully scanned. In January 1943 the *Chūō kōron* started serializing Tanizaki Jun'ichirō's novel *Sasameyuki* (The Makioka Sisters), which was to appear every other month. After the second instalment was printed in the March edition, the army expressed its anger that the magazine was serializing such an 'effeminate' novel, so out of tune with the martial spirit of the war. The magazine yielded to the army's pressure and the serialization was discontinued. This was not Tanizaki's first brush with the authorities. In 1940 his translation of the classic *Genji monogatari* (Tale of Genji) into modern Japanese was allowed to be published only after he had removed all disrespectful allusions to emperors, which abounded in the original. Not all of the magazine's readers lamented the disappearance of Tanizaki's novel from the pages of the *Chūō kōron*. Professor Yabe Sadaji wrote in his diary in April 1943 that the first instalments had made him realize 'how morbid was the period when such novels were popular'.[27]

The June 1943 issue of *Chūō kōron*, which announced the

discontinuation of Tanizaki's novel, also carried the play *Kaeraji-to* (I Shall Not Return) by Kishida Kunio. Kishida, one of the founders of modern Japanese drama, was a known supporter of the war and until July 1942 had been head of the Culture Department of the IRAA. In 1943 he published a book, *Chikara toshite-no bunka* (Culture as Strength), in which he called on all writers to support the war. Nevertheless, the army authorities claimed that Kishida's play ridiculed the draft and they rebuked the *Chūō kōron* for publishing it. Trying to avoid further friction, but unwilling to succumb to army pressure, Hatanaka decided not to publish the July issue. This action infuriated the authorities. In August Hatanaka was summoned to the Information Bureau and ordered to resign together with his whole editorial board. They were replaced by other men from the magazine's staff.[28]

The *Kaizō* did not fare any better. In August and September 1942 the magazine carried the article 'Sekai-shi no dōkō to Nihon' (Trends in World History and Japan) by Hosokawa Karoku. The author, a former socialist who had espoused nationalism and later served as a member of the *Shōwa kenkyū-kai*, expressed the opinion that Japan should not repeat the mistakes of Western colonialists, who had oppressed the peoples of East Asia, but should instead learn from the Soviet Union how to grant freedom to other nations, while keeping them bound together within a common political framework. Although the article had been cleared by the censors, the army was outraged by such a display of homage to Moscow. Hosokawa was arrested in early September 1942 on charges of communism, and the editor of the *Kaizō*, Ōmori Naomichi, was ordered to resign together with his whole editorial staff.

Other arrests followed. Then, during the search of a suspect's house in Yokohama in May 1943, the police found a group photograph of several men in their summer *yukata*, with Hosokawa at the centre. The other men in the picture were a former editor of the *Kaizō* (Kimura Tōru) and several members of the Research Department of the South Manchuria Railway Company. The police claimed that the photograph was taken at a secret meeting at which the banned Japan Communist Party was re-established. Actually it had been taken at a reunion of Hosokawa and his friends at a summer resort in Tomari,

Toyama Prefecture. In the following month all the men who appeared in the picture, as well as other connected with them, were detained. In the first months of 1944 Hatanaka Shigeo and Ōmori Naomichi, the two dismissed magazine editors, were arrested together with other employees of their magazines. Altogether forty-nine people were detained in this affair, including eight from *Kaizō*, six from *Chūō kōron*, five from *Nihon hyōron*, two from the Iwanami publishing house, and one from the *Asahi shimbun*.

The Yokohama Incident, as the affair came to be known, provided the authorities with an excuse to crack down on the serious magazines, but it took some time before they dared to do so. On 10 July 1944, one week before Tōjō's resignation, the Information Bureau instructed the *Chūō kōron* and *Kaizō* to dissolve themselves 'voluntarily' for failing to guide public opinion in time of war. There was no way the magazines could defy this order and both closed down at the end of the month.[29]

Unable to obtain evidence against the suspects, the police used torture in order to make them confess. As a result, four of them died in gaol and two died shortly after their release. In February 1945, seventeen of the prisoners were released and the others were indicted on charges of violating the Peace Preservation Law. Their trial, which started at the Yokohama District Court in the summer of 1945, continued even after Japan had surrendered. The sentences were handed down in early September, three weeks *after* the end of the war. All defendants were found guilty and given prison terms with hard labour. But the sentences were suspended and the prisoners were released, into a country already under American occupation.[30]

3. COMPLIANCE AND DISSENT

Postwar Japanese historians have tried hard to uncover evidence of 'resistance' in wartime Japan, but they had to reconcile themselves to the fact that there were neither underground organizations which fought the regime nor noteworthy instances of open defiance. After the first burst of wartime enthusiasm had died down, and when military setbacks began to occur, some intellectuals felt uneasy about the war and the regime, but their discontent did not amount to organized opposition. According to Maruyama Masao, most

Japanese intellectuals abhorred the wartime regime but felt unable to do anything about it. Ienaga Saburō claims that many intellectuals expressed passive resistance by simply continuing their normal activities in total disregard of the war, or by withdrawing completely from any public activity.[31]

However, the pursuit of one's scholarly or literary work in time of war does not necessarily signify protest. It may serve the goals of a repressive regime interested in maintaining a business-as-usual atmosphere. Both Maruyama and Ienaga, for example, continued their scholarly work as long as it was possible, despite their inner objections to the war and the regime. Maruyama's essays on Tokugawa thought were published in the wartime editions of the *Kokka gakkai zasshi*; Ienaga published two books on Buddhism and religious thought, and was in the midst of preparations for a third book, on Japanese painting, when the war ended.[32]

Most scholars did the same. Minobe Tatsukichi, whose works on the constitution had been discredited in 1935, continued to edit the year-book *Kōhō hanrei hyōshaku* (Commentary on Public Law Cases) throughout the war, and published a book on economic legislation in 1944. The journalist Kiyosawa Kiyoshi, barred from writing for magazines because of his liberal views, published two books during the war, a biography of Ōkubo Toshimichi and a non-conformist two-volume history of Japanese diplomacy. Nishida Kitarō, despite his advanced age, continued to contribute essays for the magazine *Shisō*, and a collection of his articles was published by Iwanami in 1944. Miki Kiyoshi published two books during the war, in addition to various articles, despite the fact that many of his prewar writings had been banned.[33] The ethnologist Yanagita Kunio pursued his research and prolific writing on Japanese folklore, and published ten new books during the war. His students took advantage of the extended conquests and went to China to collect ethnographic material. Sinologists like Tachibana Shiraki found new opportunities for research and even the left-wing sinologist Nakae Ushikichi, son of the Meiji radical Nakae Chōmin, was engaged in academic work in Peking.[34]

The literary muses were not quiescent either. Novels, poems, plays, and short stories, besides those concerned with the war, continued to be published in great numbers. Kawabata

Yasunari's novel *Kōgen* (Heights) appeared in 1942, his novel *Kokoku* (Homeland) was serialized in the magazine *Bungei* from 1943 until 1945, and in 1944 he was awarded the Kikuchi Kan literary prize. Tanizaki Jun'ichirō wrote his masterpiece *Sasameyuki* in 1943, and when *Chūō kōron* stopped its serialization in the spring of that year, he published the first half of the novel privately. Dazai Osamu published two novels during the war, *Seigi to bishō* (Justice and Smile) and *Udaijin Sanetomo* (Sanetomo the Minister of the Right), in addition to essays and short stories. Mishima Yukio's first novel, *Hanazakari no mori* (The Forest in Full Bloom), was published in 1944, and his first short stories appeared in the wartime editions of the magazine *Bungei bunka*. Serizawa Kōjirō's novel *Pari ni shisu* (To Die in Paris) was serialized in the women's magazine *Fujin kōron* in 1943. Itō Sei (Hitoshi) had two of his novels published during the war, *Tokunō monogatari* (Tokunō's Story) and *Dōji no zō* (Figure of a Child). Yosano Akiko's last collection of poems, *Hakuō-shū* (A Collection of the White Cherry Blossom), was published in September 1942, four months after her death. In the field of cricitism there were Kobayashi Hideo, who wrote books and articles on literature; Takami Jun, who continued writing for the *Kaizō*; and Yashiro Yukio, who published his popular book *Nihon bijutsu no tokushitsu* (Characteristics of Japanese Art) in 1943.[35]

Those who preferred to be quiet were not harassed. Unlike writers in most totalitarian states, those in Japan had the freedom to remain silent, although very few took advantage of it. Among those who preferred to do so was the novelist Nagai Kafū, who refused to join the Literary Patriotic Association and published nothing during the war. But he did not stop writing: his three novels, *Ukishizumi* (Floating and Sinking), *Odoriko* (Dancing Girl), and *Towazugatari* (A Tale No One Asked For), which he wrote in those years, were published shortly after the war. The case of the novelist Shiga Naoya was somewhat different. Shiga was at first enthusiastic about the war, and a collection of his patriotic essays, under the name *Sōshun* (Early Spring), appeared in 1942. But he later changed his mind and published nothing more. Yet he too continued to write and his wartime novel *Hairo no tsuki* (Gray Moon) appeared in the autumn of 1945.[36]

No scholar or writer fled Japan before or during the war, and no one was forced to do so.[37] The prospects of literary activity abroad were nil, while at home writers remained respected citizens within their social milieu. Some of those who were not allowed to publish changed their occupations: the essayist Ishikawa Sanshirō became a farmer, and the socialist historian Hattori Shisō joined the Kaō soap factory as the company's historian. But most of the silenced writers remained in the metropolitan areas, where they could maintain contacts with other intellectuals and wait for better days to come. They were not subjected to any kind of ostracism. Kiyosawa reveals in his diary that in July 1944 the navy consulted a group of intellectuals, including the disgraced Baba Tsunego, about ways to raise the fighting spirit of the people.[38] Baba later admitted that during the war he continued to visit Prince Chichibu and to receive letters from Prince Konoe.[39]

Most of the 'internal émigrés' as the alienated intellectuals later called themselves, kept diaries in which they recorded their growing disenchantment with the regime. Had the police discovered these diaries, their writers would have been in trouble. But the fact that such diaries were kept in the first place shows that the danger of a police search was not considered great. Some diaries, like Kiyosawa's *Ankoku nikki* (Diary of Dark Days), were published after the war. Kiyosawa, who died of pneumonia in May 1945, was not afraid of ridiculing the regime. In his entry on 10 March 1944 he quoted a Tokyo Imperial University professor (later identified as Tatsuno Yutaka, professor of French literature), who said that Tōjō had the intelligence of a junior high school student. On 13 April 1944 he wrote: 'Tōjō took advantage of the emperor's trust to make himself Prime Minister, Army Minister, Munitions Minister, and now also Chief of Staff. He has become a real dictator.'[40]

Nagai Kafū also kept a diary that would have surprised the police. In June 1943, he wrote that Japan was ruled by its worst government in history. In December 1944 he noted: 'The year 1944 ends, and we face a forlorn New Year. We have not faced such another since the founding of the country, and for this fact we may thank the militarists. Let their crimes be recorded for eternity.' Takami Jun, the former communist novelist and critic, wrote in his diary on 10 March 1945: 'Around my house, nay, around the whole of Japan hangs an air of collapse. Could I imagine that this would happen when I was in Burma or in China? Could I imagine it even three months ago?'[41]

Some poets, who had been jubilant when the war first broke out, became pessimistic as it dragged on. Their change of mood can be detected in the poems published during the latter half of the war. Horiguchi Daigaku, who had written 'The Joy of Fighting and Dying' after Pearl Harbor, contributed a different kind of poem to the 1943 collection *Kokumin-shi* (National Poetry). Entitled *Rekishi* (History), it said in part:

> There were no fires, but there was an earthquake,
> No one was sick, but there was war,
> Life was lived at intervals.
> The country grew bigger and bigger,
> But the path of life became steeper,
> The roses ceased to bloom.[42]

Others wrote poems that could not be published at the time. One of them, Kaneko Mitsuharu, who had toured Malaya at the beginning of the war, wrote the 'Song of Loneliness' in May 1945, which said in part:

> Loneliness made us shoulder guns,
> Loneliness lured us towards the fluttering flag . . .
> All blinded by the emperor's name,
> Set out bustling with joy like mischievous children.
> While those left behind are in constant fear . . .
> Women silently endure in lines,
> Like beggars, waiting for their rations.
> In their looks, growing sadder day by day,
> Never before have I seen a loneliness,
> So pressing and so deep.[43]

Although the censors were strict with major magazines and newspapers, they were not so vigilant with the smaller magazines. Least affected were the 'private journals' (*kojin zasshi*) which were distributed only to subscribers by mail. Writers who were barred from the regular magazines could express their views in these smaller ones. One such private journal, *Tazan no ishi* (Food for Thought), was established by the journalist Kiryū Yūyū after his dismissal from the newspaper *Shinano mainichi* in 1933. Kiryū's magazine, which expressed non-conformist views, was printed regularly until the editor's death in 1941. Another such journal was the small Christian magazine *Tsūshin* (Correspondence), edited and published by Yanaihara Tadao, professor of economics at Tokyo Imperial University. In 1937, after the magazine had criticized the army's actions in China, Yanaihara was dismissed from the university and ordered to close *Tsūshin*. But he changed the name of the journal to *Kashin* (Good News), and this ostensibly new magazine was not suppressed. Yanaihara was a disciple of the pacifist Christian scholar Uchimura Kanzō, who in 1891 had refused to bow before Emperor Meiji's portrait, and he continued his teacher's example of adherence to moral principles. In 1940 the magazine protested against the invitation of General Matsui Iwane to a Christian meeting, on the grounds that Matsui was responsible for the Nanking atrocities. In 1941 Yanaihara's name was put on the black list of commentators whose articles could not be published by the major magazines, but his private journal was not suppressed. After the outbreak of the Pacific War, he was sent on an official tour of Manchuria and North China. In 1944 the police finally ordered Yanaihara to close his magazine, but again he changed its name into *Kashin kaihō* (Good News Bulletin), and this bulletin appeared until the end of the war.[44]

Another nonconformist small magazine was *Chikaki-yori* (From Nearby), edited and published by the lawyer Masaki Hiroshi. Masaki was a colourful figure: a graduate of Tokyo Imperial University, he worked first as a painter and then as a schoolteacher, a journalist, and a lawyer. His private magazine had a circulation of about 3,000 copies, and among its subscribers were well-known figures such as retired General Ugaki Kazushige; the president of NHK Dr Shimomura Hiroshi; the liberal commentators Baba Tsunego and Kiyosawa Kiyoshi, and even the right-wing writers Yasuoka Masaatsu and Tsukui Tatsuo.

Masaki eluded the censors by employing customary expressions of patriotism and loyalty to mask the satire and innuendo with which he attacked the arbitrariness and stupidity of the regime. Thus, the September 1943 issue of the *Chikaki-yori* carried a review of the adventure book *The New Hebrides: An*

Account of the Cannibals' Manners by Martin E. Johnson. The review described the strange habits of the cannibals' land, where tribal leaders oppressed their people and sometimes even ate them up, and it ended with the sarcastic remark, 'When we read this book, we feel grateful that we were born in a civilized country were such things never happen.' Among Masaki's witticisms were: 'Once the samurai leaders of this country were ready to commit *seppuku*, today they prefer *manpuku* (full stomach).' Or, 'the important thing to remember about wars is that rich cowards stay alive, while brave idealists die in battle'.

Masaki's subtle technique of attacking the government was also illustrated in the November 1942 issue of his magazine. The title of the leading article seemd innocuous enough: 'Don't be Misled by Erroneous Opinions.' Yet the article unexpectedly went on to say. 'On 7th October Vice-President of the Information Bureau Okumura, in a speech to the students of Waseda University, said that Japan's aim in the war was to destroy the Western principle of liberalism. . . . But let us read again the Imperial Proclamation of War, and let us not be led astray by such erroneous opinions.'[45]

The February 1943 issue of the magazine carried the article 'Learn Responsibility' (*Sekinin o shire*), which ridiculed Tōjō's speech in the House of Peers on 29 January. In the speech the Prime Minister said that he was not afraid of defeat, because defeat could come only as a result of a strife between the army and the navy, or breakdown of the people's morale. Masaki wrote: 'The speech made me very angry. First of all, it was based on a logical contradiction. Secondly, the enemy could use it in his propaganda against us. Thirdly, it violated the idea of the national polity (*kokutai*). Fourthly, it revealed a lack of responsibility. Fifthly, it showed a lack of imagination.' He criticized Tōjō for having raised the possibility of a rift between the army and the navy, and as for the people, Masaki wrote, 'if their morale ever broke down, it would only be a result of a military defeat, and never the reason for such a defeat'.[46]

This article upset the censor and the entire issue was banned. But Masaki's friends at the post office saw to it that the issue was posted to the subscribers before the ban was imposed. Kiyosawa Kiyoshi, one of those who received the issue, remarked in his diary that he admired the courage of the man who wrote the article and was surprised that such views could be published in wartime. Kiyosawa called Masaki 'a real democrat who knows how to write'.[47] The magazine continued to appear regularly until the end of the war, although some issues were occasionally banned. Probably the reason the authorities did not shut down the *Chikaki-yori* was that Masaki paid constant lip-service to the war and maintained good connections with important people, whose views he occasionally published. When he was denied newsprint, Masaki obtained paper from his friend Iwanami Shigeo, the president of the Iwanami publishing house.[48]

Ienaga relates a grisly story about Masaki. In January 1944 Masaki learned that that police in Ibaraki Prefecture had tortured a suspect to death. He went to Ibaraki, unearthed the man's corpse, severed the head and took it back, by train, to Professor Furuhata Tanemoto, an expert on forensic medicine at Tokyo Imperial University. Furuhata established the fact that the man had died of injuries and Masaki sued the police sergeant who was responsible for the interrogation. The policeman was put on trial, but acquitted.[49]

When Japan started using suicide tactics to ward off the approaching Americans, Masaki dared to doubt the spiritual value of the kamikaze. In the combined February–March 1945 issue of his magazine he wrote: 'Is this spiritual strength? Or is it something like compressed air put into a torpedo? Instead of sending tubes of compressed air, they now send men with special valour. Material has been substituted by spirit.'[50]

However, the small magazines had little influence. Their dissent was expressed in a vague and circumspect way, and they had a very limited circulation. Only a few knew of their existence, and only a handful of writers used them as a means for criticizing the government. The majority of Japanese intellectuals supported the war or kept silent.

East versus West

If the culture of Great East Asia does not overcome
the Western scientific spirit it will be doomed.
Novelist Yokomitsu Riichi, November 1942.

I. SPIRIT VERSUS MACHINES

At the outbreak of the Pacific War Japan possessed some of the
most advanced aircraft and warships in the world.[1] Nevertheless, victories were attributed to the courage, resourcefulness,
and spiritual superiority of the nation rather than to its sophisticated weaponry. When the tide of war turned and the
Americans were advancing on all fronts, it was again stressed
that only the bold spirit of soldiers and civilians, ready to
endure any hardship and suffer any sacrifice, could overcome
the enemy's superiority in armaments and fire-power. As the
military setbacks became more obvious, the more strident
became the voices proclaiming that ultimate victory would be
determined by strength and purity of spirit.

For almost a century, the Japanese had been looking with
envy at the strong and prosperous West and trying to imitate its
patterns. The astonishing victories at the beginning of the war
seemed to prove that Japan, possessing higher spiritual qualities, had at last overtaken the West and no longer had any
reason to feel inferior.

The novelist Shiga Naoya, by no means a supporter of the
regime, expressed this new mood in an essay on the fall of
Singapore, published in 1942, in which he wrote: 'The
Americans are boasting of their economic power and huge
military budgets. . . . But how much poorer are they in spiritual
power compared to Japan!'[2]

Reserve General Suzuki Teiichi, President of the Planning
Board, told reporters in November 1942:

The key to final victory lies not in the material fighting strength of the
nation, but in the spirit which infuses strength in all directions. There

are some who are rather pessimistic in view of the enormous national resources of the US. However, material wealth does not decide the outcome of a war. . . . The side with a great productive power can be compared to a bulky adversary in a duel. . . . It is not difficult to recognize a difference in spirit between the Anglo-Americans and the Japanese. They have been brought up with the ideology of individualism and democracy while we, the Japanese, have been raised with sacred spiritual ideas. . . . Should we be determined to sink every enemy ship, then we have nothing to fear, regardless of the great number of enemy warships. . . . The mightier the enemy forces are, the greater Japan's victory will be.[3]

Such an ardent belief in the importance of spirit could also be found in Tōjō's speeches. Addressing the rally of mobilized students in December 1943, he declared: 'A combat must be fought with spirit against spirit; guns only serve as a means for fighting, but you can fight without them.'[4]

This ideology reached a climax with the formation of the kamikaze units. The suicidal attacks were described as the ultimate manifestation of Japan's spiritual superiority over the materially richer enemy. The kamikaze were expected to reverse the trend of the war, by demonstrating the unlimited powers of patriotism and courage. After the war General Kawabe Masakazu, head of the Japanese air command at the end of the war, told his American interrogators: 'I wish to explain something which is a difficult thing and which you may not be able to understand. The Japanese, to the very end, believed that by spiritual means they could fight on equal terms with you. . . . We believed our spiritual confidence in victory would balance any scientific advantages.'[5]

Even after the war was lost, officials tended to attribute Japan's defeat to inadequate spiritual efforts. Following the surrender, Education Minister Maeda Tamon issued a memorandum to school principals which said: 'We should reflect upon the fact that defeat occurred as a result of insufficient efforts and a lack of true patriotism on our part, so that in the future we shall be better able to exercise our duties as His Majesty's loyal subjects.'[6] Prime Minister Higashikuni blamed the wartime bureaucratic regulations for having destroyed the people's fighting morale.[7]

The spiritual energy of the nation was based on the superhuman power of the gods (*kami*), which included the deceased emperors and the spirits of all fallen soldiers. These gods were expected to defend Japan in her moment of peril as they had done before. The editorial of the *Japan Times and Advertiser* on 15 December 1942 remarked: 'Japan has never lost a war in her history, and she will surely win the one which she is fighting, for not only is her cause absolutely just, but she is protected by a hallowed spirit of the Imperial Ancestors.'

On 24 August 1943, the *Asahi* and the *Nippon Times* carried the following story:

A number of miraculous and mysterious events, transcending the existing limits of science, are reported to have occurred in the Kiska area, which many soldiers on the spot believe to this day had been worked by the deified souls of the heroes, who went down fighting to the last man at Attu. Miracles, mysterious occurrences . . . have been reported as occurring on the battlefield. . . . There are no longer any Japanese forces at Kiska . . . but it seems that in their place the heroic spirits of Attu landed. Foreign reports reveal that the American forces fought intensely and bitterly against this army of spirits over a period of three weeks. . . . In the South Pacific sector too, spirits of the Japanese troops have got hold of the enemy.

The search for good omens, always popular in Japan, intensified during the war years. On 23 September 1942 a reader wrote to the *Japan Times and Advertiser*: 'Can it be a mere coincidence that the attempted Mongol invasion of the Japanese mainland took place in the 1941st year after the founding of the Japanese Empire . . . and that the current war against America broke out in 1941 of the Christian Era? . . . The figure 8 for the Japanese is an auspicious symbol, used in such words as *Hakkō ichiu*. . . . The War of Great East Asia was declared on December 8th. These coincidences presage a final victory of the Japanese.' There were no astrological comments on 5 February 1943, when a full solar eclipse which occurs once every ninety-two years was visible throughout the country, nor when major earthquakes struck Japan on 10 September 1943 in Tottori Prefecture, and on 7 December 1944 in Shizuoka, Aichi, and Mie Prefectures, causing thousands of deaths. Traditionally eclipses and earthquakes were omens that presaged future trouble.[8]

The concept that spirit was superior to machines did not

generate a contempt for science. Although science and technology were products of the 'materialistic West', Japan could
not do without them in war or peace. The relationship between
science and spirit was discussed in the *Chūō Kōron* symposium of
April 1942. One of the participants, the philosopher Kōyama
Iwao, revealed that he was often asked 'how will science be
reconciled with the Japanese spirit in the New Japan?' Another
philosopher, Nishitani Keiji, replied: 'The battle of Hawaii [i.e.
the attack on Pearl Harbor] has already provided the answer. It
is the combination of science and spirit that yields these
wonderful results. . . . One cannot separate the two and claim
that it was a result of only science or only spirit. It was the result
of both.'[9]

The same newspapers that insisted that spirit was more
important than machines went to great lengths to explain that
machines were, after all, vital for winning the war. On 22 May
1942 the *Miyako* conceded: 'Some people are apt to put the
fighting spirit of the officers and men above arms and ammuni-
tion. To make light of these arms is dangerous. . . . It should not
be forgotten that the great victories won by the imperial forces
thus far are in large measure due to the superior arms at their
disposal.'[10] On 4 January 1943 the *Mainichi* commented: 'Of
course, the outcome of the war is not to be decided only by the
strength of science and technique, for in the long run spiritual
power is the final key to victory. Yet it is wrong to neglect
science, for when science and technique are lacking, it is impossible to win a modern war.' On 2 February 1943 the industrial-
ists' organ *Jitsugyō no Nihon* wrote: 'Modern wars are decided by
the power and efficiency of the optical and wireless instruments,
aircraft, tanks, and other modern arms. Any country not fully
equipped with these cannot defeat the enemy.' On 1 June 1944
the *Asahi* warned: 'To expect a victory without sending ships or
aircraft to the front is to expect a miracle, but wars are not won
by miracles,'[11]

Prime Minister Tōjō, who often emphasized the superiority
of Japanese spirit over Western arms also felt obliged to stress
the importance of technology and increased production. At a
governors' conference on 22 December 1943 he declared:
'Whether or not we can send aircraft in adequate quantities to
the front will decide the outcome of the war.'[12]

It was indeed ironic that in an attempt to encourage applied research, the Japanese government discouraged theoretical science, especially nuclear physics. On 16 April 1943 the *Asahi* editorial discussed the subject of atomic research in Japan: 'Up to only a few years ago the tendency among our scientists was to concentrate on the study of the atomic nucleus. . . . But in times like the present, with the whole world plunged into war, it has become quite undesirable that the bulk of the nation's physicists should be crowded into a single field. . . . Since modern war is a science war, it is of vital importance that physicists should spread out into all fields of research.'[13] Obviously the writer could not imagine the impact that nuclear physics would have on the outcome of the war and on his country.

The high prestige accorded to science produced the phenomenon, known in some totalitarian countries, of attributing various inventions and discoveries to native scientists. In June 1942 the *Japan Times and Advertiser* informed its readers that the electric light-bulb and the telephone were both invented by Japanese scientists in the Meiji era. The same newspaper also revealed that a Japanese engineer, Asano Ōsuke, was the first to build a wireless set, and that modern explosives were developed by a Japanese naval engineer, Shimose Masachika, on the eve of the Russo-Japanese War. In May 1943 the readers of the *Nippon Times* learned that a Japanese pilot was the first in the world to fly an aeroplane. In March 1944, Tanigawa Ryotarō, who had built the first Japanese aeroplane in 1907, explained to a reporter: 'The Japanese people are more science-minded and more creative than the Westerners; but the latter have succeeded in commercializing their inventions.'[14]

The importance accorded to science was also reflected in the school curriculum. Although the elementary National Schools (*kokumin gakkō*) emphasized such 'national studies' as Japanese language, history, geography, and morals (*shūshin*), the higher one climbed the educational ladder, the more science one encountered. During the war, the number of hours devoted to science in high schools and universities was greatly increased.[15] In 1942 a special Science Bureau was set up in the Ministry of Education to promote science education. All universities were ordered to set up science and engineering departments, and many liberal arts schools were converted into science colleges.

When university students were mobilized in the autumn of 1943, science students were exempt from conscription. On 1 May 1944 the government reported that for the first time the number of university students in science courses equalled the number of students in liberal arts courses. The result of this policy was that between the years 1941 and 1945 as many as 100,000 students (or 23 per cent of all graduates) graduated from science and engineering departments, as compared to only 30,000 students (or 15 per cent of all graduates) who had graduated from the departments of science, engineering, *and* agriculture between the years 1931 and 1935. The number of higher technical schools jumped from 11 to 1935 to 413 in 1945, and the number of students enrolled in them rose from 45,527 in 1935 to 285,178 in 1945, an increase of about 600 per cent.[16]

The industrial achievements of wartime Japan were also impressive, paving the way for the phenomenal postwar developments in technology. Notwithstanding the ideological belief that spirit was more important than machines, from 1941 to 1945 Japanese factories produced about 70,000 aeroplanes and 4,500 tanks. The 60,000-ton battleship *Musashi*, one of the largest and most sophisticated of its kind, was launched in August 1942. By the end of the war Japanese scientists were working on jet-propelled aeroplanes and rocket-powered missiles which came too late to be of operational use. In the civilian sector, construction of merchant ships, which amounted to only 230,000 tons a year in 1941, jumped to 1,600,000 tons a year in 1944, before both ships and shipyards were annihilated.[17] The Kannon Tunnel, connecting the islands of Honshū and Kyūshū, was completed in November 1942, well ahead of schedule, and in December 1943 a second tunnel between the two islands was opened. While city transport remained inadequate and congested, Japanese engineers were working on the construction of a super-express 'bullet-train' that would connect Tokyo with Shimonoseki and Nagasaki, similar to the *Shinkansen* that was constructed some twenty years later. Other planned projects included a canal to link Lake Biwa with the Sea of Japan and the Pacific Ocean, and a tunnel under the Yang-tse River in China. There was even a plan to construct an Asia–Europe railway, which would connect Berlin with Tokyo via Peking and Iraq.[18] Japan wished to lead East Asia in a scientific as well as a spiritual awakening. As the *Nippon Times* of 30 August 1943 put it: 'Indeed it is not too much to say that, stimulated to unprecedented heights by the exigencies of war, the present progressive investigations and phenomenal development of resources . . . are bringing about a Great East Asia scientific revolution.'

Was it possible to extricate science from its Western context and base it upon Eastern attitudes to nature and life? In the *Chūō kōron* symposium of January 1942 the philosopher Kōyama Iwao claimed that Japan's modernization was not a product of the Western impact. Preceding the 'modernization school' of Western historians by some twenty years, he argued that during the Tokugawa period there were already internal and endogenous developments which prepared Japan for the Meiji reforms. When the gates of the country were opened in the nineteenth century, he went on, an indiscriminate adoption of Western culture and techniques began, and the Japanese developed an erroneous opinion of the superiority of the West. But the Pacific War finally gave Japan the opportunity to correct that mistake and to rediscover the modern elements inherent in her own tradition.[19]

This trend of thought was pursued further by the literary magazine *Bungakukai*, which in September and October 1942 carried a symposium on the topic of 'overcoming modernity' (*kindai no chōkoku*). The symposium was conducted by Kobayashi Hideo and among the participants were the philosophers Nishitani Keiji, Suzuki Shigetaka, and Shimomura Toratarō; the writers Hayashi Fusao, Kamei Katsuichirō, Kawakami Tetsutarō, and Nakamura Mitsuo; the poet Miyoshi Tatsuji; the film critic Tsumura Hideo; the theologian Yoshimitsu Yoshihiko; the nuclear physicist Kikuchi Masashi; and the composer Moroi Saburō. They all agreed that Japan should 'overcome' modernity, by aspiring to a higher stage of development than just matching the accomplishments of the West, and that by doing so she should set a model for the rest of Asia. But they were divided on the meaning of 'modernity' and on the ways in which it should be overcome. Nishitani suggested that the unifying principle for civilization should be based on the Buddhist concept of Nothingness (*mu*), as elaborated in the writings of Nishida Kitarō. Shimomura recommended a spiritual awakening that would enhance moral progress. Kamei called for the purging of decadent Western influences from Japan. Tsumura complained that the importance of science had been exaggerated. Hayashi advocated a return to the traditional values of loyalty and patriotism.[20] No new formula for a Japanese-style modernization emerged from this or any other symposium. The vision of progress without Westernization remained attractive, but no one knew exactly how such a goal could be achieved.

2. ERADICATING WESTERN CULTURE

On 12 December 1941, four days after the outbreak of the Pacific War, the Information Bureau announced: 'The present war against the US and Britain, including the Sino-Japanese conflict, shall from now on be called the Great East Asia War (*Daitōa sensō*).'[21] This name, which became standard, signified that the Pacific War was, from its beginning, conceived in terms of constructing a new East Asian world. The abbreviated word *Daitōa* (Great East Asia) now replaced the former term *kyokutō* (Far East). On 15 December 1941 the government declared that the 'obnoxious word Far East . . . derived from the conception of the British that England was the centre of the world', would not be used any more.[22]

The exact limits of Great East Asia were never clearly defined. However, it usually included Japan, Korea, Manchoukuo, and those parts of China and Southeast Asia that had been brought under Japanese control. These were the countries in which the bulk of the peoples of Mongol and Malay stock lived. But sometimes the term designated a wider area, including countries not yet under Japanese control, such as India, Australia, New Zealand, and Eastern Siberia, populated by other races. In either case the name implied that these areas should form an autonomous Great East Asia Co-Prosperity Sphere (*Dai tōa kyōeiken*) under Japanese leadership.[23]

East Asia was regarded as a distinct cultural region which had been exploited by Western colonialism until its redemption by Japan. The ethnic diversity of East and Southeast Asia seemed less significant than the underlying similarities. According to a wartime sixth grade textbook, all these countries produced rice and therefore would join Japan, which was also a rice producer. The same textbook explained that the islands of Indonesia resembled Japan, the inhabitants of Celebes had the same ancestry as the Japanese, and the Filipinos, although still 'inclined to laziness', would soon be enlightened.[24]

The idea that Japanese culture stood at the apex of Eastern civilization and therefore was superior to the 'decadent' Western civilization, had often been preached by nationalistic thinkers in the past. Kita Ikki, the ideological mentor of the Young Officers in the 1920s and 1930s, wrote in 1919 that, following an apocalyptic World War II, a new Asian culture based on the Buddhist scriptures and the sword of Japan would emerge to be recognized as 'the second coming of Christ'.[25]

The moral superiority of Japan was attributed to *kokutai*, her unique national polity as a family nation with the emperor as its father. Western civilization was repudiated as materialistic, egoistic, and founded on exploitation and personal profit, while Japanese culture was praised as spiritual, harmonious, and based on justice and collective welfare. Professor Fujisawa Chikao of Kyūshū Imperial University wrote in 1932: 'The Japanese empire is a huge family and the people are tied by close blood-relationships into a tight spiritual unity. It is thus quite different from states in Europe and America that have been organized to meet the rational needs of the people. . . . Instead of the principles of freedom and equality for individuals, held essential in occidental states, the Japanese rely on parental love and deep affection among brothers and sisters.'[26] The 1937 guidelines for teachers, *Kokutai no hongi* (Principles of National Polity), warned against the adoption of 'bad Western values' such as individualism and materialism, and explained that Japan's mission was to build a new culture, based on *kokutai* as well as the positive elements of the West.[27]

The outbreak of the Pacific War brought this rhetoric to a new pitch. Following the attack on Pearl Harbor, the poet Takamura Kōtarō wrote in the *Yomiuri*:

> We are standing for justice and life,
> While they are standing for profits,
> We are defending justice,
> While they are attacking for profits.
> They raise their heads in arrogance,
> While we are constructing the Great East Asia family.[28]

Japan's victories on land and sea seemed to prove her moral superiority. The sudden collapse of the British, American, and Dutch empires in East Asia was regarded as heralding a new epoch in world history. In the 1942 New Year issue of *Bungei shunjū* a group of nationalistic writers, including Hanami Tatsuji, Izawa Hiroshi, Mitsuda Iwao, and Nomura Shigeomi, heralded the beginning of 'the Japanese century', a new era in which the world would be united 'under one roof', with the guidance of Japan.[29]

Before the new East Asia civilization could be constructed, the disruptive influences of the West had to be eradicated. In January 1942, the essayist Hasegawa Nyozekan wrote in the *Nichi nichi*: 'With the War of Great East Asia as the starting-point, the races of East Asia are going to establish a united cultural sphere, like the one the Europeans have created since the medieval age. As the first step . . . the influences of the occidental peoples . . . in East Asia must be driven away.'[30] Tokutomi Sohō, in his 1942 commentary on the imperial declaration of war, struck a similar note when he wrote: 'We must show the races of East Asia that the order, tranquillity, peace, happiness, and contentment of East Asia can be gained only by eradicating the evil precedent of the encroachment and extortion of the Anglo-Saxons in East Asia.' Okumura Hideo, the Vice-President of the Information Bureau, in his speech to students at Waseda University on 7 October 1942, claimed that the war was a struggle to free Japan of the 'evil ideology' of Western liberalism. It is therefore not surprising that the Great East Asia Literary Conference that met in Tokyo in August 1943 adopted a resolution 'to destroy American and British culture in East Asia, and create a new culture common to all East Asian nations'.[31]

However, expelling Western influence from Japan was easier said than done. After four generations of intensive contact with the West and exposure to Western ideas, Japanese society could not extricate itself from European and American culture. The need to make the country strong and prosperous precluded the giving-up of Western science and techniques. No matter how much Western civilization was condemned and derided, the Japanese still needed it to win the war. The military could denounce the 'decadent' West, but it was anxious not to lag

behind it in any way. The anti-Western movement was therefore limited to such harmless fields as arts and entertainment,
and even there a fine distinction was drawn between Anglo-
Saxon culture, which was deemed bad, and 'friendly' Western
cultures which could be tolerated.

When the Pacific War broke out, cinemas were ordered to
stop showing American and British films. German and French
films were allowed, but the love scenes were cut out, in order not
to spoil the martial atmosphere. On 2 January 1942 the Information Bureau banned all 'enemy music', except for melodies
that were the basis for Japanese songs, such as *Hotaru no hikari*
(The Light of Fireflies), a famous primary-school graduation
song, which was sung to the tune of 'Auld Lang Syne'. Popular
'sexy' songs, like *Wasurechaiyayo* (Don't Forget) by the woman
singer Watanabe Hamako, were also banned. Jazz music was
considered decadent and therefore forbidden. In January 1943
the Nippon Music Culture Association, the Nippon Record
Music Culture Association, and the Musicians' Association
jointly announced that they would 'weed Japan of the influence
of American jazz' which, they admitted, had widely permeated
into the daily life of Japan. The announcement said that every
third Friday would be set aside to discuss ways of 'ousting the
degenerate American jazz music'. In April 1944 musical instruments used for playing jazz, such as electric guitars, banjo, and
ukulele were also banned.[32]

The public, however, and especially the young, were not so
easily coerced into giving up jazz. John Morris, a British
teacher of English in Tokyo Imperial Univeristy who lived
in Japan until his evacuation in mid-1942, noticed that when
the ban on jazz was first announced, the gramophones in
the numerous little tea and coffee shops, which used to play
such music, were silent for a few days. Then the records started
being played again, but very softly. Gradually the volume was
increased, as people began to realize that the police could not
distinguish between Duke Ellington and Mozart. Even within
the military itself, some 'enemy music' survived. A kamikaze
pilot, describing his last hours before take-off, wrote: '. . . how
funny to listen to jazz music on the night before going out to kill
the jazzy Americans.'[33]

Baseball, introduced from the US in the liberal 1920s, had

become very popular before the war, and the authorities did not suppress it until the spring of 1943, when the baseball league was dissolved and the games banned. However, when the government started mobilizing university students in the autumn of that year, the best farewell present that the universities of Waseda and Keiō could think of for their departing students was a baseball match between the two universities. The game, which took place on 16 October, attracted a huge crowd from both universities, and when it ended (with the victory of Waseda), the whole audience rose and sang the farewell martial song 'Umi yukaba' (When sailing away).[34]

The wartime textbooks presented a sinister image of the US, which had allegedly been Japan's mortal enemy for almost a century. Schools put up posters which said 'Kill the American devils', and pupils practised charging attacks against pictures of Roosevelt and Churchill. In February 1943 teachers and officials were debating what to do with the 12,000 'blue-eyed sleeping dolls', which had been presented in 1927 by American charity organizations to Japanese schools as a gesture of international good will. In a poll taken in the Nishi Tsugaru district of Aomori Prefecture, out of 336 children above the fifth grade in one elementary school, 133 children favoured burning the dolls, 89 preferred breaking them, 44 suggested sending them back to the US, 33 were for casting them into the sea, 31 wanted to display and torment them, 5 were for decorating them with a white flag, and one child suggested using them as models for identifying American spies. Finally, the Ministry of Education instructed all schools in Japan to remove or destroy the American dolls in their possession.[35]

The press played an active role in the vilification campaign, carrying lengthy articles about the depravity, degeneration, corruption, and inhumanity of the Americans. Columnists reminded the readers of the 'vicious designs' the US had been harbouring against Japan since Perry and his gunboats. Newspapers often referred to the 'American and British devils' (*Kichiku Bei-Ei*), and the *Yomiuri-Hōchi* used to spell the words 'America' and 'England' with pejorative Chinese characters that had animal connotations. Sometimes American flags were painted on sidewalks, so that people could tread on them.[36]

In the first months of the war the enemy was derided. American and British pilots were said to be afraid to fight and the soldiers were portrayed as all too willing to surrender. But as the war intensified, that cowardly image was replaced by one of a relentless and savage foe. In September 1942, Reserve Admiral Takahashi San'kichi told reporters: 'The US and Britain are not the weak enemy that some think.' On 19 August 1943, after the fall of Guadalcanal and Attu, the *Yomiuri-Hōchi* admitted: 'The Americans as a people are individualistic and hedonist, easily roused to enthusiasm and as easily cooled, but once they get into the swing, they develop unexpected strength. . . . Thus it has been thought that a war of endurance, like the one now being fought through the jungle islands, was not suited to their temper. But in the course of recent battles they have shown a fighting spirit little expected of them.'[37]

The Americans were described as vicious, wicked, bereft of moral standards, lacking in martial spirit, and devoid of any chivalry. The indiscriminate bombings of Japanese cities and sinking of Japanese hospital ships were held up as proofs of American moral depravity, although no one mentioned that the Japanese had done the same to the Chinese. In August 1944 the newspapers reported that American GIs were sending skulls of Japanese soldiers home as souvenirs. Commenting on this story, the economic newspaper *Nippon sangyō keizai* wrote in its editorial on 5 August 1944:

The barbarism of the Americans is a conspicuous characteristic of American history. If one considers the atrocities which they have committed against the American Indians, the Negroes, and the Chinese, one is amazed at their presumption in wearing the mask of civilization. . . . And now come dispatches from Zurich that American soldiers have sent skulls and bones of our officers and men to their homeland as souvenirs. . .[38]

As no humanity could be expected from such an enemy, it was better to die fighting than to surrender to the bestial Americans. Kiyosawa Kiyoshi wrote in his diary that when he was on a trip in Hokkaidō in the spring of 1944, some 'patriotic volunteers' boarded the train near Urakawa, and one of them gave a speech to the passengers in which he said that Roosevelt and Churchill had decided to kill all Japanese, male and female, except for a few slaves who would be castrated, so that the Japanese nation would be obliterated for ever.[39]

American victories in the Pacific were dismissed as temporary setbacks, reminiscent of the initial Mongol conquests off Kyūshū Island in the thirteenth century, which merely preceded the eventual Japanese triumph, borne by the heavenly wind (*kamikaze*). Mori Yasotarō wrote in the *Nippon Times* of 20 August 1944: 'It is not without reason that the Pacific War should readily remind the people of Nippon of the elaborate but abortive Mongol invasion. . . . The American replica of the Mongol chief now in the White House, a puny mortal of ordinary clay, puffed up with the lust of world conquest . . . has been following the same fatal trail that the Mongol chief blazed.' When that 'Mongol Chief', President Roosevelt, died in April 1945, the editorial of the *Mainichi* said: 'Roosevelt has died. It is Heaven's punishment!'. Professor Koizumi Shinzō President of Keiō University and the postwar tutor of Crown Prince Akihito, wrote in the June 1945 issue of the magazine *Shūkan asahi*:

That Roosevelt was allowed to die in his bed, instead of being killed by a Japanese shell or bomb, may be a cause of regret for Japanese officers and men. But they can draw some consolation from the fact that his death was not unconnected with their brave fighting. . . . It is not too much to say that it was the Japanese forces that killed him. His death can be counted among the biggest war results scored by the imperial forces.[40]

Despite the barrage of anti-American rhetoric, it was not easy to persuade the public to hate the Americans. The Japanese had been taught for years to admire the US and Britain for their technological and cultural achievements, and it was impossible to change these feelings at one stroke. On 4 December 1942, Lieutenant-Colonel Akiyama Kunio of the army's press section, in a radio broadcast rebuked an 'upper-class Tokyo lady', who had exclaimed *kawaisō!* (poor fellows) when she saw American prisoners of war being led in the street.[41] In April 1943, the army scolded *Chūō kōron* for mentioning the existence of positive elements in the American heritage. Postwar film critics have observed that American and British characters in wartime Japanese movies were portrayed as human beings, in marked contrast to the squat and lustful yellow dwarfs who represented Japanese characters in American films of that time. When the air raids started, Tokyo residents were reported to express curiosity rather than hatred towards the American bombers, even referring to them as 'Mr Enemy' (*teki-san*), or 'Guests from America' (*Amerika no okyaku-san*).[42]

The ambivalent feelings towards the West were also apparent in the ambiguous attitude towards the English language during the war. Since it was the language of the 'decadent Anglo-Saxon enemy', English had to be obliterated from the life of Japan. But English had been the main foreign language in Japan for a long time; it was the language of science and technology, and it was the only language in which Japan could communicate with the 'liberated' nations of Asia. This created a dilemma which no amount of sophistry could solve.

On 4 March 1942 the *Japan Times and Advertiser* reported that 'because it is spoken by Japan's enemy nations, the English language has fallen into discredit and there is even an outcry for its abolition'. It was ironic that this statement should appear in the semi-official English-language newspaper, which continued to appear throughout the war, along with other English publications, such as *Contemporary Japan, Nippon Today and Tomorrow, Cultural Nippon*, and *The Oriental Economist*.

Certain English expressions were purged from the official vocabulary. 'Radio' was considered to be Latin, and thus permitted to remain, but 'announcer' (*anaunsaa*) and 'news' (*nyūsu*) were replaced by *hōsōin* and *hōdō* respectively, and the baseball terms 'out' and 'strike' became *dame* and *yoshi*. When the island of Singapore fell in February 1942 its name was changed to *Shōnan* (*shō* being the first character of the era name Shōwa, and *nan* meaning South). Similarly, the name of the Japan Alps, adopted at the height of Westernization in the Meiji era, was changed into *Chūbu sangaku* (Central Mountains). English signs in railway stations and other public places were removed. Vernacular newspapers and magazines that sported foreign names were advised to 'Japanize'; in 1943 the monthly magazine *King* became *Fuji*, the weekly *Sunday Mainichi* became *Shūkan mainichi*, and the English daily *Japan Times and Advertiser* became the *Nippon Times*. Even such private family words as *Mamma* and *Papa*, introduced in the Taishō era, were strongly discouraged.[43]

The question of whether or not to continue the teaching of

English in middle and high schools was discussed at the beginning of the war by a conference of high school principals, which finally recommended reducing the hours devoted to English in high schools. This recommendation was assailed by Ichikawa Sanki, professor of English literature at Tokyo Imperial University, who declared that, as the international language of East Asia, English was essential for Japan. Another professor of English literature, Honda Kenshō, an expert on Shakespeare from Hōsei University, wrote in the September 1942 issue of *Chūō kōron* that although harmful foreign influences had to be driven out, Japan should not discard the good together with the bad. 'English literature must not be cast off. . . . We must not create a purely Japanese culture by carving away everything that is foreign. . . . The tragedy of the scholars of English literature should be a tragedy in which the principal actor does not die.'[44]

The Ministry of Education vacillated between the two views. At first, English was made optional in middle schools, and students could formally choose one out of five foreign languages: English, German, French, Chinese, and Malay. But most schools concentrated on English, and there was little instruction in the other languages. Nevertheless the number of hours allocated to English was reduced, and Western-oriented textbooks gave way to nationalistic ones, in which even the common characters of Tom and Mary were replaced by the more familiar Tarō and Hanako. The fashionable aversion to the teaching of English was exemplified in a wartime cartoon, which showed a boy, with his head bent over a rubbish bin, and his mouth practising 'It is a dog', while his mother, standing near by, says: 'When you finish, I shall sprinkle salt over it.' The caption said: 'Dirty things in dirty places.'[45]

However, the English-language newspaper *Japan Times and Advertiser*, which addressed itself to the foreign community in Japan and to English-speaking readers in the occupied territories, was also read by many Japanese, presumably for practising the language. In September 1942 the newspaper announced a contest for selecting an English slogan which would express 'the united determination of Japan's hundred million in the execution of the War of Great East Asia'. The response was immense. Nearly twenty thousand readers, most of them

Japanese, sent contributions. Among the slogans which were selected were: 'Japanese action spells construction, enemy action spells self-destruction' and 'Victory for Japan is victory for East Asia'.[46]

Few Japanese authors wrote in English. One of those who did was the poet Noguchi Yonejirō, who published a poem in English in the *Nippon Times* on 26 October 1943 called 'Marching to Delhi'. It ended with the words:

> Lo, the anti-British war-men go in majestic line,—
> The crusaders to take liberty by force are they!
> Ah, what enemy can defy Heaven's will?

The Great East Asian literary conferences, dedicated to the destruction of Anglo-Saxon culture, were conducted in English, and the Asian leaders who assembled in Tokyo in December 1943 for the Great East Asia Conference had to use English, since they had no other common language. According to the diary of Kiyosawa Kiyoshi, this fact was resented by many Japanese, and Tōjō, who chaired the conference, found it particularly embarrassing.[47]

Despite the anti-British and anti-American propaganda, English culture and the English language continued to hold a special fascination for those who had received their education in the late nineteenth or early twentieth century, when Britain ruled the seas. In his election-campaign brochure of 1942, Ozaki Yukio wrote that those who criticized him for his attachment to English culture and institutions should remember that Emperor Meiji had signed a treaty with Great Britain and praised her regime, while Emperor Taishō had sent his son Prince Chichibu to study in England. Therefore the people who were attacking the English way of life were contradicting the views of these two emperors. As for the language, he wrote: 'I received my education by means of Chinese characters and the English language, therefore I feel more at home in Chinese and English than I do in German or Italian.'[48]

The government hoped that in due time Japanese would become the *lingua franca* of the Co-Prosperity Sphere, but this could not be achieved overnight. A major obstacle to the teaching of Japanese to Southeast Asians was the fact that more than 4,000 Chinese characters were used in writing the language. In June 1942 the National Language Council (*Kokugo shingikai*) recommended reducing the number of characters to 2,028. This provoked an angry outcry from conservatives, and Tōyama Mitsuru, the eighty-seven-year-old doyen of right-wing agitators, organized a protest against the proposed reform. In a petition that he and fifteen others sent to the Minister of Education in July 1942, they claimed that the proposed reduction would cut off Japan from her cultural roots, impair her national polity (*kokutai*), and make it more difficult for the Japanese to communicate with the Chinese, who still used the old characters. In December 1942 the cabinet decided on 2,669 standard characters (*tōyō kanji*), which would be used for all official and daily purposes; but the implementation of that reform could not be carried out before the end of the war.[49]

Discarding Western influences also meant getting rid of foreign luxuries, which were regarded as morally decadent and economically harmful. Under the slogan 'Luxuries are the enemy' (*zeitaku wa teki da*), the people were called to return to the simpler ways of their ancestors. The astronomer Araki Toshima wrote in the *Yomiuri-Hōchi* in January 1944:

Thanks to the War of Great East Asia, the Japanese are reverting, by degrees, to the true Japanese way of living. The life we now lead is not rich or abundant, but from day to day we are purging ourselves of American and British influences, which have been poisoning us since the end of World War I. . . . The Japanese people are returning to the simple life of their forefathers.[50]

But the simple ways of the forefathers did not meet the needs of modern Japan. Omodaka Hisataka, professor of literature at Kyoto Imperial University, writing in *Bungei shunjū* in November 1942, pointed out sarcastically that kimono-clad women were as inappropriate to modern Japan as were women in Western dresses, and therefore some combination of the two had to be found.[51]

3. THE OTHER WEST

Japan's anti-Western ideology had to come to grips with the fact that her chief ally was a first-rate Western European nation—Nazi Germany. Germany's apparent success in building a strong national state was admired by many Japanese, but only a few recommended that Japan should adopt the fascist ideology. Former Ambassador to Sweden Shiratori Toshio wrote in *Contemporary Japan* in March 1938:

It is a marvel of the present century that Germany and Italy have created afresh totalitarian formulae of government . . . that may be traced to the ancient philosophy of the orient. . . . It makes our hearts warm to see ideas that have influenced our race for centuries in the past embroiled in the systems of the modern states of Europe.

Professor Fujisawa Chikao, in a book he published in 1940, claimed that Hitler had been influenced by Confucianism through the works of Voltaire and Frederick the Great.[52]

From 8 December 1941, Japan and Germany were fighting the US and Britain as full-fledged allies, but being geographically and culturally far apart there was little co-ordination between them. Mutual suspicion was always rife. The President of the Privy Council, Baron Hara Yoshimichi, speaking at the Imperial Conference of 5 November 1941 warned:

I fear . . . that . . . Germany and Great Britain, and Germany and the US., will come to terms, leaving Japan by herself. That is, we must be prepared for the possibility that hatred of the yellow race might shift the hatred now being directed against Germany to Japan.

He concluded with the call: 'Don't let hatred of Japan become stronger than hatred of Hitler, so that everybody will in name and in fact gang up on Japan.' According to Foreign Minister Tōgō Shigenori, Japanese cabinet ministers throughout the war regarded Germany as a potential rival and were reluctant to share war materials with her.[53]

The press tended to emphasize that Japan's military exploits did not fall behind those of the Germans. On 12 December 1941 the *Dōmei* news agency reported from Berlin that Japan's destruction of the two British battleships, the *Prince of Wales* and the *Repulse*, within thirty minutes of each other, had been hailed by the Germans as 'the greatest feat of naval history'. Two months later, the same news agency reported from Berlin: 'The secret of Japan's overwhelming victories ever since the outbreak of the Great East Asia War can be attributed to the spiritual strength of the Japanese. This is the final answer which satisfies the German people, who have been unable to solve the riddle of Japan's fighting power.' Japanese commentators were more explicit; they compared Japan's martial feats with those of

Germany and found Japan's to be the better. On the day following the attack on Pearl Harbor, Retired Major-General Oba Yahei explained: 'These large-scale bombardments are unprecedented since history began. Even the German Luft-waffe did not dare attempt such an epochal venture.'[54]

Japanese residents in Germany were exempt from racial restrictions, and some of them, like Tōgō himself, had married German women. But they knew that in the Nazi order of things they belonged to the lesser breeds.[55] Indeed, when Japan attacked Pearl Harbor, Hitler, though first elated, remarked to General Gause: 'It means the loss of a whole continent, and one must regret it for it's the white race which is the loser.'[56] The Japanese authorities tried hard to prevent the public from learning the extent of Hitler's racial ideas. The full translation of *Mein Kampf*, which was done in 1942, was classified as 'secret', and the president of the Asia Research Institute which published it, Baron Ōkura Kimmochi, wrote in the introduction that it was decided not to make the full translation available to the general public, 'in order to avoid an unfavourable impact which the book might have on Japanese–German relations'.[57] Nevertheless, the arrogant attitude of the Germans to all other, and especially non-white, races was well known in Japan and could not be hidden or glossed over. The philosophers Nishitani Keiji and Suzuki Shigetaka, who discussed the war in the 1942 symposium in *Chūō kōron*, pointed at Hitler's racial prejudices against Japan as a proof of the Europeans' basic bias against Asians.[58]

As long as the war in Europe continued, the press praised the 'courageous Germans' and expressed confidence in their ultimate victory. But when Germany collapsed, long-buried feelings of resentment surfaced. Germany lost the war, it was alleged, because she did not fight as gallantly as Japan did. *Kokutai* and *bushidō* were proven, after all, to surpass anything the West could produce, including National Socialism. Prime Minister Suzuki, addressing a press conference on 14 June 1945, blamed Germany's defeat on lack of fighting spirit. He pointed out that few officers had been found among the German war dead in the last stages of the war, contrary to the situation in Saipan and Iwo Jima where Japanese officers had died bravely with their men. 'Our fighting men cannot understand', he said, 'how Germany, left with such a big army, did not persist until the end.' The *Nippon keizai shimbun*, criticizing the demoralized spirit of the German troops, revealed that in the last months of the war in Europe about 10,000 German soldiers surrendered daily to the Allies.[59]

Professor Koizumi Shinzō, President of Keiō University, blamed the older generation in Germany for the defeat. On 9 May 1945 he told a reporter: 'The courageous fighting of the German youth in the present war deserves praise, but it is regrettable that among the older Germans . . . there were some who hoped for a cheap peace. This was manifested in the disorder which prevailed in Germany after the death of Hitler.' Referring to his former students who had become kamikaze pilots he concluded: 'One should never lose spirit, victory comes only to those who fight to the end with confidence. . . . When the Americans meet the full force of our Special Attack planes, they will realize that their invasion into Japan is only a dream.'[60]

Disappointment at Germany's defeat led to open criticism of the Nazi ideology. On 7 May 1945 the *Asahi* urged that Japan 'discard the ideology of the Axis'. On 5 July the *Yomiuri-Hōchi* wrote that Hitler's obsession with the idea of blood-and-earth turned Nazism into a 'narrow-minded national ideology, incompatible with the establishment of a new order in Europe'. Nazi ideology, the newspaper explained, had failed not only in attracting other nations in Europe, but also in inspiring the German people themselves. 'Politics were entrusted to the instinct of a few talented men, and the masses were regarded as having no wisdom of their own. As a result, the evil of bureaucracy prevailed, and a deep rift was created between the government and the people.'[61] The implication was that because no such narrow-mindedness existed in Japan she could expect victory, or at least an honourable peace.

Italy, the other partner in the Axis, received less attention in Japan. Mussolini was praised as a far-sighted and courageous leader, 'the only head of a government able to pilot a plane'. But Italy's collapse in 1943 drew comments of anger and contempt. On 13 August 1944 the *Tōkyō shimbun* wrote: 'Italy has been defeated because the Italian people, in pursuit of their personal pleasures, lost sight of the difficulties besetting the Italian soldiers on the front.'[62]

France had for a long time enjoyed a positive image in Japan, because of her culture and art. Although she remained a Western colonial power, Vichy France was an ally of Hitler and was therefore spared the opprobrium directed towards the US and Britain. French literature was not banned, but books by authors like Maupassant, who was regarded as decadent, were withdrawn from the shops. French nationals in Japan were treated well. One of them, the journalist Robert Guillain, wrote later: 'During the war, the Japanese could hardly hide their dislike for the haughty Germans. But they liked the French, whom they associated with the achievements of French culture.'[63]

The attitude towards Africa was ambivalent. On the one hand, Japan sided with the struggle of the non-white races against Western colonialism, but on the other she sympathized with the anti-British racist government of South Africa, and French colonialism was not mentioned at all. This ambivalence was reflected in an article by Miyashita Hideo in *Taiheiyō* of September 1942, which said: 'The history of Africa is one of extreme sorrow. . . . The continent has been mercilessly partitioned by the imperialistic urges of the European nations. The peoples of Africa are eagerly awaiting the day when the Axis powers will crush the British . . . and the Boers' dream of a free South Africa will be realized.'[64]

Russia was a special case. As a near and dangerous power, with whom Japan had fought a bloody war forty years earlier, and whose ideology the Japanese authorities feared and abhorred, Russia was hated and dreaded. But it was vitally important not to provoke her. Throughout the war, Japanese diplomats stayed in the Soviet Union and Soviet diplomats stayed in Japan. From the standpoint of Japan, Germany should not have attacked Russia, but should have concentrated her blows against the common Anglo-Saxon enemy. On 22 June 1943 the *Mainichi*, commenting on the second anniversary of the outbreak of the German–Soviet War, wrote: 'From our point of view, we regret the fact that our neighbour the Soviet Union should be standing on the same front with the US and Britain to fight our allies Germany and Italy. We also regret that Germany and Italy must devote much of their energies to the war with the Soviet Union, instead of concentrating on the task of smashing Britain and the US.'[65] In May 1944 Prince Takamatsu, the emperor's young brother, even suggested to Hosokawa Morisada, the son-in-law of Prince Konoe, that the three countries Germany, Japan, and Russia, 'having developed similar economic structures', should form an alliance.[66]

The valiant resistance of the Russians to Hitler's armoured columns did not leave the martial Japanese indifferent. The editorial of *Nichi nichi* of 4 October 1942 admitted: 'How the Red Army defenders stick to their posts is enough to surprise even the Japanese nation, the valour and patriotism of which is unprecedented in the world.' Two years later, on 1 September 1944, the *Asahi* called on the Japanese to learn from the Russians, who, although having lost a great part of their territory, a great deal of their industries and raw materials, and millions of human lives, refused to surrender and continued to fight.

Significantly, Russia's military achievements were attributed to her 'Asian' background. After signing the neutrality treaty with Japan, in April 1941, Stalin told Japan's Foreign Minister Matsuoka: 'You are an Asian, so am I.'[67] When Germany was defeated, the *Yomiuri-Hōchi* described it as a victory for Asia:

The victory of the Soviets over the Gremans is none other than the victory of the Asian spirit over that of the Europeans. It may sound strange to call the Soviets Asians, but geographically they can easily be called so. . . . Even Hitler, who thought that he knew the Russians well, was after all a European, unable to understand the spirit of Asia. He therefore underestimated Premier Stalin, who is an Asian.[68]

Less than three months after that article was printed the Soviet Union declared war on Japan.

4. THE IMAGINARY DEVIL: JAPANESE ANTI-SEMITISM

A bizarre element in the anti-Western ideology of wartime Japan was the flirtation with anti-Semitism. Although there had been no Jews in Japan until the middle of the nineteenth century, and no reference to Jews existed in Japanese tradition, in the Meiji era certain translations of Western literary works, like *The Merchant of Venice*, established the image of the Jew as a greedy and domineering businessman. During the Siberian Intervention of 1918–22 some Japanese officers were influenced by their White Russian counterparts, who blamed the Jews for the Bolshevik Revolution. When these officers returned to Japan, they spread this view, quoting from the forged Tsarist document *The Protocols of the Elders of Zion* (1903) to prove that the Jews were conspiring to dominate the world. Japanese anti-Semitism was thus, at first, part of the anti-communist campaign, conducted by the military and the right wing.[69] On the other hand, those liberal intellectuals, such as Professor Yoshino Sakuzō of Tokyo Imperial University, who opposed militarism and virulent nationalism, also objected to the anti-Semitic propaganda.[70]

The second wave of anti-Semitism in Japan started in the 1930s, following the growing Nazi influence of that time. In *Mein Kampf*, parts of which were first translated into Japanese in 1925, Hitler divided all human beings into three categories: the creators of culture, as represented by the Germans, the preservers (or carriers) of culture, as represented by the Japanese; and the destroyers of culture, as represented by the Jews. In this world order the Germans, Japanese, and Jews exemplified three categorically distinct types of nations, of which the last had to be exterminated. Hitler devoted a special section of his book to Jewish designs on Japan. He wrote:

Now, a Jew knows only too well that in his thousand years of adaptation, he may have been able to undermine European peoples . . . but that he would scarcely be in a position to subject an Asiatic national state like Japan to this fate. . . . In his millennial Jewish empire, he dreads a Japanese national state and therefore desires its annihilation even before establishing his own dictatorship. And so he incites the nations against Japan, as he once did against Germany.[71]

Hitler's concept of the Japanese as a second-rate race was not accepted in Japan, but his theory about an international conspiracy against Japan, directed by greedy manipulators in Western capitals, gained many adherents. During the 1930s various societies and 'research institutes' on Jews sprang up in Japan; the largest one being the *Kokusai seikei gakkai* (International Political and Economic Affairs Study Group), which was established in 1937 with support from the Foreign Ministry. The society published a year-book, *Kokusai himitsu-*

ryoku kenkyū (Research in International Conspiracy), which in 1940 became a monthly journal, *Yudaya kenkyū* (Jewish Research).[72] Its leading figure was Shiōden Nobutaka.

Books and articles on Jews, mostly of an anti-Semitic nature, proliferated in the late 1930s. In 1938, for instance, twenty-eight books and thirty-three articles on Jews were published in Japan, dealing with such subjects as 'The Jewish Attack on Japan', 'The International Jewish Front', and 'The World Israel League'. There were also translations from German, like the book *Der Kampf zwischen Juda und Japan* (The Struggle between Jews and Japan) by the German naval commander Alfred Stoss, who accused the Jews and the Freemasons of trying to strangle Japan through their 'puppets', the Western states and China. Needless to say, the notion that most Japanese had of the Freemasons was as vague as that of the Jews, and many thought the two were synonymous.[73]

The anti-Semitic propaganda intensified after the outbreak of the Pacific War. In December 1942 the IRAA recommended that Japan expel 'Freemasonry, the Rotary Club, and everything else tinted with Judaism'. In January 1943 an exhibition of 'Freemasonry, the Secret International Society of the Jews' was opened at the Matsuya Department Store in Tokyo, under the sponsorship of the Information Bureau and .the *Mainichi* newspaper. Among its exhibits was 'a complete lodge of Freemasonry, captured intact in Southeast Asia by Japanese forces'. Another Tokyo department store, the Mitsukoshi of Shinjuku, held an exhibition on 'American films and the ideological war', which exposed 'the sinister Jewish influence on American films and morals . . . as exemplified by Charlie Chaplin'.[74]

In Japan, in contrast to Germany, anti-Semitism was never an official ideology. Neither Tōjō nor any of his cabinet members attacked the Jews in speech or writing. The leaders of the anti-Semitic movement were all second-rate figures, many of them retired officers or bureaucrats, or right-wing intellectuals. The most prominent was Reserve Brigadier-General Shiōden Nobutaka, founder and director of the *Kokusai seikei gakkai*. Shiōden was first attracted to anti-Semitism when he served as military attaché in Paris during World War I. Later he participated in the Siberian Expedition and was influenced by White Russian officers. He retired in 1928 and in 1938 attended an anti-Semitic conference in Germany where he met Julius Streicher, editor of the notoriously anti-Semitic journal *Der Stürmer*. As a result of that meeting, the June 1939 issue of *Der Stürmer* praised General Shiōden as the great leader of Japanese anti-Semitism. On his return to Japan Shiōden wrote the book *Yudaya shisō oyobi undō* (Jewish Thought and Action), in which he accused the Jews of plotting to dominate the world. In that book he rejected the theory, first propounded by the Scottish missionary N. McLeod in the nineteenth century, that the Japanese were descendants of the Ten Lost Tribes of Israel. He then dismissed the argument that the Jews were, as some had claimed, kind and helpful. Jewish kindness, Shiōden wrote, was only a cover for their sinister schemes, and any country that let them in took an immense risk.[75] In 1942 General Shiōden, using anti-Semitic propaganda in his election campaign in Tokyo, was elected to the Diet by the highest number of votes in the whole country.

The peculiar character of Japanese anti-Semitism was illustrated in the words of retired General Nakaoka Yatsutaka. Writing in the magazine *Hankyō jōhō* (Anti-Communist News) in March 1943, he claimed: 'The Jews, detestable as they are, possess a strong spirit. . . . Only Japan, which has a strong spirit of her own, dating back to the foundation of the country, can confront them in battle. In the present war, the champion of the East and the champion of the West are pitted against each other.'[76] In this scenario the Jews are not considered to be the enemies of Western civilization, as Hitler claimed they were. On the contrary, they are depicted as the very personification of the West engaged in a fateful struggle with the East.

Shiratori Toshio, a member of the House of Representatives and former Ambassador to Sweden and to Italy, wrote in the *Yomiuri-Hōchi* in September 1942:

The aim of the Jews is to establish hegemony over the world, by the grace of *Jehovah* their racial god, in order to force mankind to worship that deity. . . . This scheme is absolutely incompatible with our imperial institution, which seeks to bring the world under one roof (*hakkō ichiu*). . . . The present war is therefore a struggle between the Japanese and the Jews.[77]

Shiratori's obsession with the Jewish threat was reflected the following year in a statement he made to an *Asahi* reporter. Commenting on the Allied summit meeting in Cairo in December 1943, he accused the Jews of having perpetrated the war:

Some Japanese refuse to take notice of the warnings about the Jews, but they are mistaken. . . . To fathom the true character of the enemy, we must acquaint ourselves with the devilish character of the Jews, who manipulate the enemy camp. There is no democracy in the US, and the American masses know nothing. A clique of Jews, numbering less than twenty and headed by Roosevelt, has been running the US for the last twelve years. England too is an oligarchy administered by Jewish interests. . . . The Jews wish to become the leaders of the world. Having found Japan a serious obstacle to their scheme, they have decided to strike against her. Should Japan be defeated, the world would fall into the hands of the Jews and the future of humanity would be bleak.[78]

In July 1943 a public conference on Jews was held in Tokyo, under the auspices of the Great Japan Patriotic Writers' Association and the *Mainichi* newspaper, in which 500 people participated. The programme included the following speakers and topics:

Shiōden Nobutaka: 'Exposing the International Wire-Pullers'
Shiratori Toshio: 'Imperial-way Japan and the Jews'
Hasegawa Yasuzō: 'The Financial Power of the Jews'
Masuda Masao: 'The Present War and the Jewish Problem'
Uehara Torashige: 'Jewish Power and the Press'
Atago Hokusan: 'The Secret Writings of the Talmud and the
                          Kabbalah'.[79]

In January 1944 the League for the Observance of the Imperial Rescript on Education (*Kyōiku chokugo o mamoru remmei*) held a conference in Tokyo on the theme of 'Jewish Intrigues'. The chairman was the president of the League, Prince Ichijō Sanetaka, and among the participants were the Vice-Minister of the Imperial Household Baron Shirane Matsusuke, Reserve Brigadier-General Hata Shinji, Reserve Brigadier-General Shiōden Nobutaka, Reserve Admiral Yamamoto Eisuke, and Shiratori Toshio.[80]

Tokutomi Sohō, the leading Japanese commentator of the time, was one of the exponents of wartime anti-Semitism. In his book *Hisshō kokumin dokuhon* (Reader for the People Determined to Win), published in 1944, he wrote: 'The Jews are the curse of mankind. Under the guise of democracy they wield their pluto-cratic hegemony in the United States. American democracy has become a Jewish den.'[81] Another writer, Takeda Seigo, in a book called *Shimbun to Yudayajin* (The Press and the Jews) published in the same year, described the American and British press as a Jewish instrument. He called upon Japan to cleanse herself of 'Jewish culture' as exemplified in jazz, sex films, mixed dances, permissiveness, and communism.[82]

Some intellectuals were attracted by the simplistic theory which attributed all the evils of the world to one cause, the avaricious Jews. The former proletarian writer Itō Ken claimed, in the January 1940 issue of *Kokusai chishiki oyobi hyōron* (International Information and Review), that the war in Europe was not a struggle between 'haves' and 'have-nots', as some had thought it to be, but a fight between those who had come under Jewish influence and those who opposed it.[83] The postwar historian Irokawa Daikichi, who was then a graduate student at Tokyo Imperial University, remembers that he was deeply moved by Shiōden's writings. He wrote in his wartime diary: 'Stalin, Chiang Kai-shek, Roosevelt, and Churchill are all international clowns of the Jews. Their intrigues stem from the secret associations of the Jews. . . . The Nazis fight them in order to save the world from the Jews.'[84]

But there were also other intellectuals whose liberal back-ground had made them immune to this sort of propaganda. The most outstanding among these was the writer Kiyosawa Kiyoshi. In his wartime diary Kiyosawa quoted many of the anti-Semitic expressions that he had encountered in news-papers and magazines, dismissing them as 'childish' and a 'disgrace to Japanese intellectuals'.[85]

The press played an active role in the attacks on Jews, as part of the over-all propaganda campaign against the US and Britain. The most outspoken newspaper was the *Mainichi*. In 1942 one of its editors, Hōjō Seiichi, published a book which depicted the Jew as Japan's 'ideological enemy'. On 6 March 1943 the newspaper's editorial lamented the fact that the US had fallen into the hands of the Jews who were flooding the country with their vending machines and ready-made foods.

On 15 March 1944 the *Mainichi* carried an editorial under the heading 'Inferior America', which said in part:

Those who know the US realize that ordinary Americans are uneducated, uncultured, and ill-mannered people. This fact has enabled the smarter Jews to fan the Americans' childish desire for adventure, and then send the Americans to the front to be slaughtered there. . . . Naturally the Jews do not care about the death of gentiles.[86]

Other newspapers voiced similar views. The *Tōkyō shimbun* wrote on 17 December 1942: 'Democracy in the US and Britain is just another name for Jewish plutocracy. . . . Roosevelt is the running dog of Jewish imperialists.'[87]

The wartime press did not hesitate to print the most bizarre allegations against Jews. On 22 January 1942 the *Yomiuri-Hōchi* quoted Baron Akita Shigetoki's accusation that Jewish doctors were spreading the flu epidemic in Europe and the US in order to weaken Western society.[88] On 21 April 1944 the *Asahi* printed an article by the commander of the Kure naval hospital, Admiral Dr Fukui Nobutaka, which blamed Jewish doctors for Germany's defeat in World War I. The naval doctor explained that the system of calculating calories in food, invented by the 'Jewish scientist' Max Rubner, had wreaked havoc with German war supplies. 'Therefore before starting the present war, Germany had expelled more than 10,000 Jewish doctors, and so improved the quality of German life.'[89]

The Japanese public had no knowledge of the holocaust that the Nazis were inflicting upon the Jews throughout Europe, but the propaganda organs sometimes took the trouble to deny the rumours about it. On 24 March 1943 the Japanese radio station in Batavia broadcast: '"The Jews are being exterminated!" goes out the parrot cry. Don't you believe it! When this present war of emotion has passed there will still be millions of Jews carrying on their dirty tricks.'[90]

Strangely enough, the image of the Jews as powerful world manipulators convinced some practical-minded Japanese that it might be in the best interests of Japan to befriend the Jews, in order to benefit from their power and wealth. In an article, 'The Jews and the Co-Prosperity Sphere', which appeared in the *Kokumin shimbun* in June 1942, Shiōden explained that he opposed the killing of Jews because it was better to use them.

Reversing his previous view that it was dangerous for any country to admit Jews, he wrote:

At present, there are only about 100,000 Jews in East Asia. . . . They can be utilized for the construction of the Great East Asia Co-Prosperity Sphere. Some of them have already offered their co-operation and others have expressed a desire to become Japanese subjects. Such behaviour is natural and praiseworthy.[91]

As contemporary writers sometimes pointed out, the Jewish financier Jacob Schiff had once helped Japan to win the Russo-Japanese War, by raising the loans which were necessary to finance the war. In his book *Tōa to Yudaya mondai* (East Asia and the Jewish Problem), published in 1941, Koyama Takeo argued that Jewish merchants all over the world contributed to Japan's economy by trading with her. His pragmatic conclusion was that Japan should treat the Jews well, since such treatment would benefit Japan. Koyama was quick to add that Japan had always shown magnanimity towards foreigners: 'Since ancient times the Japanese have treated well those whom they ruled and never massacred those who surrendered to them. We have always welcomed foreigners and tried to develop harmonious relations with them.'[92]

The problem of the Japanese anti-Semites was that as the self-declared champion of racial equality, Japan could not embrace an ideology which sanctioned the persecution of an ethnic group. Discrimination against Jews in Western countries was sometimes described as a symptom of Western racism; as the *Nippon Times* wrote on 12 December 1943:

The Americans like to boast about their tolerance towards the Jews. . . . But the fact is that they have imposed social barriers against the Jews that are only slightly less rigid than those imposed on the negroes and orientals. . . . And the same holds true for the Anglo-American attitude towards all other racial minorities. That is the way the Anglo-Saxons intend to rule the world.[93]

In some quarters there was even a genuine admiration for Jewish achievements and contributions. In the book *Nihon seishin to Nihon gakujutsu* (Japanese Spirit and Japanese Science), published in 1944, the famous astronomer, Professor Araki Toshima of Kyoto Imperial University, discussed various national attitudes towards science. The British, he wrote, were interested in science as a means for increasing their wealth; the French wanted science to expand knowledge; the Americans regarded science as the quickest way to achieve first place in everything; while the Jews saw science as a means for promoting human happiness.[94] This was only a passing remark in an essay about science, but it revealed a sympathetic attitude towards Jews, which the author was not afraid to express and the editor did not hesitate to publish.

Zionism too had some admirers among Japanese Christians, who were the only ones who could understand the link between the Jews and Palestine. One of them was Bishop Nakada Jūji who, together with an American couple had founded the Japan Holiness Church in 1901. In 1933 Nakada set up his own *Kiyome kyōkai* (Purification Church) and published a book, in which he predicted that a second world war was approaching. In that war, he wrote, the Jews would suffer terribly, but Japan would come to their rescue and lead them back to their ancient homeland in Palestine. This act would herald the Second Coming of Christ.[95]

Nakada died in September 1939, shortly after the outbreak of World War II in Europe, and his group split into two, but both sects continued to propagate his views. After Pearl Harbor, some of his disciples were arrested because they had equated Japan's mission in East Asia with the return of the Jews to Palestine as parts of the same divine scheme. In June 1942 the police arrested 554 members of the *Kiyome kyōkai*, together with members of other new religious sects, and this crack-down put an end to the group's wartime activities.[96]

The theory that the Japanese were descendants of the Ten Lost Tribes of Israel found adherents not only among Christians, but also among some right-wing intellectuals eager to find the noble roots of their nation. One of them was Professor Fujisawa Chikao, who claimed that Emperor Jimmu was a descendant of King David. Another was Mitsukawa Kametarō, a colleague of Kita Ikki and Ōkawa Shūmei, who in 1929 wrote the book *Yudayaka no meimō* (The Fallacy of the Jewish Peril), in which he praised the Jewish contribution to civilization and dismissed the anti-Semitic accusations.[97] Thus nationalism and anti-Semitism did not necessarily go together in Japan.

The behaviour of the Japanese authorities towards the Jews

who lived in Japan or in the occupied territories was tolerant, despite the great number of anti-Semitic writings. There were several reasons for this. The number of Jews in East Asia remained small, the distinction between Jew and gentile was not intelligible to most Japanese, the official proclamations about harmony between nations and races did not allow the exclusion of one nation from the family of mankind, and the belief in Jewish power made some Japanese officials interested in enlisting that power for the benefit of Japan.

There were no Japanese Jews. All the Jews who lived in Japan and in the territories under her control were Western foreigners who had settled there with other Westerners of different creeds and nationalities. Since the Japanese were used to Christians of different denominations in their midst, they regarded the Jews as just another Christian sect. Against the background of Shintō and Buddhism, the differences between Judaism and Christianity lost their significance. The Jews were therefore treated according to their passports, and not according to their faith or origin, and a man like Wilfried Fleisher, for many years the editor of the *Japan Advertiser*, was regarded as an American and not as a Jew.

On the eve of the Pacific War, there were only a few hundred Jews living in Japan. Most of them were merchants of Russian or Midlde Eastern origin, but some were professionals who had fled the racial persecutions in Germany. As the latter were carrying German passports, the Japanese treated them as German citizens, despite the protestations of the German embassy. Thus the Polish-born Jewish pianist Joseph Rosenstock, who conducted German orchestras until 1933, arrived in Japan in 1936, and was appointed conductor of the Nippon Philharmonic Orchestra. Although the Germans protested and boycotted his concerts, the Japanese liked his music, and so he conducted, and gave piano recitals in Japan throughout the Pacific War.[98]

After Pearl Harbor, Jews who carried American or British passports were detained and later exchanged, together with other nationals of enemy countries. Most of the Russian Jews were deported to Shanghai, where there was a considerable Jewish community. But some Jews remained in Japan and were not harmed.

On the eve of World War II there were about 6,000 Jews in
Manchuria, most of them in Harbin. These were Russian Jews,
some of whom had settled there in the late nineteenth century,
when the Trans-Siberian Railway was constructed, but most of
whom had fled there after the upheavals of World War I and the
Russian Revolution. When Japan seized Manchuria in 1931,
there were about 10,000 Jews living there. The Kwantung
Army wanted them to stay and help develop the new Manchoukuo. In 1933 the Special Branch (*tokumu kikan*) of the
Kwantung Army, which was in charge of political affairs,
recommended that the Jews be treated well, so that 'their
enormous economic power and their covert political influence'
could be harnessed for the good of Japan.[99]

Yet the severance of Manchuria from China and the law-
lessness which accompanied the military and political changes
there caused many Jews to leave the region and settle in North
China or Shanghai, where business opportunities were better.

Shanghai, for long the commercial capital of China, was very
attractive to Jewish businessmen and immigrants. Some
famous Jewish family concerns, like those of the Sassoons
and Kadoories, both of Middle Eastern origin, had been based
there before the war. In 1937 there were about 5,000 Jews in
Shanghai, and they constituted 10 per cent of the foreign
community.[100]

In 1938 thousands of Jewish refugees, first from Germany
and later from German-occupied territories in eastern Europe,
started arriving in East Asia. The Kwantung Army allowed the
refugees to settle in Manchuria despite the protests from the
German Ambassador to Japan, General Eugen Ott. According
to Miyazawa, Major-General Higuchi Kiichirō, Commander of
the Kwantung Army's Special Branch, replied that since the
refugees had been expelled from Germany, the Germans had no
authority over them. He added that Japan did not belong to
Germany and Manchuria did not belong to Japan, and therefore the Empire of Manchoukuo was free to admit whomever
she wished. This blunt answer, conveyed through the
Commander of the Kwantung Army General Ueda Ken'kichi
to the army's general staff, was endorsed by Vice-Minister
General Tōjō Hideki and passed through the Foreign Ministry,
to the German embassy.[101]

In 1939 the Japanese consul in Lithuania, Sugihara Sempō, issued thousands of transit visas to Jewish refugees, enabling them to take the Trans-Siberian Railway to Vladivostok and sail from there to Japan, formally *en route* to Curaçao, a place which did not require entry visas. The refugees who arrived at the port of Suruga in western Japan was sent to Kobe, where the local Jewish community, with the assistance of American relief organizations, helped them until they could continue to other countries. Most of them had nowhere to go and were allowed to proceed to Shanghai. During the years 1939–41 about 5,000 Jewish refugees passed in this way through Kobe. The most exotic of them were the 300 teachers and students of the *Yeshiva* of Mir, Lithuania, whose long beards and traditional black robes perplexed the local Japanese. The refugees encountered no hostility in Japan. Although their transit visas were valid for only two weeks, they were allowed to stay for up to a year, until they could find a safe place to go to. The attitude of the local population was a mixture of curiosity and sympathy. Members of the *Kiyome kyōkai* sect in Kobe welcomed them with baskets of food, a Hebrew-speaking Japanese professor came to visit them, and a Japanese doctor provided them with free medical care.[102]

Many other refugees arrived in Shanghai directly from Europe. From 1938 until the outbreak of the Pacific War, about 17,000 Jewish refugees from central and eastern Europe settled in Shanghai, mainly in the Japanese-controlled section of the International Settlement, Hongkew, where housing was cheapest. Most of them were poor and jobless and they were helped by the American Joint Distribution Committee. The financial assistance from the US, coming through neutral countries, was allowed to continue even after the outbreak of the Pacific War.[103] An American journalist, Hallett Abend, visiting Shanghai in the winter of 1940–1, noted: 'Of all the groups of Jewish refugees scattered over the world today . . . those in Shanghai are probably enduring the most difficult immediate present and are facing the most uncertain and perilous future.'[104] But what Abend could not know at that time was that the Shanghai Jews, despite their economic difficulties, were spared the much worse fate that awaited their brethren in Europe.

The army maintained an expert on Jewish affairs, Colonel Yasue Norihiro, who had taken part in the Siberian Intervention and, like others, had been influenced by White Russian anti-Semitism. With the army's support, he devoted himself to the study of the 'Jewish question', and in 1927, on his way to Europe, he visited Palestine and met with Jewish leaders there. In 1934 he wrote the book *Yudaya no hitobito* (The Jews), in which he 'exposed' the Jewish control over capitalist and communist countries alike. The book was published by the Military Club (*gunjin kaikan*) and a former Army Minister, General Minami Jirō, wrote the introduction. Although basically anti-Semitic, the book also included some favourable passages about the Jews, such as positive descriptions of the new settlements in Palestine. Yasue acknowledged the fact that the Jewish financier Jacob Schiff had helped Japan during the Russo-Japanese War, but argued that this was done only because of hatred for Russia and that it actually prolonged the war. Yasue dismissed the theory that the Japanese were descendants of Israel, but admitted that there were similarities between the two peoples. The Old Testament, he wrote, was more meaningful to Japanese than to Europeans, because many Jewish customs resembled Japanese customs, and the ancient Hebrews, like the Japanese, believed in the 'unity of religion and state' (*saisei itchi*). In addition, both nations regarded the family very highly and Jewish family life resembled the family life of Japan. Among the Jews, he noted, 'parents are kind to children, and children respect their parents, ancestors are revered, and men are superior to women', all of which reminded him of Japan. The book warned against the 'sinister machinations' of the Jews, but noted that there were many Jews who were neither capitalists nor revolutionaries, 'like the pious Orthodox Jews praying at the Wailing Wall in Jerusalem, or the energetic pioneers building the new villages in Palestine'. His conclusion was that some of the Jews were dangerous to Japan, some were harmless, and some could be utilized.[105] As an adviser to the Kwantung Army in the late 1930s, Yasue helped Jewish refugees to settle in Manchuria, and because of that his name was entered in the Golden Book of the Jewish National Fund in Jerusalem on 14 July 1941.[106]

The navy's expert on Jewish affairs was Captain Inuzuka

Koreshige, who represented a similar combination of ideological anti-Semitism and practical friendship for the Jews. In 1939 he published a book, *Yudaya mondai to Nihon* (The Jewish Problem and Japan), under the pen-name of Utsunomiya Kiyo, in which he too 'exposed' the Jewish machinations to dominate the world and exploit Japan. 'Japan's Jewish peril did not start with the China Incident', he wrote. 'Long ago, the Jewish explorer Marco Polo made Japan known as an earthly paradise in the Eastern Ocean, blossoming with gold, and his yearning for this golden Japan was the inspiration for the discovery of America by another Jew, Columbus.' Inuzuka warned that although there were few Jews in Japan, 'destructive Jewish ideologies', like communism and liberalism, were threatening her national foundations. His conclusion was that the Jews should be utilized by Japan. For a while, he wrote, they had regarded Palestine as their haven, but the British policy of favouring the Arabs in order to obtain their oil had closed the doors of Palestine to them. Therefore, they were turning east and looking for a new haven. This was a historic opportunity for Japan. The Jews 'returning to Asia' should be invited to settle in East Asia. Once they had learned the Japanese language and became familiar with Japanese culture, they would acknowledge the leadership of Japan and co-operate with the Co-Prosperity Sphere. Japan should not be afraid to take the risk of such an invitation. 'Our tolerant attitude towards the Jews, the like of which cannot be found in Europe, has already evoked favourable reactions among them.' The concluding chapter, entitled 'An Appeal to the Leading Class of the Jewish People', stated that Japan, as the leader of East Asia, understood the feelings that the Jews had developed during two thousand years of exile, and was calling on them to accept her principle of the world under one roof (*hakkō ichiu*), in order to establish together the New Order in East Asia on the basis of Japan's traditional tolerance towards all human beings.[107]

In a report written in 1939, Inuzuka compared the Jews to a globe fish (*fugu*). 'When you eat it, it is delicious; but if you do not know how to fry it, it may kill you.'[108] The captain proved that he knew how to fry his fish. He helped Jewish refugees to settle in the Japanese-controlled part of Shanghai, and designed a plan for attracting Jewish investments there.[109] In

1939 a three-man committee, made up of Colonel Yasue, Captain Inuzuka, and Ishiguro Shirō of the Foreign Ministry, recommended that Jewish refugees be invited to settle in Shangahi, as a gesture of goodwill to American Jews, 'who control the US government'.[110] In a broadcast on Shanghai radio in 1940, Inuzuka praised Jewish contributions towards the rebuilding of the city, and promised that no harm would be done to them as long as they remained loyal to Japan. He ended his speech by declaring that the old Jewish dream of 'returning to the East' was being realized by the Jewish settlement in Shanghai.[111] Inuzuka's help to the refugees was acknowledged in March 1941, when he received a silver cigarette-case from Rabbi Frank Newman, in the name of the Union of Orthodox Rabbis in the US, with an inscription thanking him for his services to the Jewish people. This cigarette-case was instrumental in saving Captain Inuzuka from being tried as a war criminal in the Philippines in 1946.[112]

While the navy was trying to settle the Jewish refugees in Shanghai, the army wanted to impress the US by its benevolent treatment of the Jews in Manchuria. On the initiative of Major-General Higuchi and Colonel Yasue, three Far East Jewish Conferences were held in Harbin between 1937 and 1939, with Jewish representatives from all parts of Manchuria. They were headed by Dr Abraham Kaufmann, a Russian-born physician who was president of the Jewish community in Harbin. The hall in which the conferences took place was decorated by Japanese, Manchoukuo, and Jewish national flags, and the guard of honour was made up of members of the para-military Zionist organization Beitar, wearing their uniforms. Major-General Higuchi, who greeted the second meeting, praised the Jewish national aspirations to return to their 'ancient homeland' in Palestine.[113]

In 1939 Dr Kaufman was invited to Tokyo, where he met Foreign Minister Arita, Home Minister Kido, and Finance Minister Ikeda. They promised him that Japan would not harm the Jews, and asked him to help attract Jewish investments to Manchuria. On 27 February 1939 Foreign Minister Arita declared at the House of Peers that the government would not discriminate against Jews in Japan or in any areas under her control.[114] In December 1940 the new Foreign Minister,

Matsuoka Yōsuke, told a Jewish businessman from Manchuria: 'Anti-Semitism will never be adopted by Japan. I have concluded a treaty with Hitler, but I never promised him to be an anti-Semite. I lived fifteen years in the US and I know how unjust people are to Jews. This is not only my personal opinion, but the opinion of the Japanese government.'[115] That year special prayers for the welfare of the emperor were said in all synagogues in Japan and Manchuria, on the occasion of the 2,600th anniversary of the founding of the Japanese empire.[116]

During the war the 22,000 Jews of Shanghai, most of them stateless, constituted the largest Western ethnic group in the city. Their situation deteriorated in February 1943, when all the stateless refugees there were ordered to transfer their residences and businesses to the Hongkew suburb. The proclamation did not mention the Jews by name and did not apply to the local Russian Jews or to Jewish refugees in North China, Manchuria, and other parts of East Asia. The Hongkew area was closed off and those who wished to leave had to obtain passes, but often a Jewish *pao-chia* (neighbourhood policeman) manned the gates. This state of affairs continued until the end of the war.[117] Hongkew was a ghetto, but it was different from the ghettoes of Europe. Not all the Shanghai Jews were interned there, and residents could obtain passes to leave during daytime. Living conditions were difficult and those who needed passes were at the mercy of petty officials, but there were no labour camps and no executions. Jewish educational and cultural institutions, as well as an active Zionist movement, functioned in Shanghai openly throughout the war.

Conclusion

Having experienced the agony and humiliation of defeat, post-war Japanese historians saw the Pacific War as the central event in their country's modern history. They traced its roots to prewar values and institutions, and blamed the ultra-nationalistic, emperor-centred ideology, as well as the 'absolutist' structure of government, for the ever-growing suppression at home and aggression abroad.[1]

Western historians, writing in the prosperous 1960s and 1970s, took a different view. They saw modernization as the central theme, and treated the war as a temporary diversion from the positive and praiseworthy road taken by the Meiji leaders and pursued again in the post-war years. To them the war was not a result of in-built values and institutions, but an aberration perpetrated by irresponsible leaders, who had taken advantage of the country's crises and dilemmas of growth.[2]

Both groups of historians have described the war years as a period of unmitigated evil, an abyss of lunatic aggression, wanton repression, and senseless suffering. The chief culprits in their view were the irresponsible military, who had engineered the war and oppressed the people. However, on closer analysis of those years it is difficult to sustain the contention that Japan was a military dictatorship, or that she was led by lunatics.

The senior position of the Japanese military, rooted in the samurai tradition and reaffirmed by the Meiji Constitution, was greatly enhanced by the international crises of the 1930s and 1940s, for which the army and navy of Japan themselves were partly responsible. During the Pacific War, when Japan was embroiled in the greatest struggle of her history and had to mobilize all human and material resources, her military leaders were the chief decision-makers, determining government policy and trying to suppress any sign of opposition at home.

But the Japanese military machine was not a monolithic body. Its two branches—the army and the navy—remained independent of each other and competed for influence and resources. The emperor, who was formally the Supreme Commander, did not exercise his power of over-all command and did not delegate it to others. There was, therefore, no way in which any individual could control the entire military machine. Each service had its own minister and chief of staff, who enjoyed equal status and equal access to the throne. Combined operations were co-ordinated by Imperial Headquarters, which were composed of the general staffs of the two services, but no unified command ever emerged. Within each service leadership was, as always, collective, and all officers were periodically shifted.

During the Pacific War, the army played the leading role in the state, but did not become the sole arbiter. Other power élites, such as the navy, the bureaucracy, the imperial court, businessmen, and politicians, retained degrees of independence that often enabled them to thwart the wishes of the army. Tōjō's removal in 1944, the nomination of Suzuki in 1945, and finally the decision to surrender, were all carried out despite initial opposition from the army. Moreover, the Home Ministry succeeded in blocking all the army-backed mass organizations which seemed to endanger the authority of the civilian government.

While all the other major belligerents in World War II were led by towering personalities—Hitler, Mussolini, Stalin, Chaing Kai-shek, Roosevelt, and Churchill—who made the important decisions and personified the national aspirations, Japan was ruled by a coalition of military officers and bureaucrats, none of whom attained a pre-eminent position. General Tōjō wielded more power than his predecessors, but his failure to control the navy, the bureaucracy, or the imperial court paved the way for his ultimate fall.

Although overt opposition to the government was not allowed during the war, Tōjō's rivals remained free, and some of them even held key military posts. The police suppressed communists and pacifists, but not the senior statesmen who eventually engineered Tōjō's downfall. Despite a tradition of political violence and the extraordinary circumstances of total war, power-holders in Japan did not kill their opponents, and political competitors did not resort to assassination, as has often happened in other countries.

The previous established rules of the game were still observed. Cabinets came and went, ministers succeeded each other, and important government positions changed hands with remarkable smoothness. Ministers who disagreed with the prime minister had to resign, but they were not punished and remained available for future appointments. Prime ministers who lost the support of their peers had to step down, but were not abused by their successors and continued to play an important role in the selection of new prime ministers.

The emperor remained the sole source of authority and the single focus of allegiance, but his special position as a semi-constitutional monarch prevented him from exercising actual leadership. Hirohito dutifully sanctioned the decisions of the cabinet and the Imperial Headquarters, as his father and grandfather had done. Only when the nation faced virtual destruction were his personal views solicited and obeyed. The emperor was not a prisoner of the military. His sacred status provided him with a degree of freedom and immunity, which he enjoyed together with the imperial princes and court officials. Therefore when the war situation grew worse, the court became the rallying point for opposition to both the government and the war.

The wartime pressure for conformity was strong, but the power of the authorities to enforce it was limited. Despite the existence of a single, officially endorsed, list of candidates for the general election of 1942, many candidates ran as independents, and eighty-five of them were elected to the Diet. Although the courts of justice were part of the oppressive system, the government could not dictate to them, and sometimes they ruled against the authorities, even on such sensitive issues as the legality of elections. The press, though usually docile, was not uniformly so. On several occasions newspapers printed critical comments, and the authorities were unable to suppress them.

Some scholars have argued that Japan did not need to *become* totalitarian, as she already *was* so. As a country where social obligations and occupational conformity kept the population in place, the argument goes, the state did not need the kind of massive framework of police suppression that was established in the totalitarian countries of the West.[3]

But one should not overlook the important difference

between conformity achieved by physical or legal coercion, and that which is the result of social pressures and conventions. Though the latter may be inhibiting, it is less demanding and more diffused than the former. Moreover, the social obligations which at an earlier stage had stifled non-conformism, also proved to be efficient blocks against arbitrary rule, protecting political opponents as long as they observed the rules of the game. Thus, although social, occupational, and residential pressures for conformity were strong, and only a few could dare defy them, the constant need for consensus prevented Tōjō from becoming a dictator and provided his critics with the kind of security which they could never enjoy in a dictatorship.

The wartime regime had no distinct ideological basis and lacked even a name. It was not an 'ism', but a temporary adaptation of the prewar political structure to the extraordinary circumstances of total war. While the government had no particular appeal for the masses or the intellectuals, there was tremendous enthusiasm for the military victories and for Japan's declared mission of liberating Asia from the domination and exploitation of the white man. This vision fired the imagination of both traditionalists and progressives, and was a goal that right and left could support. The sight of the arrogant colonial powers crumbling before the onslaught of the imperial army and navy in the vast areas of East and Southeast Asia evoked an enthusiastic response from most quarters of the Japanese public, including the suppressed liberals who had strong reservations about the regime.

The intellectuals had little esteem for Tōjō or the other power-holders, but admired the courage and martial feats of the soldiers at the front. As they themselves could not join the troops in combat, they led the ideological war (*shisōsen*) at home, spurring their compatriots to greater efforts, fomenting hatred of the enemy, and dispelling fears and doubts. After several decades of alienation, scholars and writers could once again identify themselves with the establishment.

Not all the intellectuals joined in this campaign. Some were arrested on charges of communism, and others were barred from the universities and the media by government orders. A few preferred to keep silent or retreated into areas that were unrelated to current affairs. But most of them adapted quickly to the new circumstances, praising the war and explaining its significance.

Many intellectuals believed that the Pacific War had shattered the cultural superiority of the West, ushering in a new era, in which a reborn Asia, based on the traditional values of the East and the modern techniques of the West, would assume its rightful place in the world. Eastern 'spirit', as represented by the martial prowess of Japan, was expected to prevail over Western 'matter', as exemplified by America's abundant resources. Military successes were to be followed by a cultural revolution, in which Japan would discard the decadent influences of the West and reaffirm the moral values of her past.

But this goal proved illusory. By 1941 Japan was already deeply steeped in Western culture, and the war itself accelerated the Westernization process by emphasizing the importance of advanced technology and heavy industry. Eastern values had their sentimental appeal, but the country needed more technology. Even the English language, discredited as the language of the enemy, proved indispensable. The attempt to transfer the traditional admiration for Britain and the US to Nazi Germany did not succeed, because respect for the West could not be obliterated while Germany's racism and arrogance offended so many Japanese.

The ambivalent attitude towards the West reached its peak in the curious phenomenon of Japanese anti-Semitism. Exposed to White Russian and German propaganda, many Japanese came to accept the existence of an international conspiracy against their country, directed by the inscrutable Jews. Whereas Hitler saw the Jews as an alien, oriental element that threatened European civilization, the Japanese regarded them as the very embodiment of the West. Thus the image of the cosmopolitan, rich, and greedy Jew was merely a caricature of the cosmopolitan, rich, and greedy West that had been confronting Japan since her opening-up in the nineteenth century. The Japanese hated and admired the Jews, just as they hated and admired the Western world.

Had Japan taken the side of the Western Allies in World War II, as she had done in World War I, or had she remained neutral, as she had been before Pearl Harbor, her prewar attempts at establishing a regional hegemony and her wartime violations of human rights might have subsequently been condoned in the context of the Cold War, as was the case with many Asian countries. They could even have been dismissed as overreaction to the real or imaginary dangers of those years. But by joining the Axis and attacking the US and Britain, Japan committed the ultimate crime that sealed her fate and gained her the stigma of a fascist, totalitarian dictatorship.

A closer observation of the wartime years has shown that Japan was not an ideological disciple of the Axis. Although militarily allied to totalitarian powers, her society was, in many respects, freer than those of the Soviet Union or Kuomintang China, both of which ostensibly fought on the side of democracy. The Japanese regime was restrictive, narrow-minded, and stifling, but it was not a dictatorship. Intellectuals and writers were subjected to many pressures, but they still retained a degree of independence. Western culture, although denigrated and vilified, continued to exert a fascination, and these pro-Western feelings, which could not be erased, were soon to surface from the ashes of defeat.

Abbreviations used in the Notes

CJ:	*Contemporary Japan*
ChK:	*Chūō kōron*
DE:	*Developing Economies*
GSS:	*Gendai-shi shiryō*
JAS:	*Journal of Asian Studies*
JI:	*Japan Interpreter*
JQ:	*Japan Quarterly*
JT:	*Japan Times*
JT&A:	*Japan Times and Advertiser*
MN:	*Monumenta Nipponica*
NT:	*Nippon Times*

Dates of newspapers, unless otherwise indicated, refer to morning editions

Notes

Introduction

1 For standard biographies of Konoe, see Yabe Sadaji, *Konoe Fumimaro* (Jiji Tsūshin, 1958), and Oka Yoshitake, *Konoe Fumimaro* (Iwanami Shinsho, 1972).

2 Gordon Mark Berger, *Parties Out of Power in Japan, 1931–1941* (Princeton University Press, 1977), p. 293.

3 Nihon Seiji Gakkai (ed.), *'Konoe shintaisei' no kenkyū* (Iwanami Shoten, 1972); Hayashi Shigeru, *Taiheiyō sensō* (Nihon no rekishi, XXV, Chūō Kōronsha, 1967), pp. 171–2. The designation of the IRAA as a 'public' and not a 'political' organization enabled teachers, women, and students to join it. *Gendai-shi shiryō*, XLIII–IV; *Kokka-sōdōin* (Misuzu Shobō, 1974).

4 *JT&A*, 21· Dec. 1941; Akimoto Ritsuo, *Sensō to minshū* (Gakuyō Shobō, 1974), pp. 48–100; Waseda Daigaku Shakai Kenkyūjo, Fuashizumu Kenkyū Bukai, *Nihon no fuashizumu* (Waseda Daigaku Shuppanbu, 1974), II, 87–120; *Dokyumento taiheiyō sensō* (Sekibunsha, 1975), II, 227–56; Suzuki Ka'ichi, *Tonarigumi to jōkai* (Seibundō, Shinkōsha, 1940); *Tonarigumi dokuhon* (Hibonkaku, 1940); Shigetomi Hozumi, 'The *Tonarigumi* of Japan', *CJ*, XII, 8 (Aug. 1943), pp. 984–90. Further evidence that the *tonarigumi* was primarily an administrative and not a political organization is the fact that after the war the Allied occupation authorities did not disband it, and it continued to function until May 1947.

5 Jerome B. Cohen, *Japan's Economy in War and Reconstruction* (University of Minnesota Press, 1949), pp. 28–73, 271–352; Takahashi Makoto, 'The development of wartime economic controls', *DE*, V, 4 (Dec. 1967), pp. 648–65.

6 Among the standard books on the wartime period, in addition to those mentioned above, are: Ienaga Saburō, *Taiheiyō sensō* (Iwanami Shoten, 1968); Rekishigaku Kenkyūkai, *Taiheiyō sensō-shi* (Suzuki Shoten, 1972); Hattori Takushirō, *Daitōa sensō zenshi* (Hara Shobō, 1965). Ienaga's book was translated into English: Ienaga Saburo, *The Pacific War: World War II and the Japanese, 1931–1945* (Pantheon Books, 1978). For the political background of the 1930s see: Hata Ikuhiko, *Gun fuashizumu undō-shi* (Kawade Shobō, 1962); Nakamura Kikuo, *Tennō-sei fuashizumu-ron* (Hara Shobō, 1967).

Chapter 1

1 Imai Seiichi, 'Cabinet, Emperor, and Senior Statesmen', in Dorothy Borg and Shumpei Okamoto (eds.), *Pearl Harbor as History: Japanese–American Relations 1931–1941* (Columbia University Press, 1973), pp. 53–79.

2 Kido Kōichi, *Kido Kōichi nikki* (Tōkyō Daigaku Shuppankai, 1966). II, 817: Kido Nikki Kenyūkai (ed.), *Kido Kōichi kankei monjo* (Tōkyō Daigaku Shuppankai, 1966), pp. 481–8. Tōjō's candidate for the post of prime minister was General Prince Higashikuni. Matsuoka Hideo, 'Tōjō Hideki-ron', in Mainichi Shimbunsha, *Ichioku-nin no shōwa-shi* (Mainichi Shimbunsha, 1976), III, 243–7. The requirement that only generals and admirals on the active list could fill the posts of the army and navy ministers or vice-ministers was abolished in 1913 but re-established in May 1936, following the 26 February rebellion.

3 Nobutaka Ike (ed.), *Japan's Decision for War* (Stanford University Press, 1967); Robert J. C. Butow, *Tōjō and the Coming of the War* (Princeton University Press, 1961).

4 Ōki Misao, *Ōki nikki* (Asahi Shimbunsha, 1969), pp. 21–2; for descriptions of Tōjō, see Jōhō Yoshio (ed.), *Tōjō Hideki* (Fuyō Shoten, 1974); Matsumura Hideyasu, *Sensen kara shūsen made* (Nihon Shūhōsha, 1964); Takamiya Tahei, *Shōwa no shōsui* (Tosho Shuppansha, 1973); Butow, *Tōjō*.

5 *NT*, 5 Feb. 1943; Masao Maruyama, *Thought and Behavior in Modern Japanese Politics* (Oxford University Press, 1963), p. 17.

6 Matsuo Hiroshi, *Chian ijihō* (Shin Nihon Shuppansha, 1971); *GSS*, XLV, *Chian-ijihō* (Misuzu Shobō, 1973); Richard H. Mitchell, *Thought Control in Prewar Japan* (Cornell University Press, 1976).

7 Akashi Hirotaka and Matsuura Sōzō, *Shōwa tokkō dan'atsu-shi* (Taihei Shuppansha, 1975), I, II; *GSS*, XL: *Masumedeya tōsei* (Misuzu Shobō, 1973); Richard H. Mitchell, *Censorship in Imperial Japan* (Princeton University Press, 1983).

8 Hayashi, *Taiheiyō*, p. 314.

9 Naimushō Keihokyoku, *Shakai undō no jōkyō* (San'ichi Shobō, 1972), XIII, 1; XIV, 1–2.

10 Ike, *Japan's Decision*, p. 273.

11 *NT*, 2 Feb. 1943.

12 Ōhara Shakai Mondai Kenkyūjo (ed.), *Taiheiyō sensō-ka no rōdō undō* (Nihon Rōdō Nenkan, 1965), p. 131; *GSS*, XL, 646–9. There are slight differences between the figures of these two sources. See also C. Johnson, *Conspiracy at Matsukawa* (University of California Press, 1972), p. 15.

13 Details about the Sorge affair are found in: *GSS*, I–III; *Zoruge*

jiken (Misuzu Shobō, 1962); F. W. Deakin and G. R. Storry, *The Case of Richard Sorge* (Chatto and Windus, 1966); C. Johnson, *An Instance of Treason* (Stanford University Press, 1964). Sorge and Ozaki were arrested on 18 October 1941, sentenced to death on 29 September 1943, and executed on 7 November 1944. Two members of the Sorge ring died in prison.

14 For an analysis of the official policy towards political offenders, see: Mitchell, *Thought Control*, pp. 98–102, 127, 136; Kazuko Tsurumi, *Social Change and the Individual* (Princeton University Press, 1970), p. 42 n. 22. According to sources cited by Mitchell, out of 2,710 people prosecuted for violating the Peace Preservation Law between 1928 and March 1943, 2,631 people recanted and got shorter prison terms (p. 147). For a dissenting view on this matter see: H. P. Bix, 'Kawakami Hajime and the Organic Law of Japanese Fascism', *JI*, XII, 1 (Winter 1978), pp. 118–33.

15 Rekishigaku, *Taiheiyō*, V, 136–41; *NT*, 10 Feb. 1944. On the eve of the Pacific War there were 42 million registered Buddhists and 17 million registered Shintōists of various sects in Japan. The number of Christians was 311,000, or less than a half per cent of the population. Of the Christians, 205,000 were Protestants, 94,000 were Roman Catholics, and 12,000 were Greek Orthodox: Masaharu Anesaki, *Religious Life of the Japanese People* (Kokusai Bunka Shinkokai, 1938).

16 Naimushō, *Shakai undō*, XIII, 5, XIV, 5–6; Akashi, *Shōwa tokkō*, III, 105–31, IV, 154–80.

17 Akashi, *Shōwa tokkō*, IV, 184–241; D. C. Holtom, *Modern Japan and Shinto Nationalism* (University of Chicago Press, 1943), pp. 100–23.

18 Kosaka Keisuke, *Tokkō* (Raifu-sha, 1956).

19 Mitchell, *Thought Control*, pp. 19–39, 97–127.

20 Ōtani Keijirō, *Shōwa kempei-shi* (Misuzu Shobō, 1966), pp. 403–73.

21 *JT&A*, 11 Jan. 1942; Ōtani, *Kempei*, pp. 442–50.

22 The Home Ministers of Japan between October 1941 and August 1945 were: Tōjō Hideki (1941); Yuzawa Michio (1942); Andō Kisaburō (1943); Ōdachi Shigeo (1944); and Abe Genki (1945).

23 They were Generals Nakamura Aketo (1941); Katō Hakujirō (1943); Ōki Shigeru (1943); and Ōkido Sanji (1944).

24 See, for example, Ōuchi Tsutomu, *Fuashizumu e no michi (Nihon no rekishi* XXIV, Chūō Kōronsha, 1967); Kinoshita Hanji, *Nihon fuashizumu-shi* (Iwasaki Shoten, 1951). Maruyama distinguishes between fascism from below, which failed, and fascism from above, which triumphed. See Maruyama, *Thought and Behavior*, pp. 25–83. Japanese historians also speak about 'military

fascism', as in Hata, *Gun fuashizumu*; or 'imperial-system fascism', as in Nakamura, *Tennō-sei*. For a discussion of the problem of Japanese fascism see G. M. Wilson, 'A New Look at the Problem of Japanese Fascism', *Comparative Studies in Society and History*, X, 4 (July 1968), pp. 401–13.

25 J. L. Talmon, *The Origins of Totalitarian Democracy* (Praeger, 1961), pp. 2–3.

26 H. Arendt, *The Origins of Totalitarianism* (Meridian Books, 1958), pp. 321, 436–40, 460–6; see also Z. K. Brzezinski, *Ideology and Power in Soviet Politics* (Praeger, 1967), pp. 46–7.

27 F. Neumann, *The Democratic and Authoritarian State* (The Free Press of Glencoe, 1957), p. 245.

28 K. Popper, *The Open Society and its Enemies* (Princeton University Press, 1963), pp. 1–2. For a description of Japanese society during the war, see: T. R. H. Havens, *The Valley of Darkness* (Norton, 1978); Tsurumi, *Social Change*.

29 Inoue Kiyoshi, *Nihon no rekishi* (Iwanami Shinsho, 1966), II, 149–210: Tōyama Shigeki, Imai Seiichi, Fujiwara Akira, *Shōwa-shi*, new edn. (Iwanami Shinsho, 1959), pp. 112–42. As early as 1934, the Soviet commentator Karl Radek claimed that Japan was a fascist country; see his introduction to O. Tanin and E. Yohan (pseuds.), *Militarism and Fascism in Japan* (Martin Lawrence, 1934).

30 Ernst Nolte, *Three Faces of Fascism* (Holt, 1965), pp. 20–1.

31 In cases of urgency, when the Diet was not in session, the emperor could issue an imperial ordinance which carried the power of law until the following session of the Diet. The Diet had then the option of making it into law or cancelling it.

32 For a negative appraisal of the prewar parties see Robert A. Scalapino, *Democracy and the Party Movement in Prewar Japan* (University of California Press, 1953). For a more positive approach see Berger, *Parties Out of Power*.

33 *Gikai seidō nanajūnenshi* (Shūgiin, Sangiin, 1963), III, 524–6; Kōno Tsukasa, *Ni ni roku jiken* (Nihon Shūhōsha, 1957), pp. 522–33. As Tokyo was then still under martial law, Saitō's speech was not published by the press, but was reported, in a censored form, a few months later.

34 *Gikai seidō*, III, 557–9; *Nihon kindaishi jiten* (Tōyō Keizai Shimpōsha, 1958), p. 769; Hata, *Gun fuashizumu*, pp. 301–3.

35 The cabinet portfolios that usually went to party men were those of Railways, Communication, and Agriculture. In the first Konoe cabinet, Nagai Ryūtarō of the *Minseitō* served as Minister of Communications, and Nakajima Chikuhei of the *Seiyūkai* served as Railways Minister: *Gikai seidō*, III, 707; Berger, *Parties*

Out of Power, pp. 123, 204, 224.

36 *Gikai seidō*, III, 664, 724; VI, 605, 621; VII, 194–5; *GSS*, XIII: *Nitchū sensō* (Misuzu Shobō, 1966), I, 336–44; Hayashi, *Taiheiyō*, p. 86–7, 135–9; Berger, *Parties Out of Power*, pp. 156, 247; Masuo Kato, *The Lost War* (Knopf, 1946), pp. 99–100.

37 *Gikai seidō*, VI, 609–14; Berger, *Parties Out of Power*, pp. 327–41. Altogether 435 Diet members joined the club.

38 *Gikai seidō*, III, 615–19; Hayasaka Jirō, 'Gakudō o hōmuru mono wa?', *Shakai oyobi kokka*, April 1937, p. 38. For a biography of Ozaki see Isa Hideo, *Ozaki Yukio* (Yoshikawa Kōbunkan, 1960).

39 *Gikai seidō*, VI, 618–19; Hayashi, *Taiheiyō*, pp. 312–13.

40 *Gikai seidō*, 451–68; III, 803–1015. A 'special session' was the first session after a general election. Several Diet members were drafted for military service and one of them, Matsuoka Hideo of the House of Representatives, was killed in battle in Burma in April 1944.

41 Ōtani, *Kempei*, p. 472.

42 *Gikai seidō*, III, 816–17, 927–37; Hayashi, *Taiheiyō*, p. 314; *NT*, 4 and 27 Oct. 1943.

43 *JT&A*, 19 Feb. 1942; Imai Seiichi, 'Ōkō shita rokotsuna kanshō, yokusan senkyo', *Shōwa-shi no shunkan* (Asahi Shimbunsha, 1974), II, 27.

44 *JT&A*, 20 Feb. 1942; Hayashi, *Taiheiyō*, pp. 302–4; Nakatani Takeyo, *Senji gikai-shi* (Minzoku to Seijisha, 1975), pp. 80–2.

45 Hayashi, *Taiheiyō*, pp. 304–7.

46 Imai, 'Ōkō', p. 31; *JT&A*, 21 April 1942. There were 826 candidates in the general election of 1937. The previous record of 965 candidates was in the general election of 1928. For an analysis of the wartime election see E. J. Drea, *The 1942 Japanese General Election: Political Mobilization in Wartime Japan* (The University of Kansas, Center for East Asian Studies, 1979). Drea's conclusion from the record number of candidates is that professional politicians may have been held in low esteem, but the institution of the Diet was not (p. 82).

47 *GSS*, XLII: *Shisō tōsei* (Misuzu Shobō, 1976), p. 1090; Imai, 'Ōkō', p. 31.

48 Nakano Yasuo, *Seijika Nakano Seigō* (Shinkōkaku Shoten, 1971), II, 600–6, 816–37; Tōkyō Jūni Channeru Hōdōbu, *Shōgen watakushi no shōwa-shi* (Gakugei Shorin, 1969), p. 126; Abe Genki, *Shōwa dōran no shinsō* (Hara Shobō, 1977), p. 310.

49 Ōtani, *Kempei*, pp. 450–1; Imai, 'Ōkō', p. 30. Y5,000 was $1,172.

50 Rekishigaku, *Taiheiyō*, IV, 207–9; Imai, 'Ōkō', pp. 29–30. This may explain why no government interference in the election was found in the rural prefecture of Akita in north-east Japan, as

observed by R. L. Sims, 'National Elections and Electioneering in Akita Ken, 1930–1942', in W. G. Beasley (ed.), *Modern Japan, Aspects of History, Literature and Society* (Allen and Unwin, 1975), pp. 105–6. Out of the 4,353 campaign rallies that were held in Tokyo, 128 were suspended by the police. Drea, *General Election*, p. 58.

51 *JT&A*, 11 March and 5 April 1942; Hayashi, *Taiheiyō*, pp. 307–8.

52 Hayashi, *Taiheiyō*, p. 308; Imai, 'Ōkō', p. 30; Rekishigaku, *Taiheiyō*, IV, 213–15. '*Sōnen*' can also be translated as 'Adults' or 'Young Adults'.

53 Sugihara Masami, *Atarashii shōwa-shi* (Shinkigensha, 1958), pp. 282–4.

54 Hayashi, *Taiheiyō*, pp. 309–10; Imai, 'Ōkō', pp. 30–1; Rekishigaku, *Taiheiyō*, IV, 209.

55 In 1898, when Ozaki was Minister of Education, he made a 'republican slip of the tongue' when he joked that if Japan were a republic, Mitsui and Mitsubishi would become candidates for President. Because of that remark, he had to resign from the cabinet. Isa, *Ozaki*, pp. 232–6: Ozaki's speech of 12 April is reproduced in *GSS*, XLII, 1098–106. See also Ōtani, *Kempei*, pp. 451–2.

56 For the previous elections see Shinobu Seizaburō, *Gendai seiji-shi nempyō* (San'ichi Shobō, 1960), pp. 62–136; Robert A. Scalapino, 'Elections and Political Modernization in Prewar Japan', in R. E. Ward (ed.), *Political Development in Modern Japan* (Princeton University Press, 1968), pp. 249–91.

57 *Nichi nichi*, 21 April 1942; Imai, 'Ōkō', p. 29; *JT&A*, 19 and 21 April 1942.

58 Hayashi, *Taiheiyō*, pp. 301–2, 310–11; Imai, 'Ōkō', p. 31.

59 Hayashi, *Taiheiyō*, pp. 312–13. There were 2,597 spoilt ballot papers which contained various messages. Some of them praised Tōjō, while others called on him to resign or commit suicide. Inagaki Masami, *Tennō no sensō to shomin* (Kokusho Kankōkai, 1975), pp. 147–50; Drea, *General Election*, pp. 133–9.

60 Imai, 'Ōkō', p. 31. In the general elections of 1936 and 1937 the fifth electoral district of Tokyo, which comprised the wards of Shibuya, Suginami, Nakano, and Ōmori, had elected Katō Kanjū of the Japan Proletarian Party as number one, with Asō Hisashi of the Social Mass Party running second. But Asō had died in 1940 and Katō was in gaol for an attempt to set up a Popular Front. Also among the newly-elected members was Reserve Admiral Mazaki Katsuji, the younger brother of the disgraced General Mazaki Jinzaburō.

61 Nakano, *Seijika*, p. 610; Isa, *Ozaki*, pp. 235–6; Tōkyō, *Shōgen*, III,

208. Inukai was suspected for his links with Ozaki Hotsumi.

62 *Gikai seidō*, I, 454; VI, 626–30: Nakatani, *Senji*, pp. 94–8.

63 *Gikai seidō*, III, 859; VI, 631, 637: Isa Hideo, *Ozaki Yukio-den* (Ozaki Yukio-den Kankōkai, 1951), pp. 1168–72.

64 *JT&A*, 3 and 10 June 1942.

65 *Asahi shimbun*, 16 Dec. 1942; *Mainichi shimbun*, 4 March 1943; *Gikai seidō*, I, 456; Nakatani, *Senji*, pp. 129–54; Hayashi, *Taiheiyō*, p. 329.

66 *Gikai seidō*, III, 888–9.

67 Oki Misao, who was secretary of the House of Representatives during the war, later admitted that behind the façade of unanimity, internal discord continued to exist in the same manner as before the war: Tōkyō, *Shōgen*, II, 52–3. See also Borg and Okamoto (eds.), *Pearl Harbor*, p. 332; Berger, *Parties Out of Power*, pp. 232–7, 294–5, 343–7; G. M. Berger, 'Recent Japan in Historical Revisionism', *JAS*, XXXIV, 2 (Feb. 1975), p. 481; Nakatani, *Senji*, pp. 4–5, 101.

68 Quoted in Dan Kurzman, *Kishi and Japan* (Ivan Obolensky, 1960), p. 185 n. See also the views of R. M. Spaulding and Kentarō Hayashi in J. W. Morley (ed.), *Dilemmas of Growth in Prewar Japan* (Princeton University Press, 1971), pp. 76–7, 483–4; Takeyama Michio, *Shōwa no seishin-shi* (Shinchōsha, 1958), pp. 130–6.

69 E. H. Norman, *Japan's Emergence as a Modern State* (Institute of Pacific Relations, 1940), p. 206; Hillis Lory, *Japan's Military Masters* (Viking Press, 1943), p. 132.

70 In November 1943 the Ministry of Agriculture and Forestry merged with part of the Ministry of Commerce and Industry to become the Ministry of Agriculture and Commerce. At the same time two other ministries, Communication and Railways, merged into one.

71 *Asahi*, 29 Sept. 1943; *NT*, 28 Sept. and 4 Oct. 1943; Cohen, *Japan's Economy*, pp. 70–4.

72 Arisawa Hiromi, *Nihon sangyō hyakunen-shi* (Nikkei Shinsho, 1967), I, 373; Richard Rice, 'Economic Mobilizátion in Wartime Japan: Business, Bureaucracy, and Military in Conflict', *JAS* XXXVIII, 4 (August 1979), pp. 689–706.

73 *JT&A*, 2 and 22 June 1942. In the town and village elections of May 1942, 89.5 per cent of the recommended candidates were elected.

74 Hayashi, *Taiheiyō*, pp. 166–9; Borg and Okamoto (eds.), *Pearl Harbor*, p. 506.

75 *JT&A*, 8 May 1942; Rekishigaku, *Taiheiyō*, IV, p. 216.

76 Akimoto, *Sensō*, pp. 62–3. Rekishigaku, *Taiheiyō*, IV, 117–18; *NT*;

21 Apr. and 26 May 1943.

77 Akimoto, *Sensō*, pp. 149–50, Rekishigaku, *Taiheiyō*, IV, 213–15.

78 Kido, *Nikki*, II, 980–1; Satō Kenryō, *Daitōa sensō kaikoroku* (Tokuma Shoten, 1966), pp. 291–2. Shigenori Togo, *The Cause of Japan* (Simon and Schuster, 1956), pp. 248–56.

79 There were 22 executions in 1941, 11 in 1942, 13 in 1943, 25 in 1944, and 8 in 1945: *Dai Nihon hyakka jiten* (Shōgakukan, 1969), VIII, 448. For the Japanese adherence to the principle of rule *by* law, as distinct from rule *of* law, see E. K. Tipton, 'The Civil Police in the Suppression of the Prewar Japanese Left,' Indiana University Ph.D dissertation 1977, pp. 117–70.

80 *Sensōchū no kurashi no kiroku* (Kurashi no Techō, 1973), pp. 79–80; *NT*, 29 Feb. 1944; Ienaga, *Taiheiyō*, pp. 244–5.

81 Isa, *Ozaki*, pp. 236–40; Wagatsuma Sakae, *Nihon seiji saiban shiroku* (Daiichi Hōki, 1970), V, 476–94; *GSS*, XLII, 1090–174.

82 Imai, 'Ōkō', pp. 32–5; Tōkyō, *Shōgen*, III, 208–18.

83 For the roles played by the palace officials before the war, see D. A. Titus, *Palace and Politics in Prewar Japan* (Columbia University Press, 1974).

84 In an interview with *Newsweek* magazine, on the eve of his first state visit to the US in 1975, Hirohito was asked who had been the major influence on his life. He refused to name any particular person, but remarked '. . . perhaps I could cite, within my own family, my grandfather, Emperor Meiji. I always have kept his deeds in my mind', *Newsweek*, 29 Sept. 1975, p. 15. The interviewer was Bernard Krisher.

85 Kido, *Nikki*, II, 743.

86 Kido, *Nikki*, I, 464–74; II, 658–9: Honjō Shigeru, *Honjō Nikki* (Hara Shobō, 1967), pp. 160–1; Harada Kumao, *Saionjikō to seikyoku* (Iwanami Shoten, 1950–6), VII, 50–2; Ben-Ami Shillony, *Revolt in Japan* (Princeton University Press, 1973). In his above-quoted interview with *Newsweek* magazine, Hirohito explained: 'At the time of the termination of the war, I made the decision on my own. That is because the Prime Minister failed to obtain agreement in the cabinet and asked my opinion. So I stated my opinion and then made the decision according to my opinion. Now, at the time of the outbreak of the war and also before the war, when the cabinet made decisions, I could not override their decisions. I believe this was in accordance with the provisions of the Japanese constitution', *Newsweek*, 29 Sept. 1975, p. 15.

87 The expenses of the imperial household were defrayed by the national treasury separately from the government budget. The amount allocated was fixed in 1910 at 4.5 billion yen a year and

remained unchanged until 1945, despite rising prices. The emperor also drew a large income from his estates all over Japan, and his stocks and bonds. Kuroda Hisata, *Tennō-ka no zaisan* (San'ichi Shinsho, 1966); Titus, *Palace and Politics*, pp. 41–6.

88 Between 1864 and 1903 five sons of Prince Fushimi Kuniie were established as heads of new imperial-family branches. They were given the names of Princes Yamashina, Kitashirakawa, Kuni, Higashifushimi, and Kan'in. In the first decade of the twentieth century, five of his grandsons, all of them sons of Prince Kuni, were established as the Imperial Princes Nashimoto, Kaya, Asaka, and Higashikuni. A son of Prince Kitashirakawa was later established as Prince Takeda. These were not surnames, because only one man in the family could hold them, but hereditary titles. Prince Higashikuni had been on friendly terms with some of the radical officers in the 1930s. His staunch supporter in the army was Colonel Ishiwara Kanji: Shillony, *Revolt, passim.*

89 'Shōwa tennō no dokuhaku hachi jikan', *Bungei Shunjū*, Dec. 1990, p. 107.

90 Konoe's rank was the higher of the two, since his family belonged to the top five aristocratic families (*go-sekke*) that were entitled in the old days to provide regents. Saionji's family belonged to the second rank of the aristocracy, which could provide the top ministers in the old imperial system; Lesley Connors, *The Emperor's Adviser* (Croom Helm, 1987).

91 Kido's role in the palace is described in his diary: Kido, *Nikki*, II, 788–1231.

92 Kido, *Nikki*, II, 817, 918; Kido, *Kankei monjo*, pp. 481–8; Matsuoka, 'Tōjō', pp. 243–5.

93 Kido, *Nikki*, II, 917.

94 The minutes of the imperial conferences of 1941 are reproduced in Ike, *Japan's Decision*. The writer Murakami Hyōe accused the emperor of being a war criminal, in the magazine *Chūō kōron* in June 1956. The article is reproduced in Murakami Hyōe, 'Tennō no sensō sekinin', in Yoshimoto Takaaki (ed.), *Kokka no shisō* (Chikuma Shobō, 1969), pp. 300–16. Nineteen years later, the historian Inoue Kiyoshi came out with a sharp rebuke of the emperor in his book *Tennō no sensō sekinin* (Gendai Hyōronsha, 1975). In the West, David Bergamini has accused Hirohito of masterminding the war, in *Japan's Imperial Conspiracy* (William Morrow, 1971). C. D. Sheldon, in his article 'Japanese Aggression and the Emperor, 1931–1941, from Contemporary Diaries', *Modern Asian Studies*, X, 1 (Feb. 1976), pp. 1–40, takes issue with Inoue's thesis. A debate between Sheldon and Inoue was serialized in the March, April, May, and June 1977 issues of the

magazine *Shokun.* See also C. D. Sheldon, 'Scapegoat or Instigator of Japanese Aggression? Inoue Kiyoshi's Case Against the Emperor', *Modern Asian Studies*, XII, 1 (Feb. 1978), pp. 1–35; Shichihei Yamamoto, 'The Living God and His War Responsibilities', *Japan Echo*, III, 1 (Spring 1976), pp. 64–77.
95 Ike, *Japan's Decision*, p. 133; Sugiyama Hajime, *Sugiyama memo* (Haro Shobō, 1967), I. 311.
96 'Shōwa tennō no dokuhaku', pp. 119, 120, 145. For the description of the emperor as a 'portable shrine' see Maruyama, *Thought and Behavior*, pp. 128–31.
97 Kido, *Nikki*, II, 949; *JT&A*, 18 Feb. 1942; Rekishigaku, *Taiheiyō*, IV, 169.
98 *NT*, 23 Feb. 1943. The emperor's Hungaro-Arabian horse *Shirayuki* (Snow White) 'retired' in December 1942, at the age of 22, after ten years in service, and was replaced by the 9-year-old Anglo-Arabian horse *Hatsuyuki* (First Snow): *JT&A*, 26 Oct. and 16 Dec. 1942.
99 Kido, *Nikki*, II, 966–7; *Asahi*, 27 Dec. 1942; 27 Dec. 1943; 27 Dec. 1944.

Chapter 2

1 Satō Kenryō, *Tōjō Hideki to taiheiyō sensō* (Bungei Shunjū Shinsha, 1960), pp. 19–20; Jōhō, *Tōjō*, pp. 521–2.
2 For an interesting account of Ishiwara in English see M. R. Peattie, *Ishiwara Kanji and Japan's Confrontation with the West* (Princeton University Press, 1975).
3 Ibid, pp. 329–30; Higashikuni Naruhiko, *Higashikuni nikki* (Tokuma Shoten, 1968), p. 107; Kido, *Nikki*, II, 1958; Yokoyama Shimpei, *Hiroku Ishiwara Kanji* (Fuyō Shoten, 1971), pp. 371–4.
4 This incident, which occurred on 6 December 1942, did not result in any severe punishment of the outspoken general. The only repercussion was Tanaka's transfer to the Southern Command. Tanaka Shin'ichi, *Tanaka sakusen buchō shōgen* (Fuyō Shobō, 1978), pp. 407–15.
5 Higashikuni, *Nikki*, pp. 109–10; Kido, *Nikki*, II, 1087.
6 Shimmyō Takeo, *Taiheiyō sensō* (Shinjimbutsu Ōraisha, 1971), pp.102–4; Satō, *Kaikoroku*, p. 301; Kiyosawa Kiyoshi, *Ankoku nikki* (Hyōronsha, 1970), II, 62.
7 Nakano, *Seijika*, II, 635–40; Inomata Keitarō, *Nakano Seigō* (Yoshikawa Kōbunkan, 1960), pp. 190–3; Jōhō, *Tōjō*, pp. 583–8; *Asahi*, 1 Jan. 1943.
8 Higashikuni, *Nikki*, p. 120; *Gikai seidō*, VI, 641; Ōtani, *Kempei*, pp. 454–5; Kojima Noboru, *Tennō* (Bungei Shunjū, 1974), V.

54–69; Maruyama, *Thought and Behavior*, p. 75. The characters are: 英機.

9 Naimushō, *Shakai undō*, XIII, 2, 577–87; Ōtani, *Kempei*, pp. 452–3; *Gikai seidō*, VI, 640; Kido, *Nikki*, II, 1057; Fukai Eigo, *Sūmitsuin jūyōgiji oboegaki* (Iwanami Shoten, 1953), p. 228.

10 Nakano, *Seijika*, II, 789–90; Ōtani, *Kempei*, pp. 453–6; Tōkyō, *Shōgen*, IV, 132–8; Kojima, *Tennō*, V, 72–96. The exact meaning of this poem is still obscure.

11 Kojima, *Tennō*, V, 97.

12 Higashikuni, *Nikki*, p. 126; Takamiya, *Shōsui*, pp. 93–4; Kojima, *Tennō*, V, 98; Yatsugi Kazuo, *Shōwa dōran shishi* (Keizai Ōraisha, 1971), III, 421–3. Nakano's son explained later that the money had been earned from Nakano's speeches. Nakano, *Seijika*, II, 789–90. It was deposited with Ogata Taketora.

13 Higashikuni, *Nikki*, p. 126; Kojima, *Tennō*, V, 95.

14 Wakatsuki Reijoirō, *Kofūan kaikoroku* (Yomiuri Shimbunsha, 1950), pp. 421–2; Satō, *Kaikoroku*, p. 296.

15 Konoe's initial enthusiasm about the war was expressed by the special appreciative gift he sent Tōjō: a precious old sword of his family, with the words 'December 8, 1941' inscribed on it: Ōtani Keijirō, *Gumbatsu* (Tosho Shuppansha, 1971), pp. 68–9, 226–7. His pessimism was expressed by his remark to his son-in-law Hosokawa that Japan would soon lose the war: Oka, *Konoe*, 194–8. The fear that war might trigger a communist revolution was shared by the writer Kiyosawa Kiyoshi, as recorded in his diary: Kiyosawa, *Ankoku*, II, 102, 134–5.

16 Higashikuni, *Nikki*, 110–15.

17 *Okada Keisuke* (Okada Taishō Kiroku Hensankai, 1956), pp. 373–83.

18 Okada Keisuke, *Okada Keisuke kaikoroku* (Mainichi Shimbunsha, 1950), pp. 206–32.

19 Kido, *Nikki*, II, 1089–90; Jōhō, *Tōjō*, pp. 385–9, 416; *Asahi*, 22 and 23 Feb. 1944; *Gikai seidō*, III, 948–9.

20 Sugiyama, *Memo*, II, 31.

21 Ōki, *Nikki*, p. 12.

22 Okada, *Kaikoroku*, pp. 214–20; Ōtani, *Gumbatsu*, pp. 237–8.

23 Kido, *Nikki*, II, 1112–14; Konoe Fumimaro, *Konoe nikki* (Kyōdō Tsūshinsha, 1968), pp. 25–8, 41–2; *Asahi*, 29 Feb. 1944.

24 Ōki, *Nikki*, pp. 25–6; Higashikuni, *Nikki*, p. 135; Kiyosawa, *Ankoku*, II, 140.

25 *Chichibu no Miya Yasuhito Shinnō* (Chichibu no Miya o shinobukai, 1970), p. 828; Jōhō, *Tōjō*, pp. 530–3. Prince Chichibu was promoted to Major-General only in March 1945.

26 Chichibu no miya-ke, *Yasuhito Shinnō jikki* (Yoshikawa

Kōbunkan, 1972), pp. 677–8; Kojima, *Tennō*, V, 156–61.
27 Kido, *Nikki*, II, 1051, 1058, 1086.
28 Hosokawa Morisada, *Jōhō tennō ni tassezu* (Isobe Shobō, 1953), I, 43–4, 121, 222–4; Konoe, *Nikki*, p. 18 n.
29 Kido, *Nikki*, II, 927–8; Konoe, *Nikki*, pp. 18, 52, 76–7; Satō, *Kaikoroku*, p. 297. Quarrels between Hirohito and his two younger brothers concerning affairs of state had also occurred in the 1930s; see Kido, *Nikki*, I, 468.
30 Higashikuni, *Nikki*, pp. 105–9.
31 Ibid., pp. 106–19.
32 Ibid., pp. 131–3; Kido, *Nikki*, II, 1049.
33 Higashikuni, *Nikki*, pp. 112, 134–5; Konoe, *Nikki*, pp. 76–7.
34 Okada, *Kaikoroku*, pp. 217, 222; Kido, *Nikki*, II, 1094; Konoe, *Nikki*, p. 78.
35 Kido, *Nikki*, II, 1079; Konoe, *Nikki*, pp. 14–15. Indeed, in August 1945, when the government decided to surrender, the cabinet resigned and Prince Higashikuni was appointed Prime Minister.
36 Konoe, *Nikki*, pp. 19–24, 32–8; Yabe Sadaji, *Yabe Sadaji nikki* (Yomiuri Shimbunsha, 1974), I, 727; Hosokawa, *Jōhō*, I, 110.
37 'Shōwa tennō no dakuhaku', p. 123.
38 Kido, *Nikki*, II, 1020, 1050; Higashikuni, *Nikki*, p. 133 n. Field Marshals Hata and Terauchi were overseas and could not attend. Field Marshal Prince Kan'in did not come because he was ill; he died in May 1945.
39 Konoe, *Nikki*, pp. 48–9, 52–3.
40 Higashikuni, *Nikki*, pp. 135–6.
41 Kido, *Nikki*, II, 1116–18; Konoe, *Nikki*, pp. 63–4, 72–4; Yabe, *Nikki*, p. 729.
42 Kido, *Nikki*, II, 1144; Higashikuni, *Nikki*, pp. 140–4; Jōhō, *Tōjō*, p. 609–11; Ōtani, *Kempei*, pp. 468–71; *NT*, 22 July 1944; Kinoshita Hanji, *Nihon no fuashizumu* (Kokusho Kankōkai, 1975), pp. 179–80.
43 Okada, *Kaikoroku*, p. 227; Higashikuni, *Nikki*, pp. 139–40; Satō, *Kaikoroku*, pp. 301–2; Jōhō, *Tōjō*, 414–17; Nakatani, *Senji*, pp. 232–6.
44 Konoe, *Nikki*, pp. 78–86; Kido, *Nikki*, II, 1120–1; Higashikuni, *Nikki*, pp. 137–9; Yabe, *Nikki*, pp. 731–3; 'Shōwa tennō no dokuhaku', pp. 123–4.
45 Kido, *Nikki*, II, 1121; Satō, *Kaikoroku*, p. 303.
46 Kido, *Nikki*, II, 1121–7; Konoe, *Nikki*, pp. 88–96.
47 Kido, *Nikki*, II, 1127–8; Konoe, *Nikki*, pp. 101–4; Koiso Kuniaki, *Katsuzan kōsō* (Chūō Kōron Jigyō Shuppan, 1968), pp. 781–5.

48 Konoe, *Nikki*, pp. 102–9. Admiral Nomura became Commander of the Yokosuka Naval Station.

49 *Asahi*, 19 July 1944.

50 *NT*, 22 July 1944.

51 *NT*, 23 July, 3 Aug., 9 Oct. 1944; *Uchida Nobuya* (Uchida Nobuya Tsuisō-roku Henshū Iinkai, 1973), p. 207; Takamiya, *Shōsui*, 94–5.

Chapter 3

1 Ogata Taketora Denki Kankōkai, *Ogata Taketora* (Asahi Shimbunsha, 1963), pp. 112–22; *Gikai seidō*, III, 961–2.

2 Koiso, *Katsuzan*, pp. 785–96.

3 *Gikai seidō*, VII, 235; *NT*, 3 Sept., 29 Oct., 2 Nov. 1944; Sambō Hombu Shozō, *Haisen no kiroku* (Hara Shobō, 1967), pp. 193–4; Nakatani, *Senji*, 257–8.

4 Ogata, *Ogata*, pp. 122–3; Koiso, *Katsuzan*, pp. 801–3; Rekishigaku, *Taiheiyō*, V, 294–6. The rift between Koiso and the Corps was reported by the newspapers several times in January 1945 (see *NT*, 8, 21, and 22 Jan. 1945). For the previous links among Koiso, Tatekawa, and Hashimoto see *GSS*, IV, *Kokka shugi undō*, 653.

5 Kuroda Hidetoshi, *Chinurareta genron* (Gakufū Shoin, 1946), pp. 189–90; *Gikai seidō*, III, 967–8, 1002; *NT*, 25 July 1944.

6 Koiso, *Katsuzan*, pp. 796–800; *NT*, 3 Nov. 1944. Russo–Japanese relations suffered a double setback on Revolution Day, 7 November 1944. On that day Stalin denounced Japan, for the first time, as an aggressor; and on the same day Japan executed the Russian spy Richard Sorge and his Japanese accomplice Ozaki Hotsumi.

7 Hattori, *Daitōa*, pp. 690–730; Takeuchi Toshizō, *Dokyumento Tōkyō daikūshū* (Ondorisha, 1968), pp. 48–81. *Tokkōtai* suicide corps had first appeared in the Sino-Japanese War of 1894–5, but until 1944 they had been deployed on a small scale (the name 'Kamikaze' was given, before the war, to the aeroplane of the *Asahi* newspaper, which reached London in a record time of 94 hours and 17 minutes in 1937). Among the English books on the kamikaze see Rikihei Inoguchi and Tadashi Nakajima, *Kamikaze* (US Naval Institute, 1958); Hagoromo Society of Kamikaze Divine Thunderbolt Corps Survivors, *Born to Die* (Ohara Publications, 1973).

8 Kido, *Nikki*, II, 1143–4, 1163, 1169; Higashikuni, *Nikki*, pp. 149–50.

9 Kido, *Nikki*, II, 1169; Okdaa, *Kaikoroku*, p. 233; Kojima, *Tennō*, V, 262–76. Konoe's memorial is often used to prove that Japan's

leaders feared an imminent revolution. Tōyama Shigeki, 'Nihon shihaisha-sō no seiji ishiki', in Maruyama Masao *et al.*, *Nihon no nashonarizumu* (Kawade Shobō, 1953), pp. 145–67; J. W. Dower, *Empire and Aftermath: Yoshida Shigeru and the Japanese Experience 1878–1956* (Harvard University, 1979), pp. 255–65. Dower suggests that the emperor's meetings with the *jūshin* were engineered by the anti-war group around Yoshida Shigeru, which tried, in this way, to convey its views through Konoe to the emperor.

10 Bōeichō Bōei Kenshūjo Senshishitsu, *Hondo kessen jumbi* (Asagumo Shimbunsha, 1971); Koiso, *Katsuzan*, pp. 826–9; Kido, *Nikki*, II, 1179–86; *NT*, 17 March 1945. In his testament, Tōjō blamed the inability to unify the two services for Japan's defeat: Sugihara, *Atarashii*, p. 292.

11 Rekishigaku, *Taiheiyō*, V, 325–6; *NT*, 2–3 April 1945; Nakatani, *Senji*, pp. 301–12.

12 *Gikai seidō*, VI, 648–57; Nakatani, *Senji*, pp. 280–300.

13 Takeuchi, *Daikūshū*, pp. 88–95, 159–62; Hattori, *Daitō*, pp. 767–800; Kojima, *Tennō*, V, 282–3; Kanroji Osanaga, *Tennō sama* (Nichirinkaku, 1960), p. 283; Kido, *Nikki*, II, 1174; G. Daniels, 'The Great Tokyo Air Raid, 9–10 March 1945', in Beasley, *Aspects*, pp. 113–31. The baby born on that night was Atsuhiko, first son of the emperor's daughter Shigeko and Higashikuni's son Morihiro.

14 Kido, *Nikki*, II, 1182, 1185; Koiso, *Katsuzan*, pp. 811–16; Sambō, *Haisen*, pp. 239–40. See also: Yoji Akashi, 'A Botched Peace Effort: The Miao Pin *Kosaku*', in A. D. Coox and H. Conroy (eds.), *China and Japan, Search for Balance Since World War I* (ABC-Clio, 1978), pp. 265–88. Wang Ching-wei had died in Nagoya on 10 November 1944.

15 Kido, *Nikki*, II, 1186; Hattori, *Daitōa*, pp. 877–8.

16 Kido, *Nikki*, II, 1188–94; Okada, *Kaikoroku*, pp. 235–7.

17 Oki Osamuji, *Anami Korechika-den* (Kōdansha, 1970), pp. 263–77; *NT*, 20 April 1945.

18 Okada, *Kaikoroku*, p. 237; Togo, *The Cause*, pp. 269–70; Sakomizu Hisatsune, *Dai Nihon teikoku saigo no yonkagetsu* (Oriento Shobō, 1973), pp. 54–70.

19 *NT*, 9 April 1945. On 9 June Diet member Ota Masatake asked in the Diet: 'Who is leading our country in war? The Prime Minister is only responsible for co-ordination', *Gikai seidō*, III, 1009–10.

20 Kojima, *Tennō*, V, 289–93; *NT*, 9 April 1945.

21 Hirakawa Sukehiro, 'Signals of Peace not Received: Premier Suzuki Kantarō's Solitary Efforts to End the Pacific War', *Com-*

parative Studies of Culture (University of Tokyo Press, 1979), No. 18, pp. 123–5.

22 Jōhō, *Tōjō*, p. 602; US General Headquarters, Far East Command, Military Intelligence Section, Historical Division, *Statements of Japanese Officials on World War II* (microfilm, 1949–50), Doc. 62083. Marshal Pietro Badoglio was appointed Prime Minister of Italy in July 1943, and in September he surrendered to the Allies.

23 Hattori, *Daitōa*, pp. 864–72; Sambō, *Haisen*, pp. 268–9.

24 Kido, *Nikki*, II, 1130, 1221, 1224; Higashikuni, *Nikki*, pp. 131–2; Tōkyō Jūni Channeru Shakai Kyōyōbu, *Shimpen watakushi no shōwa-shi* (Gakugei Shorin, 1974), II, 138–9. Thomas Havens reports a rumour that several thousand Koreans, who had been employed on the construction of that tunnel, were later massacred to hush up the project: Havens, *Valley*, p. 106; but the book *Zainichi Kankokujin no rekishi to genjitsu* (Yōyōsha, 1970), compiled by the Korean Youth League in Japan, which describes the hardships of Korean labourers in Japan, does not mention such an allegation.

25 Kido, *Nikki*, II, 1173–4, 1204–6; Bōeichō, *Hondo*, I, 486–7; Kojima, *Tennō*, V, 302–8.

26 Bōeichō, *Hondo*, I, 293–305; Hattori, *Daitōa*, pp. 892–3; Abe, *Dōran*, p. 350; *NT*, 11 June 1945.

27 Bōeichō, *Hondo*, I, 562–8; Hattori, *Daitōa*, pp. 893–5; *Gikai seidō*, II, 1013–14; *NT*, 15 June 1945.

28 'Kaigenrei', *Nihonshi jiten* (Kadokawa Shoten, 1976).

29 *Gikai seidō*, III, 1010–12; *NT*, 11, 13, and 30 June, 3 July 1945.

30 *NT*, 14 and 25 June 1945.

31 Ōtani, *Kempei*, pp. 497–504; Shigeru Yoshida, *The Yoshida Memoirs* (Heinemann, 1961), pp. 26–9; Rekishigaku, *Taiheiyō*, V, 117, 140; Dower, *Empire*, pp. 265–72.

32 Kido, *Nikki*, II, 1212–13; Sakomizu, *Dai Nihon*, pp. 9–10.

33 Oki, *Anami*, pp. 289–329; Hattori, *Daitōa*, pp. 924–37.

34 Kido, *Nikki*, II, 1208, 1213; Hattori, *Daitōa*, pp. 908–11.

35 Abe, *Dōran*, p. 349.

36 Hattori, *Daitōa*, pp. 924–42; Kojima, *Tennō*, V, 379–411; Pacific War Research Society, *Japan's Longest Day* (Kodansha International, 1965), pp. 30–169.

37 Kadoya Fumio, *Shōwa jidai* (Gakuyō Shobō, 1973), pp. 258–9. This phrase is usually translated as 'enduring the unendurable and suffering what is insufferable'. R. J. C. Butow, *Japan's Decision to Surrender* (Stanford University Press, 1954), p. 248.

38 Sambō, *Haisen*, pp. 378–83; Bōeichō, *Hondo*, I, 580–5; Otani, *Kempei*, pp. 527–37; Kojima, *Tennō*, V, 411–28.

39 *GSS*, XXXIX, 803; Sambō, *Haisen*, p. 318.
40 Hattori, *Daitōa*, pp. 951–2. Tōjō attempted suicide when the American military police came to arrest him, but failed.
41 Kido, *Nikki*, II, 1226–7.
42 Kido, *Nikki*, II, 1227–8; *Gikai seidō*, III, 1019. Obata joined the cabinet on 19 August and Shimomura joined it on the 23rd. The two ministries were abolished on the 23rd.
43 Bōeichō, *Hondo*, pp. 587–9; Hattori, *Daitōa*, p. 948.

Chapter 4

1 During the war, 43 per cent of households had radio sets: Hayashi, *Taiheiyō*, pp. 316–17. Circulation figures for daily newspapers differ slightly from one source to another. The figures quoted here are based on the *Japan Year Book* of 1941–2 and 1942–3, and the *Nihon shimbun Hyakunen-shi* (Nihon Shimbun Remmei, 1961). See also William J. Coughlin, *Conquered Press* (Pacific Books, 1952); Peter de Mendelssohn, *Japan's Political Warfare* (Allen and Unwin, 1944); Shūichi Kato, 'The Mass Media, Japan', in Robert E. Ward and Dankwart A. Rustow (eds.), *Political Modernization in Japan and Turkey* (Princeton University Press, 1964), pp. 236–54. Each newspaper has also published its own history, cf. *Asahi shimbun no kyūjūnen* (Asahi Shimbunsha, 1969); *Mainichi shimbun shichijūnen* (Mainichi Shimbunsha, 1952); *Yomiuri shimbun hachijūnenshi* (Yomiuri Shimbunsha, 1955).
2 After the conquests of Southeast Asia, each of the major dailies was given a monopoly in an overseas area in order to develop a local press in Japanese. Thus, Java was allocated to *Asahi*, the Philippines to *Mainichi*, and Burma to *Yomiuri*.
3 *GSS*, XLI: *Masumedeya tōsei* (Misuzu Shobō, 1975), 1–50, 324, 336–41, 377–444; Matsuura Sōzō, *Senjika no genron tōsei* (Shirakawa Shoin, 1975), pp. 104–8. For the wartime media see also Gregory J. Kasza, *The State and the Mass Media in Japan 1918–1945* (University of California Press, 1988).
4 *GSS*, XL, xxviii–xxix; Ōtani, *Kempei*, pp. 471–3; Hatanaka Shigeo, *Shōwa shuppan dan'atsu shōshi* (Tosho Shimbun-sha, 1965); Kuroda Hidetoshi, *Chinurareta genron* (Gakufu Shoin, 1946); Mimasaka Tarō, Fujita Chikamasa, Watanabe Kiyoshi, *Genron no haiboku* (San-ichi Shoten, 1959); Borg and Okamato (eds.), *Pearl Harbor*, pp. 533–49.
5 *Kindai Nihon shisō-shi kōza*, I: *Rekishiteki gaikan* (Chikuma Shobō, 1959), p. 329; *Nihon shimbun hyakunen-shi*, pp. 763–4.
6 Hayashi, *Taiheiyō*, p. 323; Mendelssohn, *Warfare*, pp. 55–6. Captain Hiraide was replaced in July 1943 by Captain Kurihara

Etsuzō. Major-General Yahagi was replaced in October 1943 by
Colonel Matsuura Shuitsu.

7 *Asahi*, 11–12 June 1942, 10 Feb. and 23 May 1943, 6 May 1944;
Mainichi, 31 May and 1 June 1943; R. Guillain, *Le Peuple Japonais
et la Guerre* (Paris: Julliard, 1947), pp. 86–7, 98–9.

8 Quoted in *NT*, 31 Jan. and 13 Aug. 1944.

9 *Mainichi*, 1 and 2 Nov. 1944; *NT*, 10 May 1945.

10 Hōjō Seiichi, *Shisōsen to kokusai himitsu kessha* (Seinensha, 1942),
p. 2. See also my 'Universities and Students in Wartime Japan',
JAS, XLV, 4 (Aug. 1986), pp. 769–87.

11 Ogata, *Ogata*, pp. 3–111. Ogata led the funeral processions of
Nakano Seigō (on 31 Oct. 1943) and of Tōyama Mitsura (on 10
Oct. 1944).

12 *Mainichi shichijūnen*, pp. 347–420; Shingorō Takaishi, *Japan Speaks
Out* (The Hokuseido Press, 1938).

13 *Yomiuri hachijūnenshi*, pp. 70–2, 417–23. The president of the
Hōchi, Diet member Miki Bukichi, formerly of the *Minseitō*, was
one of the supporters of the amalgamation plan. Had Shōriki
accepted the plan, he would have become the president of the
amalgamated newspaper.

14 *Nichi nichi*, 17 Dec. 1941; *JT&A*, 11 Dec. 1941; *The Japan Times*, a
semi-official newspaper controlled by the Foreign Ministry,
purchased the *Japan Advertiser* in November 1941 from its
American owner and editor Wilfried Fleisher, and the name of
the united newspaper was changed to *The Japan Times and Advertiser*. On 1 January 1943 the newspaper changed its name again
to *The Nippon Times*: Ogata, *Ogata*, p. 103.

15 *Mainichi*, 22 March 1944.

16 Quoted in *JT&A*, 26 March and 3 May 1942; *NT*, 7 Feb 1943.

17 *JT&A*, 2 May 1942; *Asahi*, 21 May 1942; *Nichi nichi*, 30 Jan 1942;
Mainichi, 15 June 1943.

18 *Asahi*, 25 Feb. 1942; *Mainichi*, 12 Sept. 1944.

19 *Asahi*, 11 Jan. 1942; *Nichi nichi*, 26 Feb. 1942.

20 *Asahi*, 1 Jan. 1943; Jōhō, *Tōjō*, p. 586; Tōkyō, *Shōgen*, IV, 127;
Rekishigaku, *Taiheiyō*, V, 139.

21 *Mainichi*, 23 Feb. 1944. After the war Shimmyō's story appeared
in various books: Shimmyō Takeo, *Shōwa-shi tsuiseki* (Shinjimbutsu Ōraisha, 1970), Shimmyō, *Taiheiyō*; Tōkyō, *Shōgen*, IV,
162–6. See also *Mainichi shimbun hyakunen-shi* (Mainichi
Shimbunsha, 1972), pp. 199–201.

22 *Asahi*, 23 July 1944. In February 1945 the *Nippon Times* explained
to its foreign readers that whereas under Tōjō it had been necessary to impose severe restrictions on the press in order to put the
country on a war footing, under Koiso these restrictions could be

relaxed since the country had already been adjusted to the war: *NT*, 19 Feb. 1945.

23 *Asahi*, 9 Sept. 1944. A criticism of the suppression of the press during the Tōjō regime was also included in an article by Iizawa Shōji, the managing director of the Japan Newspaper Association, published in the English-language quarterly *Contemporary Japan* in late 1944: Shōji Iizawa, 'Policy of the Koiso Cabinet', *CJ*, VIII, 10–12 (Oct.–Dec. 1944), pp. 900–11.

24 Quoted in *NT*, 15 March and 12 April 1945.

25 Kato, *Lost War*, pp. 141–2.

26 *Nihon shimbun hyakunen-shi*, p. 767. On 16 June 1944, when the area of Kitakyūshū was bombed, all three local newspapers combined to issue a common local paper, the *Kyōdō gōgai*. *Mainichi shichijūnen*, pp. 410–12.

27 *Asahi*, 18 May 1945; *Mainichi*, 30 June 1945.

28 *Asahi*, 28 July 1945.

29 *Asahi*, 8 Aug. 1945; *NT*, 10 Aug. 1945.

30 *Asahi*, 9, 11, and 12 Aug. 1945; *NT*, 11 and 12 Aug. 1945. The *Mainichi* reported the dropping of the second atomic bomb on Nagasaki on 11 August, one day before the *Asahi*.

31 *Asahi*, 15 Aug. 1945; *Mainichi*, 15 Aug. 1945.

32 As quoted in *NT*, 16 Aug. 1945.

Chapter 5

An earlier version of a part of this chapter was delivered as a paper at the third annual conference of the British Association for Japanese Studies at St. Antony's College, Oxford, in April 1977, and was subsequently published in *Proceedings of the British Association for Japanese Studies*, II, edited by Gordon Daniels and Peter Lowe (University of Sheffield, Centre of Japanese Studies, 1977), Part I, pp. 90–9.

1 *Nihon shuppan nenkan* (Kyōdō Shuppansha, 1943), pp. ii, iii; *Shuppan nenkan* (Tōkyōdō, 1941), p. iii. Although the magazines appeared around the middle of the month, they carried the date of the following month. The magazines were widely advertised in daily newspapers.

2 For accounts of the *Shōwa kenkyūkai* see J. B. Crowley, 'Intellectuals as Visionaries of the New Asia Order', in Morley, *Dilemmas*, pp. 319–73; Johnson, *An Instance*; Miles Fletcher, 'Intellectuals and Fascism in Early Shōwa Japan', *JAS*, XXXIX, 1 (Nov. 1979), pp. 39–63. For the views of Miki see Miki Kiyoshi, 'Gendai Nihon ni okeru sekai-shi no igi', *Kaizō*, June 1938; Miki Kiyoshi, 'Tōa shisō no konkyo', *Kaizō*, Oct. 1938; Kiyoshi Miki, 'The China Affair and Japanese Thought',

CJ, March 1938, pp. 601–10; Shisō no Kagaku Kenkyūkai (ed.), *Kyōdō kenkyū tenkō* (Heibonsha, 1959–62), I, 367–82; William M. Fletcher, *The Search for a New Order* (University of North Carolina Press, 1982).

3 Kōsaka Masaaki, Suzuki Shigetaka, Kōyama Iwao, Nishitani Keiji, 'Sekaishi-teki tachiba to Nihon', *ChK.*, January 1942, pp. 150–92; 'Tōa kyōeiken no rinrisei to rekishisei', *ChK*, April 1942, pp. 120–61; Rekishigaku, *Taiheiyō*, IV, 257. The January 1942 issue of the magazine went on sale in mid-December 1941.

4 Arakawa Ikuo and Ikimatsu Keizō (eds.), *Kindai Nihon shisō-shi* (Yūhikaku, 1973), pp. 210–18; Furuta Hikaru, Sakuta Keiichi, Ikimatsu Keizō (eds.), *Kindai Nihon shakai shisō-shi* (Yūhikaku, 1971), II, 276–8; Yatsugi, *Shōwa dōran shishi*, III, 358–71. Furuta claims that Nishida was forced to write the draft, but, according to Yatsugi, who received the draft from Nishida, there was no intimidation involved. The draft was not included in the 18-volume *Zenshū* (Complete Works) of Nishida, published in 1953 by Iwanami Shoten.

5 *NT*, 28 Dec. 1943; *JT&A*, 20 Jan. 1942; Kinoshita Hanji, 'Sensō shidō to seiji', *ChK*, December 1942, pp. 92–100; Rekishigaku, *Taiheiyō*, IV, 258; D. Keene, 'Japanese Writers and the Greater East Asia War', *JAS*, XXIII, 2 (Feb. 1964), 223 n. 52.

6 Masao Fukushima, 'Profile of Asian Minded Man, VI: Noboru Niida', *DE*, V (1967), 180–1; H. J. Wray, 'A Study of Contrasts, Japanese School Textbooks of 1903 and 1941–5', *MN*, XXVIII, 1 (Spring 1973), 78–82; Rekishigaku, *Taiheiyō*, IV, 139–40; G. B. Bikle, *The New Jerusalem, Aspects of Utopianism in the Thought of Kagawa Toyohiko* (The University of Arizona Press, 1976), pp. 236–48; Yuzo Ota, 'Kagawa Toyohiko: A Pacifist?' in Nobuya Bamba and John F. Howes (eds.), *Pacifism in Japan* (University of British Columbia Press, 1978), pp. 169–97.

7 Hayashi, *Taiheiyō*, p. 318; Rekishigaku, *Taiheiyō*, IV, 256, 258; Saegusa Shigeo, *Genron shōwa-shi* (Nihon Hyōronsha, 1958), pp. 139–40.

8 *JT&A*, 24 Dec. 1942; Hayashi, *Taiheiyō*, p. 231; Rekishigaku, *Taiheiyō*, IV, 256; *NT*, 7 March 1943; *Asahi*, 7 March 1943 (evening edition).

9 Hayashi; *Taiheiyō*, pp. 320–4, 374; Rekishigaku, *Taiheiyō*, IV, 170; Donald Keene, 'The Barren Years, Japanese War Literature', *MN*, XXXIII, 1 (Spring 1978), pp. 67–112; Keene, 'Japanese Writers'; Atsumi Ikuko and Graeme Wilson, 'The Poetry of Takamura Kōtarō, *JQ*, XX, 3 (July–Sept, 1973), p. 316. The translation of the poem is by Atsumi and Wilson.

10 Nakajima Kenzō. *Shōwa jidai* (Iwanami Shinsho, 1957),

pp. 151–2; Tsuruoka Yoshihisa, *Taiheiyō sensōka no shi to shisō* (Shōshinsha, 1971), pp. 349–50.

11 *Gendai Nihon bungaku daijiten* (Meiji Shoin, 1965); Hayashi, *Taiheiyō*, p. 318; Keene, 'Japanese Writers', pp. 216–17; Kato, *Lost War*, p. 191; Hidaka Rokurō, *Sengo shisō no shuppatsu* (Chikuma Shobō, 1968), pp. 223–5; Kadoya, *Shōwa*, pp. 251–2; *JT&A*, 16 Sept. and 28 Dec. 1942; *NT*, 8 April 1943; *Asahi*, 9 April 1943. Kikuchi Kan also presided over a convention of a hundred novelists, poets, and critics, which met on 24 December 1941 at the IRAA headquarters to express support for the war. He is known to Western readers from his short play *Madman on the Roof*.

12 *JT&A*, 16 March 1942; *NT*, 19 Aug. 1943; Kagoya, *Shōwa*, pp. 251–3.

13 An analysis of the wartime novels of Osanagi Jirō, Shishi Bunroku, and Funabashi Seiichi has shown the use of a greater number of Chinese characters and longer sentences than before. Ishikawa Hiroyoshi and Yasumoto Yoshinori, 'Sensōka no shimbun shōsetsu', in *Bungaku*, XXIX, 8 (Aug. 1961), pp. 167–83; Keene, 'Japanese Writers', p. 220; *Synopses of Contemporary Japanese Literature* (Kokusai Bunka Shinkōkai, 1970), II, 90–2; Nakamura Mitsuo, *Contemporary Japanese Fiction* (Kokusai Bunka Shinkōkai, 1969), p. 122. For the wartime attitudes towards China see my 'Friend or Foe: The Ambivalent Images of the U.S. and China in Wartime Japan', in James W. White, Michio Umegaki, Thomas R. H. Havens (eds.), *The Ambivalence of Nationalism* (University Press of America, 1990), pp. 187–212.

14 *JT&A*, 19 Dec. 1942; Katō Shūichi, 'Sensō to chishikijin', *Kindai Nihon shiso-shi kōza*, IV, 341–8; Kuno Osamu (ed.), *Miki Kiyoshi* (*Gendai Nihon shisō taikei*, XXXIII) (Chikuma Shobō, 1966), p. 441.

15 Keene, 'Japanese Writers', pp. 217–18; *JT&A*, 4 Nov. 1942: *NT* 25 Aug. 1943 and 12 Nov. 1944.

16 *NT*, 12 Jan. and 27 Dec. 1943, 21 May and 22 June 1945. Interestingly, Osaragi's postwar novel *Kikyō* (Homecoming) ridiculed the intellectuals who had changed their views to conform to the prevailing regime: Jiro Osaragi, *Homecoming* (Eng. tr. Brewster Horwitz, Tuttle, 1955). Kurahara's poem appears in Tsuruoka, *Shi to shisō*, p. 214.

17 *NT*, 2 Feb., 6–12 March, 16–24 Nov., 16 Dec. 1942; 23–27 Jan., 27 Feb., 5–30 May 1943; 16 Jan., 28 Feb., 8 March 1944.

18 G. M. Beckman and Okubo Genji. *The Communist Party, 1922–1945* (Stanford University Press, 1964), pp. 175–7;

Mitchell, *Thought Control*, pp. 109–10; Tsurumi, *Social Change*, p. 42; P. G. Steinhoff, 'Tenkō: Ideology and Societal Integration in Prewar Japan', Harvard University Ph.D. dissertation, 1969.

19 Yabe, *Nikki*, I, 714–34; Hashikawa Bunsō, 'Antiwar Values, the Resistance in Japan', *JI*, IX, 1 (Spring 1974), pp. 90–1; *Kawai Eijrō-shū* (Sōgensha, 1953), pp. 217–18; Atsuko Hirai, *Individualism and Socialism* (Council on East Asian Studies, Harvard University, 1986).

20 Ōhara Shakai Mondai Kenkyūjo, *Taiheiyō sensō-ka rōdōsha jōtai* (Tōyō Keizai Shimbunsha, 1964), p. 219; Ōtani, *Gumbatsu*, p. 65; Rekishigaku, *Taiheiyō*, IV, 141; Matsuo, *Chian ijihō*, p. 223; *GSS*, XLII, xxiv–xxxiv, 353–1089.

21 Kiyosawa, *Ankoku*, II, 138; Rekishigaku, *Taiheiyō*, V, 141; Akashi, *Shōwa tokkō*, II, 300.

22 Katō, 'Sensō', p. 329; Hatanaka, *Shuppan*, pp. 53–4; Ōhara, *Rōdōsha*, pp. 181–3; Yabe, *Nikki*, pp. 714–20.

23 Hatanaka, *Shuppan*, pp. 57–8, 64–5, 83–8; Saegusa, *Genron*, p. 141; Mimasaka, *Genron*, pp. 70–4, 88; Katō, 'Sensō', p. 327; Kuroda, *Chinurareta*, pp. 107–8; Nakamura, *Tennō-sei*, pp. 202–4.

24 *ChK* Jan. 1942–Dec. 1942; Kiyosawa, *Ankoku*, I, 204, 'Yokusan sōsenkyo, risō to jissen', *Ch K*, April 1942, pp. 1–44, 178–85. Suzuki's article is summarized in *CJ*, Oct. 1942, pp. 1501–4.

25 Kōsaka, 'Sekaishiteki', pp. 174–7; Hayashi Kentarō, 'Rekishika no tachiba', *ChK*, Dec. 1942, pp. 57–71.

26 Hatanaka, *Shuppan*, pp. 62–5; Kuroda, *Chinurareta*, pp. 48–60, 78–9.

27 Hatanaka, *Shuppan*, p. 47; Yabe, *Nikki*, I, 611.

28 Hatanaka, *Shuppan*, pp. 79–90, 166–9; Mimasaka, *Genron*, pp. 88–9; Kuroda, *Chinurareta*, 51–8; Keene, 'Japanese Writers', pp. 220–2.

29 Hatanaka, *Shuppan*, pp. 91–6; Kishida Kunio, 'Kaerajito', in *Kishida Kunio zenshū* (Shinchōsha, 1955), III, 67–87.

30 Hatanaka, *Shuppan*, 128–32, 189–285; Tōkyō, *Shōgen*, IV, 304–16; Mimasaka, *Genron*, pp. 86–7, 103; Wagatsuma, *Seiji saiban*, pp. 495–542.

31 Maruyama, *Thought and Behavior*, pp. 25–83; Ienaga, *Taiheiyō*, pp. 235, 253–4; Hashikawa, 'Antiwar Values'. Ienaga's book was translated into English: Saburo Ienaga, *The Pacific War*.

32 Maruyama Masao, *Senchū to sengo no aida* (Misuzu Shobō, 1976); Masao Maruyama, *Studies in the Intellectual History of Tokugawa Japan* (Princeton University Press, 1974), pp. xiv–xviii; Ienaga Saburō, *Jōdai bukkyō shisō-shi kenkyū* (Sōgensha, 1942); Ienaga Saburō, *Nihon shisō-shi ni okeru shūkyōteki shizen-kan no tenkai* (Sōgensha, 1944). Ienaga pointed out his own and Maruyama's

intellectual resistance to the war in his article 'Shisōka toshiteno Maruyama Masao', in Imai Kiichirō (ed.), *Maruyama Masao chosaku nōto* (Tosho Shimbunsha, 1964), pp. 2–5; and in his book *Ichirekishi-gakusha no ayumi* (Sanshōdō, 1967), pp. 106–21. Hata Ikuhiko regards Ienaga as an outstanding example of those intellectuals who had praised the war before 1945, but later changed their views and became ardent supporters of peace and democracy. See Hata Ikuhiko and Sodei Rinjirō, *Nihon senryō hishi* (Asahi Shimbunsha, 1977), II, 102–3.

33 Kiyosawa Kiyoshi, *Nihon gaikō-shi* (Keizai Shimpōsha, 1942), *Gaiseika toshite Ōkubo Toshimichi* (Chūō Kōronsha, 1942); Mitani Taichirō, 'Changes in Japan's International Position and the Responses of Japanese Intellectuals', in Borg and Okamoto (eds.), *Pearl Harbor*, pp. 585–6. Nishida Keiji (ed.), *Nishida Kitarō* (Chikuma Shobō, 1968), p. 471; Ienaga, *Taiheiyō*, pp. 238–9, 433–5; Kuno, *Miki*, p. 441.

34 Masuda Katsumi (ed.), *Yanagita Kunio* (Chikuma Shobō, 1965), p. 407–8; R. Morse, 'Personalities and Issues in Yanagita Kunio Studies', *JQ*, XXII, 3 (July–Sept. 1975), pp. 245–8; Hideo Yamamoto, 'Profile of Asian Minded Man: Shiraki Tachibana', *DE*, IV, (1966), 400; Hashikawa, 'Antiwar Values', pp. 91–2; Fukushima, 'Niida', pp. 178–80.

35 Furuta, *Kindai*, pp. 433–5; *Synopses*, pp. xxiii–xxv, 82–5, 132; Nakamura, *Contemporary Japanese Fiction*, pp. 92, 131–2; E. Seidensticker, 'Kobayashi Hideo', in Donald H. Shively (ed.), *Tradition and Modernization in Japanese Culture* (Princeton University Press, 1971), pp. 419–61; Takami Jun-shū (*Gendai Nihon bungaku zenshū*, XLVI) (Chikuma Shobō, 1955), p. 432.

36 Katō, 'Sensō', p. 338; Keene, 'Japanese Writers', p. 211–14; E. Seidensticker, *Kafū the Scribbler* (Stanford University Press, 1965), pp. 157–64.

37 Two actors, Sugimoto Ryōkichi and Okada Yoshiko, fled to the Soviet Union in 1938, but they can hardly be called scholars or writers.

38 Ienaga, *Taiheiyō*, p. 236; Kiyosawa, *Ankoku*, II, 138.

39 Kuroda Hidetoshi, *Shōwa gumbatsu* (Tosho Shuppansha, 1979), pp. 372–3.

40 Kiyosawa, *Ankoku*, II, 43, 80.

41 Kafū's entry was translated by Seidensticker, *Kafū*, p. 167; Takami's entry appears in Takami, *Takami Jun nikki* (Keisō Shobō, 1966), III, 176; see also Keene, 'Japanese Writers', p. 222. Even government officials dared to express themselves freely in their diaries. On 1 January 1945, Kase Toshikazu, a senior official in the Foreign Ministry, wrote in his diary: 'Sad

though it is . . . we have lost the war.': Kase, *Journey to the Missouri* (Yale University Press, 1950).

42 Tōkyō, *Shimpen*, I. 246–7, translation mine.

43 Translated by Takagi Keiko, in 'Poems of Kaneko Mitsuharu', *JQ*, XXIII, 3 (July–Sept. 1976), pp. 275–83.

44 Ienaga, *Taiheiyō*, pp. 240–1; Hashikawa, 'Antiwar Values', pp. 88–9, 93–4; Naokichi Ubukata, 'Profile of Asian Minded Man: Tadao Yanaihara', *DE*, IV (1966), 100–4; Matsuura, *Senjika*, pp. 104–6. After the war Yanaihara was elected president of Tokyo Univeristy.

45 Ienaga, *Taiheiyō*, pp. 242–4; Ienaga Saburō, *Ken'ryoku-aku to no tatakai* (Kōbundō, 1964), pp. 35–93; Masaki Hiroshi, 'Tonarigumi e no kengen to hihan', *Bungei shunjū*, Sept. 1940. Martin Johnson's book was published in 1922 in London by Constable and Co. under the title *Cannibal Land, Adventures with a Camera in the New Hebrides*. Quotations are from Masaki Hiroshi, 'Chikakiyori: shō', in Tsurumi Shun'suke (ed.), *Jānarizumu no shisō* (Chikuma Shobō, 1965), pp. 320–8; and Nezu Masashi, *Tennō to shōwa-shi* (San'ichi Shobō, 1974), pp. 183–5.

46 Hashikawa, 'Antiwar Values', p. 95; Nezu, *Tennō*, pp. 185–6.

47 Ienaga, *Ken'ryoku-aku*, pp. 51–2.

48 Ibid.

49 Ibid., pp. 55–62.

50 Ienaga, *Taiheiyō*, p. 244.

Chapter 6

An earlier version of a part of this chapter was delivered as a paper at the first international conference on Japanese studies in Europe, held at the University of Zurich in September 1976, and was subsequently published in *European Studies on Japan*, edited by Ian Nish and Charles Dunn (Paul Norbury Publications, Tenterden, Kent, 1979), pp. 149–56.

1 Cf. S. E. Pelz, *Race to Pearl Harbor* (Harvard University Pres, 1974), pp. 25–40; Masatake Okumiya and Jiro Horikoshi, *Zero! The Story of the Japanese Navy Air Force 1937–1945* (Cassell, 1957); A. J. Watts and B. G. Gordon, *The Imperial Japanese Navy* (Doubleday, 1971).

2 Shiga's essay appeared in the collection 'Sōshun' (Early Spring), in *Shiga Naoya zenshū* (Iwanami Shoten, 1974), VII, 306–7.

3 *JT&A*, 18 Nov. 1942.

4 *NT* 2 Dec. 1943.

5 US Army Air Forces, Assistant Chief of Air Staff, Intelligence Headquarters, *Mission Accomplished* (US Government Printing Office, 1946), p. 35.

6 Maeda's memorandum is quoted in Ōtsuki Ken, 'Gunkoku-shugi kyōiku to kodomo', *Dokyumento taiheiyō*, p. 132.
7 Higashikuni's speech is quoted in L.D. Meo, *Japan's Radio War on Australia, 1941–1945* (Melbourne University Press, 1968), p. 30.
8 The second Mongol invasion occurred in 1281, which was the 1941st year after the legendary foundation of Japan in 660 BC. For details about the earthquakes see Mainichi Shimbunsha, *Ichioku-nin no shōwa-shi*, III, 109–43.
9 Kōsaka, 'Tōa', pp. 159–60.
10 As quoted in *JT&A*, 22 May 1942.
11 *Jitsugyō no Nihon*'s article is quoted in *NT*, 2 Feb. 1943.
12 *NT*, 22 Dec. 1943.
13 *Asahi*, 16 April 1943. For more details about the plan to develop nuclear weapons in wartime Japan see Pacific War Research Society, *The Day Man Lost* (Kodansha International, 1972), pp. 1–64. On 25 August 1944 The *Nippon Times* reported that Oda Masaharu, an assistant in the Science Department of Tokyo Imperial University, was killed in his laboratory while conducting 'experiments on utilizing atomic energy in the construction of war arms'. On 29 December 1944 the same newspaper, quoting a German source, reported that on the Western front in Europe the Germans were using 'atomic bombs' that had a tremendous blasting power and obliterated whole areas.
14 *JT&A*, 21 and 24 June 1942; *NT*, 13 May 1943 and 15 March 1944. Asano Ōsuke (1858–1940), an expert on telegraphy, had directed the laying of the first submarine cable between Nagasaki and Taiwan. Shimose Masachika (1859–1911) had invented a high-performance gunpowder, known as the 'Shimose gunpowder', which helped the Japanese win the Russo-Japanese War.
15 Waseda, *Fuashizumu*, II, 207–55; Ōtsuki, 'Gunkoku', pp. 105–34.
16 Rekishigaku, *Taiheiyō*, IV, 243–7; Cohen, *Japan's Economy*, p. 274; R. S. Anderson, *Japan, Three Epochs of Modern Education* (US Department of Health, Education and Welfare, Bulletin 11, 1959), p. 59; Japanese National Commission for UNESCO, *The Role of Education in the Social and Economic Development of Japan* (Japan Ministry of Education, 1966), p. 178; Makoto Aso and I. Amano, *Education and Japan's Modernization* (Japan Ministry of Foreign Affairs, 1972), p. 59.
17 Cohen, *Japan's Economy*, pp. 216–17, 222, 237, 240–1. Okumiya and Horikoshi, *Zero!*, pp. xv, 291. The *Musashi* was sunk in October 1944 in the Battle of Leyte Gulf. *JT&A*, 1942, *passim*; *NT*, 1943, 1944, *passim*.
18 *NT*, 30 Aug. 1943.

19 Kōsaka, 'Sekaishiteki', pp. 158–9. The negative responses of postwar Japanese intellectuals to the 'modernization' literature of Western historians in the 1960s may stem from their fear that it might once again stir nationalistic feelings. See Takeuchi Yoshimi, 'Kindai no chōkoku', in Yoshimoto, *Nashonarizumu*, pp. 377–427.

20 *Kindai Nihon shiso-shi kōza*, II, 227–81; Yoshimoto, *Nashonarizumu*, pp. 377–427. The symposium itself was held on 23 and 24 July 1942.

21 *JT&A*, 13 Dec. 1942. The term *Diatōa sensō* (Great East Asia War) was banned by the Allied Occupation of Japan on 5 December 1945. Instead, the American name *Taiheiyō sensō* (Pacific War) was adopted, although it required some effort of imagination to regard places like Burma as belonging to the Pacific region. The common translation of *Daitōa* is 'Greater East Asia', but 'Great East Asia' seems to me more accurate.

22 *JT&A*, 16 Dec. 1941. In November 1943 the Japanese Geographic Society decided on a new world map, in which Japan would be located at the centre, and not on the extreme right, as it used to be in Western maps: *NT*, 27 Nov. 1943. For attitudes towards Great East Asia see also Shunsuke Tsurumi, *An Intellectual History of Wartime Japan* (KPI, 1986).

23 The 'Draft of the Basic Plan for the Establishment of the Great East Asia Co-Prosperity Sphere', prepared by the Total War Research Institute in January 1942, distinguished between three circles of Great East Asia:
   (a) The Inner Sphere: Japan, Korea, Manchuria, North and Central China, and the Russian Maritime Province.
   (b) The Smaller Co-Prosperity Sphere: The Inner Sphere plus Eastern Siberia, South China, Indo-China, and all of Southeast Asia.
   (c) The Greater Co-Prosperity Sphere: The Smaller Co-Prosperity Sphere plus Australia, India, and the Pacific Islands.
   Ryusaku Tsunoda, et al. (eds.), *Sources of Japanese Tradition*, (Columbia University Press, 1958), pp. 801–5.

24 Wray, 'A Study of Contrasts', pp. 82–3. See also Christopher Thorne, *The Issue of War* (Oxford University Press, 1980), pp. 144–76.

25 Kita Ikki, *Kita Ikki chosaku-shū* (Misuzu Shobō, 1959), II, 342–8.

26 Chikao Fujisawa, 'Japan versus Marxism', *CJ*, Dec. 1932, p. 448.

27 R. K. Hall (ed.), *Kokutai no Hongi* (Harvard University Press, 1949), pp. 98, 183.

28 Rekishigaku, *Taiheiyō*, IV, 170. The poem was reprinted in 1944

in a collection of Takamura's poems called *Kiroku* (chronicles). Translation mine.

29 Rekishigaku, *Taiheiyō*, IV, 256. The term *hakkō ichiu* (the whole world under one roof) signified the Confucian notion of a moral unification of the world, as well as Japan's new empire in East Asia. Nevertheless, even a knowledgeable person such as former Ambassador to Japan Joseph Grew told the Ohio Affairs Council on 5 February 1943 that Japan's 'overwhelming ambition' surpassed the megalomania of Hitler, because she intended 'to invade and to conquer these United States', J. C. Grew, *Turbulent Era* (Boston Houghton Mifflin, 1952), II, 1393–4.

30 Quoted in *JT&A*, 5 Feb. 1942. Until the outbreak of the war Britain enjoyed a more favourable image among the social élite of Japan than did the US. According to Hirohito's 1946 monologue, when Tōjō showed him the declaration of war, the emperor expressed regret that Japan had to fight Britain, a country which he had loved and respected. 'Shōwa tennō no dokuhakū', p. 121.

31 Tsunoda, *Sources,* p. 800; Nezu, *Tennō*, p. 185. It was in response to this speech by Okumura that Masaki wrote the article 'Don't Be Misled by Erroneous Opinions', mentioned in the previous chapter; *NT*, 27 Aug. 1943.

32 *JT&A*, 11 December 1942; *NT*, 2 and 23 Jan. 1943; Rekishigaku, *Taiheiyō*, V, 135–6; Matsuura, *Senjika*, pp. 106–8.

33 Morris noted that programmes of Beethoven on the radio ended with the statement: 'You have been listening to a symphony by Mr Beethoven, the well-known German composer': John Morris, *Traveller from Tokyo* (Penguin, 1943), pp. 196–7. The pilot's letter is reproduced in Mainichi Daily News Staff, *Fifty Years of Light and Dark* (The Mainichi Newspapers, 1975), p. 148.

34 Tōkyō, *Shōgen*, IV, 141.

35 Ōtsuki, 'Gunkoku', II, 106, 206. The poll was reported in *NT*, 19 Feb. 1943. The story of the destroyed American dolls came back to public attention in August 1978, when the Mitsukoshi department store in Tokyo displayed 31 such dolls that had been salvaged: *JT*, 17 Aug. 1978.

36 *JT&A*, 1 Oct. 1942. The Chinese characters for 'rice' (米), and 'illustrious', (英), standardly standing for the US and Britain, were sometimes replaced by new characters produced by adding the radical 'beast' (狆, 獏). Another derogatory spelling used at that time was to write 'Meiriken' (米利犬) i.e. 'rice-advantage-dog' for American, and 'Anguro' (暗愚魯) i.e. 'dark-stupid-fool' for England: Hayashi, *Taiheiyō*, p. 376; Saegusa, *Genron*, p. 155; Roby Eunson, *100 Years* (Kodansha International, 1965), p. 133.

37 *JT&A*, 10 Sept. 1942; *NT*, 19 Aug. 1943. For the vicious image of the US in wartime Japan, see John W. Dower, *War Without Mercy* (Pantheon, 1986), pp. 234–61.

38 As quoted in *NT*, 6 Aug. 1944.

39 Kiyosawa, *Ankoku*, II, 44.

40 *NT*, 20 Aug. 1944 and 26 June 1945; *Mainichi*, 14 April 1945.

41 Asahi Shimbun Staff, *The Pacific Rivals* (Weatherhill, 1972), p. 105.

42 Hatanaka, *Shuppan*, pp. 78–82; L. Anderson and Donald Richie, *The Japanese Film* (Tuttle, 1959), pp. 134–5; Mitsuaki Kakehi, 'Tokyoites under the Raids', *CJ*, XIV (Jan.–March 1945), 75–84.

43 *JT&A*, 4 March 1922; Saegusa, *Genron*, p. 150.

44 *JT&A*, 4 March and 7 April 1942. Honda's article is quoted in *JT&A*, 31 Aug. 1942. It is interesting that Kita Ikki had favoured teaching Esperanto, rather than English, as the foreign language: Kita, *Chosakushū*, II, 321. A movement to replace foreign words by native ones also existed in Nazi Germany, although Hitler himself did not like it. On one occasion he remarked to his aides: 'The linguists who recommend these Germanizations are deadly enemies of the German language. If we follow them in that path, we'd soon be unable to express our thoughts with precision, and our language would be poorer in words. It would end—I scarcely dare to say it—by being like Japanese: such a cackling and cawing!', *Hitler's Secret Conversations, 1941–1944* (Octagon Books, 1972), p. 290.

45 *NT*, 5 March and 3 Dec. 1943, 27 January 1944; Shimizu Isao, *Taiheiyō sensōki no manga* (Bijutsu Dōjinsha, 1971), p. 65.

46 *JT&A*, 21 Sept. and 20 Nov. 1942.

47 Kiyosawa, *Ankoku*, I, 190.

48 *GSS*, XLII, 1093–4.

49 *JT&A*, 18 June and 4 Dec. 1942; Naimushō, *Shakai undō*, XIV, 377–9. It was also during the war that the left-to-right writing, in the case of horizontal inscriptions, became common, despite the official use of right-to-left. The Ministry of Education wanted to standardize the new trend, but the Ministry of Finance objected, since the new style would make it necessary to change the paper currency and all the statistical tables. *JT&A*, 13 March 1942.

50 Hayashi, *Taiheiyō*, p. 173; Takami, *Nikki*, II, 599; *NT*, 5 Jan. 1944.

51 Quoted in *CJ*, XII, 12 (Dec. 1942), pp. 1171–4.

52 Toshio Shiratori, 'Fascism versus Popular Front', *CJ*, VI, 4 (March 1938), p. 589; J. K. Wheeler, 'Rōyama Masamichi and the Search for a Middle Ground, 1932–1940', *Papers on Japan*

(East Asian Research Center, Harvard University), VI (1972), 70–101; Fujisawa Chikao, *Zentaishugi to kōdō* (Tōyō Tosho, 1940), pp. 116–17.

53 Hara's speech is quoted in Ike, *Japan's Decision*, p. 237; Togo, *The Cause*, p. 239; see also E. L. Presseisen, *Germany and Japan* (Martinus Nijhoff, 1958), pp. 322–3.

54 *JT&A*, 12 Dec. 1941, 22 Feb. and 10 Dec. 1942.

55 In October 1934 the German–Japanese Society in Berlin asked the authorities to exempt Japanese residents in Germany from the race laws, but its request was turned down by the Nazi Party's Bureau for Racial Politics. The exemption was extended to the Japanese only after the two countries signed the anti-Comintern pact in 1936: E. Friese, *Japaninstitut Berlin und Deutsch-Japanische Gesellschaft Berlin* (Occasional Papers No. 9, Social and Economic Research on Modern Japan, East Asian Institute, Free University of Berlin, 1980).

56 *Hitler's Secret Conversations*, p. 149. Hitler's attitude towards Japan was a mixture of admiration, suspicion, and contempt. On 7 January 1942 he remarked: 'It goes without saying that we have no affinities with the Japanese. They're too foreign to us, by their way of living, by their culture.' (p. 155). To the criticism that the alliance with Japan contradicted Germany's racial principles, he replied: 'The essential aim is to win, and to that end we are quite ready to make an alliance with the Devil himself' (p. 396). See also E. L. Presseisen, 'Le Racisme et les Japonais', *Revue d'Histoire de la Deuxième Guerre Mondiale*, LI (July 1963), pp. 1–14. There was much resentment against Japan in Germany because of the former's failure to join the war against the Soviet Union. On 14 April 1943 the president of the German–Japanese Society found it necessary to issue a secret circular to try and abate this criticism: Bundesarchiv Koblenz, R 64/IV, Bd. 167. Quoted in Friese, *Japaninstitut*, pp. 53–5.

57 Hittorā (Hitler), *Waga tōsō* (Mein Kampf) (Tōa Kenkyūjo, 1942), I, introduction. In 1940 the Japanese Foreign Ministry printed a classified translation of *Mein Kampf* for its own officials. The introduction to that book stated that the text included 'praiseworthy parts alongside elements that cannot be accepted by Japan and should therefore be discarded': Gaimushō Jōhōbu, *Main kampu no naiseihen* (1940), II, 1.

58 Kōsaka, 'Sekaishiteki', pp. 155–6.

59 *Asahi*, 15 June 1945; as quoted in *NT*, 3 June 1945.

60 *NT*, 10 May 1945.

61 As quoted in *NT*, 7 July 1945.

62 *NT*, 11 April 1943; as quoted in *NT*, 13 Aug. 1944.

63 Hatanaka, *Shuppan*, p. 53; Guillain, *Le Peuple*, p. 187; *JT&A*, 9
   April 1942.
64 As quoted in *JT&A*, 21 Sept. 1942.
65 *Mainichi*, 22 June 1943. For Japanese attempts to mediate
   between Germany and the Soviet Union in the years 1940–1, see
   Presseisen, *Germany and Japan*, p. 323.
66 Hosokawa, *Jōhō*, I, 196–7: Hosokawa was Prince Takamatsu's
   secretary. For an account of Soviet–Japanese relations during
   the war see G. A. Lensen, *The Strange Neutrality* (Diplomatic
   Press, 1972).
67 Stalin's remark is quoted in Otto Tolischus, *Tokyo Record*
   (Hamish Hamilton, 1943), pp. 78–9.
68 As quoted in *NT*, 16 May 1945.
69 The first anti-Semitic pamphlet in Japanese appeared in Vladivostok in the spring of 1919 and was called 'Kageki-shugi no
   seizui' (The Spirit of Radicalism): Kobayashi Masayuki,
   Yudayajin (Seiko Shobō, 1977), p. 241.
70 Yoshino Sakuzō, 'Yudayajin no sekai tempuku no imbō ni
   tsuite', *ChK*, May 1921; Yoshino Sakuzō 'Iwayuru sekai-teki
   himitsu kessha no seitai', *CHK*, June 1921.
71 Adolf Hitler, *Mein Kampf* (Eng. tr. R. Manheim, Houghton
   Mifflin, 1943), pp. 638–40; Miyazawa Masanori, *Yudayajin ronkō*
   (Shinsensha, 1973), pp. 218–22. Interestingly enough, until
   Hitler's rise to power, Jews had played an important role in
   promoting German–Japanese relations. On 24 April 1933 the
   Governor of Berlin, in a letter to the Home Ministry, complained
   that the chairman of the German–Japanese Society was a Jew by
   the name of Professor W. Haas, and that the managing director
   of the Society was a Polish Jew, Dr A. Chanoch: Archiv des
   Auswärtigen Amtes Bonn, Politik VIII, Bd. 92. Quoted in
   Friese, *Japaninstitut*, pp. 38–9.
72 Miyazawa, *Yudayajin*, pp. 86–91. Shiōden's first anti-Semitic
   article, 'Yudaya kenkyū', was published in the magazine *Kyokutō*
   (Far East) in Harbin in October 1921: Kobayashi, *Yudayajin*,
   241, 273. The monthly journal appeared from 1941 to 1943.
73 Miyazawa, *Yudayajin*, pp. 95, 220–2; Hyman Kublin, 'Star of
   David and Rising Sun', *Jewish Frontier*, XXV, 4 (April 1958), p.
   19.
74 Kase Hideaki, 'Nihon no naka no Yudayajin', *Ch K..*, May 1971,
   pp. 242–3; *JT&A*, 12 Dec. 1942; *NT*, 14 and 19 Jan. 1943.
75 Shiōden Nobutaka, *Yudaya shisō oyobi undō* (Naigai Shobō, 1941),
   pp. 350–7, *Shiōden Nobutaka kaikoroku* (Misuzu Shobō, 1964), pp.
   123–4; *Der Stürmer*, 23 (June 1939), p. 4.
76 Miyazawa, *Yudayajin*, p. 127.

77 Quoted in *JT&A*, 22 Sept. 1942.
78 *Asahi*, 9 Dec. 1943.
79 Miyazawa, *Yudayajin*, p. 193.
80 *NT*, 21 Jan. 1944.
81 Tokutomi Iichirō, *Hisshō kokumin dokuhon* (Mainichi Shimbunsha, 1944), pp. 71–124.
82 Takeda Seigo, *Shimbun to Yudayajin* (Ōa Tsūshinsha, 1944).
83 Miyazawa, *Yudayajin*, pp. 97–8.
84 Irokawa Daikichi, *Aru shōwa-shi* (Chūō Kōronsha, 1975), p. 115.
85 Kiyosawa, *Ankoku*, I, 77–8, 198–9.
86 Hōjō, *Shisōsen; Mainichi*, 6 March 1943, 15 March 1944.
87 As quoted in *JT&A*, 17 Dec. 1942.
88 Kiyosawa, *Ankoku*, II, 16.
89 *Asahi*, 21 April 1944. Max Rubner (1854–1932) was a professor at the University of Berlin.
90 Meo, *Radio*, pp. 111–15.
91 As quoted in *JT&A*, 16 June 1942. Shiōden's estimate was an exaggeration. There were only about 50,000 Jews there.
92 Miyazawa, *Yudayajin*, pp. 100–1. For an account of Jacob Schiff's role in the Russo-Japanese War see Cyrus Adler, *Jacob H. Schiff, His Life and Letters* (Doubleday, 1928), I, 212–59. In 1916 Schiff, while on a visit to Japan, was invited to dinner with the emperor and was given the Order of the Rising Sun.
93 *NT*, 12 Dec. 1943.
94 See Kawahara Hiroshi, 'Senjika ni okeru kagaku gijutsuron', in Waseda, *Fuashizumu*, II, 70.
95 Juji Nakada, *An Unknown Nation* (Japan Holiness Church, 1933).
96 Akashi, *Shōwa tokkō*, IV, 66–78, 129–53; Dōshisha Daigaku Jimbun Kagaku Kenkyūjo, *Senjika no kirisutokyō undō* (Shinkyō Shuppansha, 1972), II, 269–70.
97 See Kobayashi, *Yudayajin*, 235–60; Herman Dicker, *Wanderers and Settlers in the Far East* (Twayne, 1962), pp. 156–8.
98 The entries about Rosenstock in such reference books as *Baker's Biographical Dictionary of Musicians* (New York: Schirmer, 1971), state that he spent the war years outside Japan. However, advertisements of his concerts in Japan appeared during the war in the Japanese press. See *NT*, 11 and 16 June, 9 Nov. 1943.
99 Sugita Rokuichi, *Higashi Ajia e kita Yudayajin* (Otoha Shobō, 1967), p. 146; M. Tokayer and M. Swartz, *The Fugu Plan* (Paddington Press, 1979), pp. 44–61.
100 'Shanghai', *Encyclopedia Judaica* (Jerusalem, 1971), IV, 1293–4.
101 Miyazawa, *Yudayajin*, p. 112.
102 Kase, 'Nihon no naka', pp. 234–5; Abraham Kotsuji, *From Tokyo to Jerusalem* (Bernard Geis, 1964), pp. 159–60; Roman Bertish,

'Jewish Emigrants from Poland During World War II and the Polish Government's Attitude to Them' (in Hebrew), *Gal-Ed*, I, 251–98 (Tel Aviv: The Diaspora Research Institute, 1973); see also the testimonies of Yehoshua Bram and Shimon Bergman, Yad Vashem Central Archives, Jerusalem (03/3045).

103 For a description of the Japanese attitudes towards the Jewish refugees see D. Kranzler, *Japanese, Nazis, and Jews* (Yeshiva University Press, 1976), pp. 85–126, 169–266; Tokayer and Swartz, *Fugu*.

104 Hallett Abend, *Japan Unmasked* (Ives Washburn, 1941), pp. 280–6.

105 Yasue Norihiro, *Yudaya no hitobito* (Gunjin Kaikan Jigyōbu, 1934), pp. 76–7, 156–7. Yasue was accompanied on his visit to Palestine by the priest Sakai Shōgun, who suggested that the Zionist movement send a delegate to the coronation ceremony of Emperor Hirohito: File Z4/10–233, Central Zionist Archives.

106 Kase, 'Nihon no naka', p. 241; Dicker, *Wanderers*, pp. 77–80; Kranzler, *Japanese*, pp. 170, 207. Yasue's name was entered into the Golden Book together with the name of General Higuchi. They are listed in vol. VI, entries 4026 and 4028. Nineteen years earlier, on 12 June 1922, the Jewish community of Shanghai had entered the name of Japan's Foreign Minister Uchida Yasuya in that Golden Book, in appreciation of his favourable attitude towards the principle of a Jewish national home in Palestine, then debated at the League of Nations. It is listed in vol. II, entry 4634.

107 Utsunomiya Kiyo, *Yudaya mondai to Nihon* (Nagai Shobō, 1939), pp. 76–7, 411–24, 477–88; Inuzuka claimed after the war that his wife had written that book. Kranzler, *Japanese*, p. 251 n. 5.

108 See Kase, 'Nihon no naka', p. 242. Tokayer and Swartz claim that there existed an official plan (*The Fugu Plan*) to set up an 'Israel in Asia', but there is no evidence that the Japanese had ever contemplated a Jewish state or a Jewish autonomous region.

109 As related after Inuzuka's death by his wife. See Inuzuka Kiyoko, 'Nihon kaigun to Yudayajin', in Shinseikai, *Nihonjin kara mita Yudaya mondai* (Sanshūsha, 1975), pp. 300–1.

110 Kase 'Nihon no naka', p. 241; Dicker, *Wanderers*, pp. 86–7.

111 Kranzler, *Japanese*, pp. 326–7.

112 Ibid., p. 174. After the war Inuzuka joined a pro-Israeli organization, the *Nihon Isuraeru kyōkai* (Japan Israel Association), in which he was an active member until his death in 1965.

113 Miyazawa, *Yudayajin*, pp. 106–7; Sugita, *Higashi*, pp. 154–5; Kotsuji, *From Tokyo*, pp. 142–50; Inuzuka, 'Nihon kaigun', pp. 290–1; Dicker, *Wanderers*, pp. 45–59.

114 Testimony of Dr Abraham Kaufmann, File 03/3168, Yad Vashem Central Archives.
115 Miyazawa, *Yudayajin*, p. 112; Sugita, *Higashi*, pp. 153–4; Kranzler, *Japanese*, pp. 229–34, 331–2.
116 Dicker, *Wanderers*, p. 59.
117 A detailed account of Jewish life in wartime Shanghai is found in Kranzler, *Japanese*, pp. 521–77.

Conclusion

1 See Maruyama Masao. *Gendai seiji no shisō to kōdō* (Miraisha, 1956); Inoue Kiyoshi, *Nihon no rekishi* (Iwanami Shinsho, 1966), III; Tōyama, *Shōwa-shi*.
2 See E. O. Reischauer, 'What Went Wrong?' in Morley, *Dilemmas of Growth*, pp. 489–510; James B. Crowley, 'Imperial Japan and its Modern Discontents: The State and the Military in Prewar Japan', in Harold Z. Schiffrin (ed.), *Military and State in Modern Asia* (Jerusalem Academic Press, 1976), pp. 31–59; Nobutaka Ike, 'War and Modernization', in Ward, *Political Development*, pp. 189–211.
3 See J. M. Maki, *Government and Politics in Japan* (Praeger, 1962); Ienaga, *Taiheiyō*, p. 140; Mainichi, *Fifty Years*, p. 111.

Bibliography

Japanese Language
(All publishers are in Tokyo unless otherwise indicated)

Abe Genki, *Shōwa dōran no shinsō* (Hara Shobō, 1977).
Akashi Hirotaka and Matsuura Sōzō, *Shōwa tokkō dan'atsu-shi* (Taihei Shuppansha, 1975), 8 vols.
Akazawa Shirō, *Taisei yokusankai* (Tokyo: Ōtsuki Shoten, 1984).
Akimoto Ritsuo, *Senso to minshū* (Gakuyō Shobō, 1974).
Arakawa Ikuo and Ikimatsu Keizō (eds.), *Kindai Nihon shisō-shi* (Yūhikaku, 1973).
Arisawa Hiromi, *Nihon sangyō hyakunen-shi* (Nikkei Shinsho, 1967), 2 vols.
Asahi nenkan, 1940–5.
Asahi shimbun, 1940–5.
Asahi shimbun no kyūjūnen (Asahi Shimbunsha, 1969).
Bōeichō Bōei Kenshūjo Senshishitsu, *Hondo kessen jumbi* (Asagumo Shimbunsha, 1971), 2 vols.
Chichibu no miya-ke, *Yasuhito Shinnō jikki* (Yoshikawa Kōbunkan, 1972).
Chichibu no Miya Yasuhito Shinnō (Chichibu no Miya o shinobukai, 1970).
Chichibu no Miya Yasuhito Shinnō Denka, Setsuko Hidenka, *Gotemba seiwa* (Sekai no Nihonsha, 1948).
Chikamori Haruyoshi, *Jimbutsu Nihon shimbun-shi* (Shin Jimbutsu Ōraisha, 1970).
Chō Bunren, *Haisen hishi, senso sekinin oboegaki* (Jiyū Shobō, 1946).
Dai Nihon hyakka jiten (Shōgakukan, 1969), 23 vols.
Daitōa senshi (Fuji Shoen, 1969), 10 vols.
Dokyumento taiheiyō senso (Sekibunsha, 1975), 5 vols.
Dōshisha Daigaku Jimbun Kagaku Kenkyūjo, *Senjika no kirisutokyō undō* (Shinkyō Shuppansha, 1972), 3 vols.
Dōshisha Daigaku Jimbun Kagaku Kenkyūjo, *Senjika teikō no kenkyū* (Misuzu Shobō, 1968), 2 vols.
Eguchi Bokurō, *Teikokushugi to minzoku* (Tōkyō Daigaku Shuppankai, 1954).
Fujimoto Haruki, *Ishiwara Kanji* (Jiji Tsūshinsha, 1964).
Fujisawa Chikao, *Zentaishugi to kōdō* (Tōyō Tosho, 1940).
Fujiwara Akira, Imai Seiichi, Ōe Shinobu (eds.), *Kindai Nihon-shi no*

212   *Bibliography*

kisō chishiki (Yūhikaku, 1972).

Fukai Eigo, *Sūmitsuin jūyōgiji oboegaki* (Iwanami Shoten, 1953).

Fukuda Tsuneari (ed.), *Han-kindai no shisō* (*Gendai Nihon shisō taikei*, XXIII) (Chikuma Shobō, 1965).

Furuta Hikaru, Sakuta Keiichi, Ikimatsu Keizō (eds.), *Kindai Nihon shakai shisō-shi* (Yūhikaku, 1971), 2 vols.

Gaimushō, *Shūsen shiroku* (Hokuyōsha, 1977), 6 vols.

Gaimushō Jōhōbu, *Main kampu no naiseihen* (1940).

Gendai Nihon bungaku daijiten (Meiji Shoin, 1965).

Gendai-shi shiryō (Misuzu Shobō, 1962–75):

vols. I, II, III, XXIV	: *Zoruge jiken*
vols. IV, V, XXIII	: *Kokkashugi undō*
vol. XIII	: *Nitchū sensō*
vols. XXXIV, XXXIX	: *Taiheiyō sensō*
vols. XL, XLI	: *Masumedeya tōsei*
vol. XLII	: *Shisō tōsei*
vols. XLIII, XLIV	: *Kokka sōdōin*
vol. XLV	: *Chian ijihō*

Gikai seidō nanajūnenshi (Shūgiin, Sangiin, 1963):

vol. I	: *Kenseishi gaikan*
vol. III	: *Teikoku gikai-shi, gekan*
vol. VI	: *Seitō kaiha-hen*
vol. VII	: *Gikai-shi nempyō*
vol. VIII	: *Shūgiin giin meikan*

Gomikawa Jumpei, *Sensō to ningen* (San'ichi Shoten, 1965–7), 9 vols.

——, *Gozen kaigi* (Bungei Shunjū, 1978).

Hani Gorō, *Nihon jimmin no rekishi* (Iwanami Shinsho, 1950).

Hara Keigo, *Dōran no shōwa-shi* (Kōdansha, 1968).

Harada Kumao, *Saionjikō to seikyoku* (Iwanami Shoten, 1950–6), 8 vols.

Haruhara Akihiko, *Nihon shimbun tsūshi* (Gendai Jānarizumu Shuppankai, 1969).

Hashikawa Bunsō (ed.), *Chōkokka-shugi* (*Gendai Nihon shisō taikei*, XXXI) (Chikuma Shobō, 1964).

Hata Ikuhiko, *Nitchū sensō-shi* (Kawade Shobō, 1961).

——, *Gun fuashizumu undō-shi* (Kawade Shobō, 1962).

Hata Ikuhiko and Sodei Rinjirō, *Nihon senryō hishi* (Asahi Shimbunsha, 1977), 2 vols.

Hatanaka Shigeo, *Shōwa shuppan dan'atsu shōshi* (Tosho Shimbunsha, 1965).

Hattori Takushiro, *Daitōa sensō zenshi* (Hara Shobō 1965).

Hayasaka Jirō, 'Gakudō o hōmuru mono wa?', *Shakai oyobi kokka*, April 1937.

Hayashi Fusao, *Daitōa sensō kōtei-ron* (Banchō Shobō, 1971).

Hayashi Heima, *Shūsen undō hiroku* (Hakubunsha, 1964).

Hayashi Kentarō. 'Rekishika no tachiba', *Chūō kōron*, December 1942, pp. 51–71.

Hayashi Masaharu, *Rikugun taishō Honjō Shigeru* (Rikugun Taishō Honjō Shigeru Denki Kankōkai, 1967).

Hayashi Shigeru, *Nihon shūsen-shi* (Yomiuri Shimbunsha, 1962), 3 vols.

——, *Taiheiyō sensō* (*Nihon no rekishi*, XXV, Chūō Kōronsha, 1967).

Hidaka Rokurō, *Sengo shisō no shuppatsu* (*Sengo Nihon shisō taikei*, I) (Chikuma Shobō, 1968).

Higashikuni Naruhiko, *Yancha kodoku* (Yomiuri Shimbunsha, 1955).

——, *Higashikuni nikki* (Tokuma Shoten, 1968).

Hirakawa Sukehiro, *Heiwa no umi to tatakai no umi: Ni-ni-roku jiken kara 'ningen sengen' made* (Tokyo: Shinchōsa, 1983).

Hōjō Seiichi, *Shisōsen to kokusai himitsu kessha* (Seinansha, 1942).

Honjō Shigeru, *Honjō Nikki* (Hara Shobō 1967).

Hosokawa Morisada, *Jōhō tennō ni tassezu* (Isobe Shobō, 1953), 2 vols.

Ichikawa Fusae, *Ichikawa Fusae jiden* (Shinjuku Shobō, 1974).

Ichikawa Muneaki, *Ichioku kokumin gyokusaika keikaku* (Nisshin Hōdō, 1975).

Ienaga Saburō, *Jōdai bukkyō shisō-shi kenkyū* (Sōgensha, 1942).

——, *Nihon shisō-shi ni okeru shūkyōteki shizen-kan no tenkai* (Sōgensha, 1964).

——, *Ken'ryoku-aku to no tatakai* (Kōbundō, 1964).

——, 'Shisōka toshiteno Maruyama Masao', in Imai Kiichirō (ed.), *Maruyama Masao chosaku nōto* (Tosho Shimbunsha, 1964), pp. 2–5.

——, *Ichirekishi-gakusha no ayumi* (Sanseidō, 1967).

——, *Taiheiyō sensō* (Iwanami Shoten, 1968).

Imai Seiichi, 'Ōkō shita rokotsuna kanshō, yokusan senkyo', *Shōwa-shi no shunkan* (Asahi Shimbunsha, 1974), II, 26–35.

Inagaki Masami, *Tennō no sensō to shomin* (Kokusho Kankōkai, 1975).

Inomata Keitarō, *Nakano Seigō* (Yoshikawa Kōbunkan, 1960).

——, *Nakano Seigō no shōgai* (Reimei Shobō, 1964).

Inoue Kiyoshi, *Nihon no rekishi* (Iwanami Shinsho, 1966), 3 vols.

——, *Nihon no 'kindaika' to gunkoku-shugi* (Shin Nihon Shinsho, 1966).

——, *Tennō no sensō sekinin* (Gendai Hyōronsha, 1975).

Inuzuka Kiyoko, 'Nihon kaigun to Yudayajin', in Shinseikai (ed.), *Nihonjin kara mita Yudaya mondai* (Sahshūsha, 1975), pp. 288–308.

Iriye Sukemasa, *Tennō-sama no kanreki* (Asahi Shimbunsha, 1962).

Irokawa Daikichi, *Aru shōwa-shi* (Chūō Kōrōnsha, 1975).

Isa Hideo, *Ozaki Yukio-den* (Ozaki Yukio-den Kankōkai, 1951).

——, *Ozaki Yukio* (Yoshikawa Kōbunkan, 1960).

Ishikawa Hiroyoshi and Yasumoto Yoshinori, 'Sensōka no shimbun shōsetsu', in *Bungaku*, XXIX, 8 (Aug. 1961), 167–83.

214 *Bibliography*

214 *Bibliography*

Itō Masanori, *Shimbun gojūnen-shi* (Masu Shobō, 1947).
——, *Gumbatsu kōbōshi* (Bungei Shunjū Shinsha, 1958).
Iwabuchi Tatsuo, *Gumbatsu no keifu* (Chūō Kōronsha, 1948).
Jiji Nenkan, 1940–5.
Jōhō Yoshio (ed.), *Tōjō Hideki* (Fuyō Shoten, 1974).
Kadoya Fumio, *Shōwa jidai* (Gakuyō Shobō, 1973).
Kagawa Saburō, 'Jōhōkyoku no kikō to sono hen'yū', *Bungaku*, XXIX, 5 (May 1961), 125–36.
Kaji Wataru, *Nihon heishi no hansen undō* (Dōseisha, 1962).
Kanroji Osanaga, *Tennō-sama* (Nichirinkaku, 1960).
Kase Hideaki, 'Nihon no naka no Yudayajin', *Chūō kōron*, May 1971, pp. 234–47.
Katō Shūichi, 'Sensō to chishikijin', *Kindai Nihon shisō-shi kōza* (Chikuma Shobō 1959), pp. 323–61.
Kawai Eijirō-shū (*Gendai zuisō zenshū*, XVII) (Sōgensha, 1953).
Keishichō-shi (Keishichō-shi Hensan Iinkai, 1961), 3 vols.
Kido Kōichi, *Kido Kōichi nikki* (Tōkyō Daigaku Shuppankai, 1966), 2 vols.
Kido Nikki Kenkyūkai (ed.), *Kido Kōichi kankei monjo* (Tōkyō Daigaku Shuppankai, 1966).
Kikkawa Manabu, *Hiroku rikugun rimen-shi* (Yamato Shobō, 1954).
Kindai Nihon shisō-shi kōza (Chikuma Shobō, 1959), 8 vols.
Kinoshita Hanji, 'Sensō shidō to seiji', *Chūō kōron*, December 1942, pp. 92–100.
——, *Nihon no fuashizumu* (Kokusho kankōkai, 1975).
——, *Nihon fuashizumu-shi* (Iwasaki Shoten, 1951), 2 vols.
Kishida Kunio, 'Kaerajito', *Kishida Kunio zenshū* (Shinchōsha, 1955), III, 67–87.
Kita Ikki, *Kita Ikki chosaku-shū* (Misuzu Shobō, 1959), 2 vols.
Kiya Ikusaburō, *Konoe-kō hibun* (Wakayama: Takanoyama Shuppansha, 1950).
Kiyosawa Kiyoshi, *Gaiseika toshite Ōkubo Toshimichi* (Chūō Kōronsha, 1942).
——, *Nihon gaikō-shi* (Keizai Shimpōsha, 1942), 2 vols.
——, *Ankoku nikki* (Hyōronsha, 1970), 3 vols.
Kobayashi Gorō, *Tokkō keisatsu hiroku* (Seikatsu Shinsha, 1952).
Kobayashi Masayuki, *Yudayajin* (Seikō Shobō, 1977).
Koiso Kuniaki, *Katsuzan kōsō* (Chūō Kōron Jigyō Shuppan, 1968).
Kojima Noboru, *Tennō* (Bungei Shunjū, 1974), 5 vols.
Kōno Tsukasa, *Ni ni-roku jiken* (Nihon Shūhōsha, 1957).
Konoe Fumimaro, *Konoe nikki* (Kyōdō Tsūshinsha, 1968).
Kōsaka Masaaki, Suzuki Shigetaka, Kōyama Iwao, Nishitani Keiji, 'Sekaishi-teki tachiba to Nihon', *Chūō kōron*, January 1942, pp. 150–92.

——, 'Tōa kyōeiken no rinrisei to rekishisei', *Chūō kōron*, April 1942, pp. 120–61.
Kosaka Keisuke, *Tokkō* (Tōkyō Raifu-sha, 1956).
Kuno Osamu (ed.), *Miki Kiyoshi* (*Gendai Nihon shisō taikei*, XXXIII), (Chikuma Shobō, 1966).
Kuno Osamu and Tsurumi Shun'suke, *Gendai Nihon no shisō* (Iwanami Shoten, 1956).
Fureki Fujio, *Gakuto shutsujin* (Asahi Shimbunsha, 1966).
Kurihara Ken, *Tennō* (Yūshindō, 1955).
Kuroda Hidetoshi, *Chinurareta genron* (Gakufu Shoin, 1946).
——, *Shōwa gumbatsu* (Tosho Shuppansha, 1979).
Kuroda Hisata, *Tennō-ka no zaisan* (San'ichi Shinsho, 1966).
Maejima Shōzō, *Nihon fuashizumu to gikai* (Hōritsu Bunka-sha, 1956).
Maeshiba Kakuzō and Naramoto Tetsuya, *Taikenteki shōwa-shi* (Yūkonsha, 1968).
Mainichi shumbun, 1940–1.
Mainichi shumbun hyakunen-shi (Mainichi Shimbunsha, 1972).
Mainichi shimbun shichijūnen (Mainichi Shumbunsha, 1952).
Mainichi Shimbunsha, *Ichioku-nin no shōwa-shi* (Mainichi Shimbunsha, 1975–6).
Maruyama Masao et al., *Nihon no nashonarizumu* (Kawade Shobō, 1953).
——, *Gendai seiji no shisō to kōdō* (Miraisha, 1956).
——, *Senchū to sengo no aida* (Misuzu Shobō, 1976).
Masaki Hiroshi, 'Tonarigumi e no kengen to hihan', *Bungei shunjū*, September 1940.
——, 'Chikakiyori: shō', in Tsurumi Shun'suke (ed.), *Jānarizumo no shisō* (Chikuma Shobō, 1965), pp. 320–8.
Masuda Katsumi (ed.), *Yanagita Kunio* (Chikuma Shobō, 1965).
Masumi Junnosuke, *Kyokoku ichi to seitō* (Tokyo: Tokyo Daigaku shuppankai, 1980).
Matsumura Hideyasu, *Sensen kara shūsen made* (Nihon Shūhōsha, 1964).
Matsuoka Hideo, 'Tōjō Hideki-ron', in Mainichi Shimbunsha, *Ichioku-nin no shōwa-shi*, III, 243–7.
Matsuo Hiroshi, *Chian ijihō* (Shin Nihon Shuppansha, 1971).
Matsuo Shōichi, *Nihon fuashizumu-shi-ron* (Hōsei Daigaku Shuppan-kyoku, 1977).
Matsushita Yoshio, *Nihon gunsei to seiji* (Kuroshiyo, 1960).
——, *Nihon riku-kaigun sōdōshi* (Tsuchiya Shobō, 1965).
——, *Nihon gumbatsu no kōbō* (Jimbutsu Ōraisha, 1967), 3 vols.
——, *Sandai hansen undō-shi* (Kōjinsha, 1973).
Matsuura Sōzō, *Senjika no genron tōsei* (Shirakawa Shoin, 1975).
Miki Kiyoshi, 'Gendai Nihon ni okeru sekai-shi no igi', *Kaizō*, June

1938.
——, 'Tōa shisō no konkyo', *Kaizō*, October 1938.
——, *Miki Kiyoshi chōsakushū* (Iwanami Shoten, 1946), 16 vols.
Mimasaka Tarō, Fujita Chikamasa, Watanabe Kiyoshi, *Genron no haiboku* (San'ichi Shoten, 1959).
Mitarai Tatsuo, *Minami Jirō* (Minami Jirō Denki Kankōkai, 1957).
Mitsuda Iwao, *Shōwa fūunroku* (Shinkigensha, 1940).
Miyazawa Masanori, *Yudayajin ronkō* (Shinsensha, 1973).
Mori Shōzō, *Sempū nijūnen* (Son'shobō, 1945), 2 vols.
Murakami Hyōe, 'Tennō no sensō sekinin', in Yoshimoto Takaaki (ed.), *Kokka no shisō* (*Sengo Nihon shisō taikei*, V) (Chikuma Shobō, 1969), pp. 300–16.
Nagano Shizuo, *Nihongun to tatakatta Nihon-hei* (Shiraishi Shoten, 1974).
Naimushō Keihokyoku, *Shakai undō no jōkyō* (San'ichi Shobō, 1972), 14 vols.
Nakajima Kenzō, *Shōwa jidai* (Iwanami Shinsho, 1957).
Nakamura Kikuo, *Tennō-sei fuashizumu-ron* (Hara Shobō, 1967).
——, *Shōwa rikugun hishi* (Banchō Shobō, 1968).
Nakano Yasuo, *Seijika Nakano Seigō* (Shinkōkaku Shoten, 1971), 2 vols.
Nakatani Takeyo, *Senji gikai-shi* (Minzoku to Seijisha, 1975).
Nezu Masashi, *Tennō to shōwa-shi* (San'ichi Shobō, 1974).
Nichi nichi shimbun, 1940–5.
Nihon Gaikō Gakkai, *Taiheiyō sensō shūketsu-ron* (Tōkyō Daigaku Shuppankai, 1958).
Nihon kindaishi jiten (Tōyō Keizai Shimpōsha, 1958).
Nihon riku-kaigun no seidō, sōshiki, jinji (Tōkyō Daigaku Shuppankai, 1972).
Nihon Seiji Gakkai (ed.), '*Konoe shintaisei' no kenkyū* (Iwanami Shoten, 1972).
Nihonshi jiten (Kadokawa Shoten, 1976).
Nihon shimbun hyakunen-shi (Nihon Shimbun Remmei, 1961).
Nihon shuppan nenkan (Kyōdō Shuppansha, 1943).
Nishida Keiji (ed.), *Nishida Kitarō* (*Gendai Nihon shisō taikei*, XXII) (Chikuma Shobō, 1968).
Ogata Taketora, *Ichigunjin no shōgai* (Bungei Shunjūsha, 1955).
Ogata Taketora Denki Kankōkai, *Ogata Taketora* (Asahi Shimbunsha, 1963).
Ōhara Shakai Mondai Kenkyūjo (ed.), *Taiheiyō sensō-ka no rōdō undō* (Nihon Rōdō Nenkan, 1965).
——, *Taiheiyō sensō-ka rōdōsha jōtai* (Tōyō Keizai Shimbunsha, 1964).
Oka Yoshitake, *Konoe Fumimaro* (Iwanami Shinsho, 1972).
Okada Keisuke (Okada Taishō Kiroku Hensankai, 1956).

Okada Keisuke, *Okada Keisuke kaikoroku* (Mainichi Shimbunsha, 1950).

Okada Takeo, *Konoe Fumimaro* (Shunjūsha, 1959).

Ōki Misao, *Ōki nikki* (Asahi Shimbunsha, 1969).

Oki Osamuji, *Yamashita Tomoyuki* (Yamashita Tomoyuki Kinenkai, 1958).

——, *Anami Korechika-den* (Kōdansha, 1970).

Ōtani Keijirō, *Shōwa kempei-shi* (Misuzu Shobō, 1966).

——, *Gumbatsu* (Tosho Shuppansha, 1971).

Ōtsuki Ken, 'Gunkoku-shugi kyōiku to kodomo', in *Dokyumento taiheiyō sensō*, II, 105–34.

Ōuchi Tsutomu, *Fuashizumu e no michi* (*Nihon no rekishi*, XXIV, Chūō Kōronsha, 1967).

Ozaki Hatsuki, *Zoruge jiken* (Chūō Kōronsha, 1963).

Ozaki Yoshiharu, *Rikugun o ugokashita hitobito* (Hachikodō Shoten, 1960).

Rekishigaku Kenkyūkai, *Taiheiyō sensō-shi* (Suzuki Shoten, 1972), 6 vols.

Saegusa Shigeo, *Genron shōwa-shi* (Nihon Hyōronsha, 1958).

Sakomizu Hisatsune, *Dai Nihon teikoku saigo no yonkagetsu* (Oriento Shobō, 1973).

Sakuda Kōtarō, *Tennō to Kido* (Heibonsha, 1948).

Sambō Hombu Shozō, *Haisen no kiroku* (Hara Shobō 1967).

Saotome Katsumoto, *Tōkyō daikūshū* (Iwanami Shinsho, 1971).

Satō Kenryō, *Tōjō Hideki to taiheiyō sensō* (Bungei Shunjū Shinsha, 1960).

——, *Daitōa sensō kaikoroku* (Tokuma Shoten, 1966).

Sensō bungaku zenshū (Mainichi Shimbunsha, 1971–2), 7 vols.

Sensōchū no kurashi no kiroku (Kurashi no Teichōsha, 1973).

Shakai Mondai Kenkyūkai (ed.), *Uyoku jiten, minzoku-ha no zembō* (Futabasha, 1971).

Shiga Naoya, *Shiga Naoya zenshū* (Iwanami Shoten, 1973–4), 12 vols.

Shigemitsu Mamoru, *Shōwa no dōran* (Chūō Kōronsha, 1952), 2 vols.

Shimamura Takashi, *Hondo kūshū* (Tosho Shuppansha, 1971).

Shimizu Isao, *Taiheiyō sensōki no manga* (Bijutsu Dōjinsha, 1971).

Shimmyō Takeo, *Shōwa-shi tsuiseki* (Shinjimbutsa Ōraisha, 1970).

——, *Taiheiyō sensō* (Shinjimbutsu Ōraisha, 1971).

Shinobu Seizaburō, *Gendai seiji-shi nempyō* (San'ichi Shobō, 1960).

Shinoda Gorō, *Tennō shūsen hishi* (Tairiku Shobō, 1978).

Shiōden Nobutaka, *Yudaya shisō oyobi undō* (Naigai Shobō, 1941).

——, *Shiōden Nobutaka kaikoroku* (Misuzu Shobō, 1964).

Shisō no Kagaku Kenkyūkai (ed.), *Kyōdō kenkyū, tenkō* (Heibonsha, 1959–62), 3 vols.

Shokun, March–June 1977.

Shōwa sensō bungaku zenshū (Shūeisha, 1964–5), 16 vols.
Shōwa-shi no shunkan (Asahi Shimbunsha, 1974), 2 vols.
'Shōwa tennō no dokuhaku hachi jikan', *Bungei Shunjū* (Dec. 1990), 94–145.
Shufu no tomo-sha no gojūnen (Shufu no tomo-sha, 1967).
Shuppan nenkan (Tōkyōdō, 1941).
Sugihara Masami, *Atarashii shōwa-shi* (Shinkigensha, 1958).
Sugita Rokuichi, *Higashi Ajia e kita Yudayajin* (Otoha Shobō, 1967).
Sugiura Maseo (ed.), *Senjichū insatsu rōdōsha no arasoi no kiroku*, 1964 (publisher not known).
Sugiyama Gensui Denki Kankōkai, *Sugiyama gensui-den* (Hara Shobō, 1969).
Sugiyama Hajime, *Sugiyama memo* (Hara Shobō, 1967), 2 vols.
Suzuki Hajime, *Tennō-sama no sain* (Mainichi Shimbunsha, 1962).
——, *Suzuki Kantarō jiden* (Jiji Tsūshinsha, 1968).
Suzuki Kaichi, *Tonarigumi to jōkai* (Seibundō Shinkōsha, 1940).
Taiheiyō sensō e no michi (Asahi Shimbunsha, 1962–3), 7 vols.
Takahashi Masae, *Shōwa no gumbatsu* (Chūō Kōronsha, 1969).
Takami Jun, *Takami Jun nikki* (Keisō Shobō, 1964–6), 7 vols.
Takami Jun-shū (*Gendai Nihon bungaku zenshū*, XLVI) (Chikuma Shobō, 1955).
Takamiya Tahei, *Gunkoku taiheiki* (Kantōsha, 1951).
——, *Tennō heika* (Kantōsha, 1951).
——, *Ningen Ogata Taketora* (Shikisha, 1958).
——, *Yonai Mitsumasa* (Jiji Tsūshinsha, 1958).
——, *Shōwa no shōsui* (Tosho Shuppansha, 1973).
Takamura Kōtarō, *Takamura Kōtarō shishū* (Iwanami Shoten, 1955).
Takeda Seigo, *Shimbun to Yudayajin* (Ōa Tsūshinsha, 1944).
Takeshita Masahiko, 'Hiraizumi shigaku to rikugun', *Gunji gakushi*, V, 1 (May 1969), 110–15.
Takeuchi Toshizō, *Dokyumento Tōkyō daikūshū* (Ondorisha, 1968).
Takeuchi Yoshimi (ed.), *Ajia-shugi* (*Gendai Nihon shisō-taikei*, IX) (Chikuma Shobō, 1963).
——, 'Kindai no chōkoku', in Yoshimoto Takaaki (ed.), *Nashonarizumu*, p. 377–427.
Takeyama Michio, *Shōwa no seishin-shi* (Shinchōsha, 1958).
Tanaka Shin'ichi, *Tanaka sakusen buchō no shōgen* (Fuyō Shobō, 1978).
Tanaka Ryūkichi, *Nihon gumbatsu antōshi* (Seiwado Shoten, 1947).
Tanaka Sōgorō, *Nihon fuashizumu-shi* (Kawade Shobō Shinsha, 1960).
Tateno Nobuyuki, *Shōwa gumbatsu* (Kōdansha, 1965), 2 vols.
Tōdai Jūhachishi-kai (ed.), *Gakuto shutsujin no kiroku* (Chūō Kōronsha, 1968).
Tokutomi Iichirō (Sohō), *Hisshō kokumin dokuhon* (Mainichi Shimbunsha, 1944).

Tōkyō Jūni Channeru Hōdōbu, *Shōgen watakushi no shōwa-shi* (Gakugei Shorin, 1969), 6 vols.

Tōkyō Jūni Channeru Shakai Kyōyōbu, *Shimpen watakushi no shōwa-shi* (Gakugei Shorin, 1974), 4 vols.

Tonarigumi dokuhon (Hibonkaku, 1940).

Tōyama Shigeki, Hattori Shisō, Maruyama Masao, *Sonjō shisō to zettaishugi* (*Tōyō bunka kōza*, II) (Hakujitsu Shoin, 1948).

Tōyama Shigeki, 'Nihon shihaisha-sō no seiji ishiki', in Maruyama Masao et al., *Nihon no nashonarizumu* (Kawade Shobō, 1953), pp. 145–67

Tōyama Shigeki, Imai Seiichi, Fujiwara Akira, *Shōwa-shi*, new edn. (Iwanami Shinsho, 1959).

Tsuji Kiyoaki, *Nihon kanryōsei no kenkyū* (Kōbundō, 1952).

Tsujimura Kōichi (ed.), *Tanabe Hajime* (Chikuma Shobō, 1965).

Tsukui Tatsuo, *Nihon kokka-shugi undōshi-ron* (Chūō Kōronsha, 1942).

Tsunoda Jun (ed.), *Ishiwara Kanji shiryō* (Hara Shobō. 1967).

Tsurumi Shun'suke, *Jānarizumu no shisō* (*Gendai Nihon shisō taikei*, XII) (Chikuma Shobō, 1965).

Tsuruoka Yoshihisa, *Taiheiyō sensōka no shi to shisō* (Shōshinsha, 1971).

Tsuzuki Shichirō, *Uyoku no rekishi* (Tsubasa Shoin, 1967).

Uchida Nobuya, *Fūsetsu gojūnen* (Jitsugyō no Nihonsha, 1951).

Uchida Nobuya (Uchida Nobuya Tsuisō-roku Henshū Iinkai, 1973).

Ugaki Kazushige, *Ugaki Nikki* (Asahi Shimbunsha, 1954).

Utsunomiya Kiyo, *Yudaya mondai to Nihon* (Naigai Shobō, 1939).

Wada Minoru, *Wadatsumi no koe kieru koto naku* (Chikuma Shobō, 1967).

Wagatsuma Sakae, *Nihon seiji saiban shiroku* (*Shōwa, go*) (Daiichi Hōki, 1970), 5 vols.

Wakatsuki Reijirō, *Kofūan kaikoroku* (Yomiuri Shimbunsha, 1950).

Waseda Daigaku Shakai Kagaku Kenkyūjo, Fuashizumu Kenkyū Bukai, *Nihon no Fuashizumu* (Waseda Daigaku Shuppanbu, 1970–4), 2 vols.

Watanabe Hiroshi, *Kiki no bungaku* (Chikuma Shobō, 1972).

Yabe Sadaji (ed.), *Konoe Fumimaro* (Konoe Fumimaro Denki Hensan Kankōkai, 1952), 2 vols.

——, *Konoe Fumimaro* (Jiji Tsūshin, 1958).

——, *Yabe Sadaji nikki* (Yomiuri Shimbunsha, 1974), 2 vols.

Yamada Fūtarō, *Senchūha fusen nikki* (Banchō Shobō, 1971).

Yamamoto Fumio, *Nihon shimbun hattatsu-shi* (Itō Shoten, 1944).

Yamamoto Katsunosuke, *Nihon o horoboshita mono* (Shōkō Shoin, 1949).

Yasuda Takeshi, *Gaguto shutsujin* (Sanshodō, 1967).

Yasue Norihiro, *Yudaya no hitobito* (Gunjin Kaikan Jigyōbu, 1934).

Yatsugi Kazuo, *Shōwa dōran shishi* (Keizai Oraisha, 1971), 3 vols.

Yokoyama Shimpei, *Hiroku Ishiwara Kanji* (Fuyō Shoten, 1971).
Yokusan kokumin undō-shi (Yokusan Undō-shi Kankōkai, 1954).
'Yokusan sōsenkyo risō to jissen', *Chūō kōron*, April 1942, pp. 1–44, 178–85.
Yomiuri Shimbun (ed.), *Shōwa-shi tennō* (Yomiuri Shimbunsha, 1967–74), 25 vols.
Yomiuri shimbun hachijūnenshi (Yomiuri Shimbunsha, 1955).
Yoneda Toshiaki, *Sensō to kajin* (Kinokuniya Shinsho, 1968).
Yoshimi Yoshiaki, *Yokusan senkyo* (Tokyo: Ōtsuki Shoten, 1983).
Yoshimoto Takaaki (ed.), *Nashonarizumu* (*Gendai Nihon shisō taikei*, IV) (Chikuma Shobō, 1964).
——, *Kokka no shisō* (*Sengo Nihon shisō taikei*, VI) (Chikuma Shobō, 1969).
Yoshino Sakuzō, 'Yudayajin no sekai tempuku no imbō ni tsuite', *Chūō kōron*, May 1921.
——, 'Iwayura sekai-teki himitsu kessha no seitai', *Chūō kōron*, June 1921.
Yui Masaomi, *Kokka-shugi undō* (Tokyo: Ōtsuki Shoten, 1981).
Zainichi Kankoku Seinen Dōmei, Chūō Hombu (ed.), *Zainichi Kankokujin no rekishi to genjitsu* (Yōyōsha, 1970).

Western Languages

Abend, Hallett, *Japan Unmasked* (New York: Ives Washburn, 1941).
Adler, Cyrus, *Jacob H. Schiff, His Life and Letters* (Garden City: Doubleday, 1928).
Akashi, Yoji, 'A Botched Peace Effort: The Miao Pin *Kosaku*', in Alvin D. Coox and Hilary Conroy (eds.), *China and Japan, Search for Balance Since World War I* (Santa Barbara: ABC-Clio, 1978), pp. 265–88.
Allardyce, G., 'What Fascism is Not: Thoughts on the Deflation of the Concept', *American Historical Review*, LXXXIV, 2 (April 1979), 367–98.
Allen, Louis, *The End of the War in Asia* (London: Hart-Davis, MacGibbon, 1976).
Anderson, L., and Richie, Donald, *The Japanese Film: Art and Industry* (Tokyo: Tuttle, 1959).
Anderson, Ronald S., *Japan, Three Epochs of Modern Education* (Washington: US Department of Health, Education and Welfare, 1959). Bulletin No. 11.
Anesaki, Masaharu, *Religious Life of the Japanese People* (Tokyo: Kokusai Bunka Shinkokai, 1938).
Arendt, Hannah, *The Origins of Totalitarianism* (New York: Meridian Books, 1958).
Arima, Tatsuo, *The Failure of Freedom, A Portrait of Modern Japanese*

Intellectuals (Cambridge: Harvard University Press, 1969).

Asahi Shimbun Staff, *The Pacific Rivals* (Tokyo: Weatherhill, 1972).

Aso, Makoto, and Amano, Ikuo, *Education and Japan's Modernization* (Tokyo: Ministry of Foreign Affairs, 1972).

Atsumi Ikuko and Wilson, Graeme, 'The Poetry of Takamura Kōtarō', *Japan Quarterly*, XX, 3 (July–Sept. 1973), 308–18.

Ayusawa, Iwao F., *A History of Labor in Modern Japan* (Honolulu: East–West Center Press, 1966).

Baty, Thomas, *Alone in Japan* (Tokyo, Maruzen, 1959).

Beasley, W. G. (ed.), *Modern Japan, Aspects of History, Literature and Society* (London: Allen and Unwin, 1975).

Beckmann, George M., and Okubo Genji, *The Japanese Communist Party, 1922–1945* (Stanford: Stanford University Press, 1964).

Benda, Harry, J., *The Crescent and the Rising Sun* (The Hague: Van Hoeve, 1958).

Bergamini, David, *Japan's Imperial Conspiracy* (New York: William Morrow, 1971).

Berger, Gordon Mark, 'Recent Japan in Historical Revisionism, Changing Historiographical Perspectives on Early Shōwa Politics: The Second Approach', *Journal of Asian Studies*, XXXIV, 2 (Feb. 1975), 473–84.

——, *Parties Out of Power in Japan, 1931–1941* (Princeton: Princeton University Press, 1977).

Bertish, Roman, 'Jewish Emigrants from Poland during World War II and the Polish Government's Attitude to Them' (in Hebrew), *Gal-Ed* (Tel-Aviv: The Diaspora Research Institute, 1973), I, 251–98.

Bikle, George B. Jr., *The New Jerusalem, Aspects of Utopianism in the Thought of Kagawa Toyohiko* (Tucson: The University of Arizona Press, 1976).

Bisson, T. A., 'The Zaibatsu's Wartime Role', *Pacific Affairs*, XVIII (Dec. 1945), 355–64.

——, *Japan's War Economy* (New York: Institute of Pacific Relations, 1945).

Bix, Herbert P., 'Kawakami Hajime and the Organic Law of Japanese Fascism', *Japan Interpreter*, XII, 1 (Winter 1978), 118–33.

Bondy, Louis, W., *Racketeers of Hatred* (London: Newman Wolsey, 1946).

Borg, Dorothy, and Okamoto Shumpei (eds.), *Pearl Harbor as History: Japanese American Relations, 1931–1941* (New York: Columbia University Press, 1973).

Brzezinski, Z. K., *Ideology and Power in Soviet Politics* (New York: Praeger, 1967).

Burrows, Robert, 'Totalitarianism, the Revised Standard Vision',

World Politics, XXI, 2 (Jan. 1969), 272–94.

Butow, Robert J. C., *Japan's Decision to Surrender* (Stanford: Stanford University Press, 1954).

——, *Tojo and the Coming of the War* (Princeton: Princeton University Press, 1961).

Byrnes, James F., *Speaking Frankly* (New York: Harper, 1958).

Cohen, Jerome B., *Japan's Economy in War and Reconstruction* (Minneapolis: University of Minnesota Press, 1949).

Connors, Lesley, *The Emperor's Adviser: Saionji Kimmochi and Prewar Japanese Politics* (London: Croom Helm, 1987).

Contemporary Japan, 1940–5.

Coox, Alvin D., *The Year of the Tiger* (Tokyo: Orient/West Press, 1964).

——, 'Zeal, Levity and the Holy War,' *The Japanese Image* (Tokyo: Orient/West Press, 1966), pp. 380–8.

——, 'Evidence of Antimilitarism in Prewar and Wartime Japan', *Pacific Affairs*, XLVI, 4 (Winter 1973–4), 502–14.

——, and Hilary Conroy (eds.), *China and Japan, Search for Balance Since World War I* (Santa Barbara: ABC-Clio, 1978).

Coughlin, William J., *Conquered Press* (California: Pacific Books, 1952).

Crowley, James B., *Japan's Quest for Autonomy: National Security and Foreign Policy 1930–1938* (Princeton: Princeton University Press, 1966).

——, 'Imperial Japan and its Modern Discontents: The State and the Military in Prewar Japan', in Harold Z. Schiffrin (ed.), *Military and State in Modern Asia* (Jerusalem: Jerusalem Academic Press, 1979), pp. 31–59.

——, 'Intellectuals as Visionaries of the New Asian Order', in J. W. Morley (ed.), *Dilemmas of Growth in Prewar Japan* (Princeton: Princeton University Press, 1971), pp. 319–73.

Daniels, Gordon, 'The Great Tokyo Air Raid, 9–10 March 1945', in W. G. Beasley (ed.), *Modern Japan, Aspects of History, Literature and Society* (London: Allen and Unwin, 1975), pp. 113–31.

Daniels, Roger, *Concentration Camps USA: Japanese Americans and World War II* (New York: Holt, Rinehart and Winston, 1971).

Deakin, F. W., and G. R. Storry, *The Case of Richard Sorge* (London: Chatto and Windus, 1966).

Dicker, Herman, *Wanderers and Settlers in the Far East* (New York: Twayne, 1962).

——, 'Jews and Japan', *Jewish Spectator*, June 1964, pp. 9–12.

Dower, J. W., 'Science, Society, and the Japanese Atomic-Bomb Project during World War II', *Bulletin of Concerned Asian Scholars*, X, 2 (1978), 41–54.

——, *Empire and Aftermath: Yoshida Shigeru and the Japanese Experience, 1878–1954* (Cambridge: Council on East Asian Studies, Harvard University, 1979).

——, *War Without Mercy: Race and Power in the Pacific War* (New York: Pantheon, 1986).

Drea, Edward J., *The 1942 Japanese General Election: Political Mobilization in Wartime Japan* (The University of Kansas: Center for East Asian Studies, 1979).

Duus, Peter, 'Nagai Ryūtarō: The Tactical Dilemmas of Reform', in Albert M. Craig and Donald H. Shively (eds.), *Personality in Japanese History* (Berkeley: University of California Press, 1970), pp. 399–424.

——, 'Nagai Ryūtarō and the 'White Peril', 1905–1944', *Journal of Asian Studies*, XXX, 1 (Nov. 1971), 41–8.

Duus, Peter, and Okimoto, Daniel I., 'Fascism and the History of Pre-War Japan: The Failure of a Concept', *Journal of Asian Studies*, XXXIX, 1 (Nov. 1979), 65–76.

Encyclopedia Judaica (Jerusalem, 1971).

Eunson, Roby, *100 Years* (Tokyo: Kodansha International, 1965).

Feis, Herbert, *The Road To Pearl Harbor: The Coming of the War Between the United States and Japan* (New York: Atheneum Press, 1965).

——, *The Atomic Bomb and the End of World War II* (Princeton: Princeton University Press, 1970).

Fleisher, Wilfried, *Volcanic Isle* (Garden City: Doubleday, 1941).

Fletcher, Miles, 'Intellectuals and Fascism in Early Shōwa Japan', *Journal of Asian Studies*, XXXIX (Nov. 1979), 39–63.

Fletcher, William M., *The Search for a New Order: Intellectuals and Fascism in Prewar Japan* (Chapel Hill: University of North Carolina Press, 1982).

Forrestal, James. *The Forrestal Diaries* (New York: Viking Press, 1951).

Friedrich, Carl J. (ed.), *Totalitarianism* (New York: Grosset and Dunlap, 1964).

Friese, Eberhart, *Japaninstitut Berlin und Deutsch-Japanische Gesellschaft Berlin* (Occasional Papers No. 9, Social and Economic Research on Modern Japan, East Asian Institute, Free University of Berlin, 1980).

Fujisawa, Chikao, 'Japan versus Marxism', *Contemporary Japan*, December 1932.

Fujita, Wakao, 'Yanaihara Tadao, Disciple of Uchimura Kanzō and Nitobe Inazo', in Nobuya Bamba and John F. Howes (eds.), *Pacifism in Japan, The Christian and Socialist Tradition* (Vancouver: University of British Columbia Press, 1978), pp. 199–219.

Fukushima, Masao, 'Profile of Asian Minded Man, VI: Noboru

Niida', *Developing Economies*, V (1967), 173–90.

Furusawa, Isojiro, 'Japan's Wartime General Elections', *Contemporary Japan*, II 5 (May 1942), 675–84.

Grew, Joseph, *Turbulent Era, A Diplomatic Record of Forty Years* (Boston: Houghton Mifflin, 1952), 2 vols.

Guillain, Robert, *Le Peuple Japonais et la Guerre* (Paris: Julliard, 1947).

——, *I Saw Tokyo Burning: An Eyewitness Narrative from Pearl Harbor to Hiroshima* (tr. William Byron, Garden City: Doubleday, 1981).

Hagoromo Society of Kamikaze Divine Thunderbolt Corps Survivors. *Born to Die* (Tokyo: Ohara Publications, 1973).

Hall, Robert King (ed.), *Kokutai no Hongi, Cardinal Principles of the National Entity of Japan* (Eng. tr. by John O. Gauntlett, Cambridge: Harvard University Press, 1949).

——, *Shūshin, The Ethics of a Defeated Nation* (New York: Columbia University, 1949).

Hashikawa Bunsō, 'Antiwar Values: The Resistance in Japan', *Japan Interpreter*, IX, 1 (Spring 1974), 86–99.

Havens, Thomas R. H., 'Frontiers of Japanese Social History During World War II', *Shakai kagaku tōkyū*, XVIII, 52 (March 1973), 1–45.

——, 'Women and War in Japan, 1937–45', *American Historical Review*, LXXX, 4 (Oct. 1975), 913–34.

——, *The Valley of Darkness* (New York: Norton, 1978).

Hayashi, Saburo, and Alvin D. Coox. *Kōgun, The Japanese Army in the Pacific War* (Quantico, Virginia; The Marine Corps Association, 1959).

Hirai, Atsuko, *Individualism and Socialism: Kawai Eijiro's Life and Thought (1891–1944)* (Cambridge: Council on East Asian Studies, Harvard University, 1986).

Hirakawa Sukehiro, 'Signals of Peace not Received: Premier Suzuki Kantarō's Solitary Efforts to End the Pacific War', *Comparative Studies of Culture*, no. 18 (University of Tokyo Press, 1979), 107–31.

Hitler, Adolf, *Mein Kampf* (Eng. tr. by Ralph Manheim, Boston: Houghton Mifflin, 1943).

Hitler's Secret Conversations, 1941–1944 (New York: Octagon Books, 1972).

Holtom, D. C., *Modern Japan and Shinto Nationalism* (Chicago: University of Chicago Press, 1943).

Hosoya, Chihiro, 'Twenty-Five Years After Pearl Harbor: A New Look at Japan's Decision for War', in Grant K. Goodman (ed.), *Imperial Japan and Asia: A Reassessment* (New York: Columbia University, Occasional Papers of the Asian Institute, 1967), pp. 52–64.

——, 'The Prewar Japanese Military in Political Decision Making', in Harold Z. Schiffrin (ed.), *Military and State in Modern Asia* (Jerusalem: Jerusalem Academic Press, 1976), pp. 19–29.

Hozumi Shigetomi, 'The Tonarigumi of Japan', *Contemporary Japan*, XII, 8 (Aug. 1943), 984–90.

Hulse, Friedrich S., 'Some Effects of the War upon Japanese Society', *Far Eastern Quarterly*, VII, 1 (Nov. 1947), 22–42.

Ienaga, Saburō, 'La Situazione degli Studi Nipponici sulla Resistenza in Giappone durante la Seconda Guerra Mondiale', *Revista Storica Italiana*, LXXXIX, 2 (1977), 263–80.

——, *The Pacific War: World War II and the Japanese, 1931–1945* (New York: Pantheon Books, 1978).

Iizawa, Shōji, 'Policy of the Koiso Cabinet', *Contemporary Japan*, VIII, 10–12 (Oct.–Dec. 1944), 900–11.

Ike, Nobutaka (ed.), *Japan's Decision for War: Records of the 1941 Policy Conferences* (Stanford: Stanford University Press, 1967).

——, 'War and Modernization', in Robert E. Ward. (ed.), *Political Development in Modern Japan* (Princeton: Princeton University Press, 1968), pp. 189–211.

Inoguchi, Rikihei, and Nakajima Tadashi, *Kamikaze* (Annapolis: US Naval Institute, 1958).

International Military Tribunal for the Far East, *Record of the Proceedings* (Tokyo: 1946–9).

Iriye, Akira, *Power and Culture: The Japanese–American War, 1941–1945* (Cambridge: Harvard University Press, 1981).

Japan Times (also *Japan Times and Advertiser*), 1940–2.

Japan Year Book (Tokyo: The Japan Times, 1940–4).

Japanese National Commission for UNESCO, *The Role of Education in the Social and Economic Development of Japan* (Tokyo: Ministry of Education, 1966).

Johnson, Chalmers, *An Instance of Treason: Ozaki Hotsumi and The Sorge Spy Ring* (Stanford: Stanford University Press, 1964).

——, *Conspiracy at Matsukawa* (Berkeley: University of California Press, 1972).

Kakehi, Mitsuaki, 'Tokyoites under Air Raids', *Contemporary Japan*, XIV, 1–3 (Jan.–March 1945), 75–84.

Kase, Toshikazu, *Journey to the Missouri* (New Haven: Yale University Press, 1950).

Kato, Masuo, *The Lost War: A Japanese Reporter's Inside Story* (New York: Knopf, 1946).

Kasza, Gregory J., *The State and the Mass Media in Japan, 1918–1945* (Berkeley: University of California Press, 1988).

Katō Shūichi, 'The Mass Media: Japan', in Robert E. Ward and Dankwart A. Rustow (eds.), *Political Modernization in Japan and Turkey* (Princeton: Princeton University Press, 1964), pp. 236–54.

Keene, David, 'Japanese Writers and the Greater East Asia War', *Journal of Asian Studies*, XXIII, 2 (Feb. 1964), 209–25.

——, 'Japanese Literature and Politics in the 1930s', *Journal of Japanese Studies*, II, 2 (Summer 1976), 225–48.

——, 'The Barren Years, Japanese War Literature', *Monumenta Nipponica*, XXXIII, 1 (Spring 1978), 67–112.

Kotsuji, Abraham, *From Tokyo to Jerusalem* (New York: Bernard Geis Associates, 1964).

Kranzler, David, *Japanese, Nazis, and Jews: the Jewish Refugee Community of Shanghai, 1938–1945* (New York: Yeshiva University Press, 1976).

——, 'Japanese Policy toward the Jews, 1938–1941', *Japan Interpreter*, XI, 4 (Spring 1977), 493–527.

Kublin, Hyman, 'Star of David and Rising Sun', *Jewish Frontier*, XXV, 4 (April 1958), 15–22.

Kurzman, Dan, *Kishi and Japan* (New York: Ivan Obolensky, 1960).

Lebra, Joyce C. (ed.), *Japan's Greater East Asia Co-Prosperity Sphere* (London: Oxford University Press, 1975).

Lensen, George Alexander, *The Strange Neutrality, Soviet–Japanese Relations during the Second World War, 1941–1945* (Tallahassee: Diplomatic Press, 1972).

Lory, Hillis, *Japan's Military Masters, the Army in Japanese Life* (New York: Viking Press, 1943).

Lu, David John (ed.), *Source of Japanese History* (New York: McGraw-Hill, 1974), 2 vols.

McLeod, N., *Japan and the Lost Tribes of Israel* (Nagasaki: The Rising Sun office, 1879).

Mainichi Daily News Staff, *Fifty Years of Light and Dark, the Hirohito Era* (Tokyo: The Mainichi Newspaper, 1975).

Maki, John M., *Government and Politics in Japan* (New York: Praeger, 1962).

Maruyama, Masao, *Thought and Behavior in Modern Japanese Politics*, edited with an introduction by Ivan Morris (London: Oxford University Press, 1963).

——, *Studies in the Intellectual History of Tokugawa Japan* (Princeton: Princeton University Press, 1974).

Mendelssohn, Peter de, *Japan's Political Warfare* (London: George Allen and Unwin, 1944).

Meo. L. D., *Japan's Radio War on Australia, 1941–1945* (London: Melbourne University Press, 1968).

Meskill, Johanna Menzel, *Hitler and Japan: The Hollow Alliance* (New York: Atherton Press, 1966).

Miki, Kiyoshi, 'The China Affair and Japanese Thought', *Contemporary Japan*, March 1938, pp. 601–10.

Minichiello, Sharon, *Retreat from Reform: Patterns of Political Behavior in Interwar Japan* (Honolulu: University of Hawaii Press, 1984).
Mitchell, Richard H., *Thought Control in Prewar Japan* (Ithaca: Cornell University Press, 1976).
——, *Censorship in Imperial Japan* (Princeton: Princeton University Press, 1983).
Moore, Barrington Jr., *Social Origins of Dictatorship and Democracy* (Boston: Beacon Press, 1966).
Morley, James William, 'The First Seven Weeks', *Japan Interpreter*, VI, 2 (Summer 1970), 151–64.
——, (ed.), *Dilemmas of Growth in Prewar Japan* (Princeton: Princeton University Press, 1971).
Morris, Ivan (ed.), *Japan 1931–1945, Militarism, Fascism, Japanism?* (Boston: D. C. Heath, Problems in Asian Civilizations, 1963).
——, *The Nobility of Failure* (London: Secker and Warburg, 1975).
Morris, John, *Traveller from Tokyo* (London: Penguin, 1943).
Morse, Ronald, 'Personalities and Issues in Yanagita Kunio Studies', *Japan Quarterly*, XXII, 3 (July–Sept. 1975), 239–54.
Murakami Hyoe, *Japan: The Years of Trial, 1919–1952* (Tokyo: Kodansha International, 1983).
Murata, Kiyoaki, *Japan's New Buddhism, An Objective Account of Sōka Gakkai* (Tokyo: Wetherhill, 1969).
Nakada, Bishop Juji, *An Unknown Nation* (Eng. tr. by Revd. B. Kida, Tokyo: The O.M.S. Japan Holiness Church, 1933).
Nakamura Mitsuo, *Contemporary Japanese Fiction* (Tokyo: Kokusai Bunka Shinkōkai, 1969).
Neumann, Franz, *The Democratic and Authoritarian State* (Chicago: The Free Press of Glencoe, 1957).
Nippon Times, 1943–5.
Nolte, Ernst, *Three Faces of Fascism* (Eng. tr. by Leila Vonnewitz, New York: Holt, Rinehart, and Winston, 1965).
Norman, E. Herbert, *Japan's Emergence as a Modern State* (New York: Institute of Pacific Relations, 1940).
Notar, Ernest J., 'Japan's Wartime Labor Policy: A Search for Method', *Journal of Asian Studies*, XLIV, 2 (Feb. 1985), 311–28.
Okumiya, Masatake and Jiro Horikoshi, with Martin Caidin, *Zero! The Story of the Japanese Navy Air Force, 1937–1945* (London: Cassell, 1957).
Osaragi, Jiro, *Homecoming* (Eng. tr. by Brewster Horwitz, Tokyo: Tuttle, 1955).
Ota, Yuzo, 'Kagawa Toyohiko: A Pacifist?', in Nobuya Bamba and John F. Howes (eds.), *Pacifism in Japan, The Christian and Social Tradition* (Vancouver: University of British Columbia Press, 1978), pp. 169–97.

Pacific War Research Society, *Japan's Longest Day* (Tokyo: Kodansha International, 1965).

———, *The Day Man Lost* (Tokyo: Kodansha International, 1972).

Peattie, Mark R., *Ishiwara Kanji and Japan's Confrontation with the West* (Princeton: Princeton University Press, 1975).

Pelz, Stephan E., *Race to Pearl Harbor* (Cambridge: Harvard University Press, 1974).

Popper, Karl, *The Open Society and its Enemies* (Princeton: Princeton University Press, 1963).

Potter, E. B., and Nimitz, Admiral Chester W., *The Great Sea War* (London: Harrap, 1961).

Presseisen, Ernst L., *Germany and Japan, a Study in Totalitarian Diplomacy, 1933–1941* (The Hague: Martinus Nijhoff, 1958).

———, 'Le Racisme et les Japonais', *Revue d'Histoire de la Deuxième Guerre Mondiale*, LI (July 1963), 1–14.

Reischauer, Edwin O., 'What Went Wrong?' in James W. Morley (ed.), *Dilemmas of Growth in Prewar Japan* (Princeton: Princeton University Press, 1971), pp. 489–510.

Rice, Richard, 'Economic Mobilization in Wartime Japan: Business, Bureaucracy, and Military in Conflict', *Journal of Asian Studies*, XXXVIII, 4 (Aug. 1979), 689–706.

Scalapino, Robert A., *Democracy and the Party Movement in Prewar Japan, the Failure of the First Attempt* (Berkeley: University of California Press, 1953).

———, *The Japanese Communist Movement, 1920–1966* (Berkeley: University of California Press, 1967).

———, 'Elections and Political Modernization in Prewar Japan', in Robert E. Ward (ed,), *Political Development in Modern Japan* (Princeton: Princeton University Press, 1968), pp. 249–91.

Schroeder, Paul W., *The Axis Alliance and Japanese–American Relations* (Ithaca: Cornell University Press, 1957).

Seidensticker, Edward, *Kafū the Scribbler* (Stanford: Stanford University Press, 1965).

———, 'Kobayashi Hideo', in Donald H. Shively (ed.), *Tradition and Modernization in Japanese Culture* (Princeton: Princeton University Press, 1971), pp. 419–61.

Sheldon, Charles D., 'Japanese Aggression and the Emperor, 1931–1941, from Contemporary Diaries', *Modern Asian Studies*, X, 1 (Feb. 1976), 1–40.

———, 'Scapegoat or Instigator of Japanese Agression? Inoue Kiyoshi's Case against the Emperor', *Modern Asian Studies*, XII, 1 (Feb. 1978), 1–35.

Shigemitsu, Mamoru, *Japan and her Destiny* (New York: Dutton, 1958).

Shillony, Ben-Ami, *Revolt in Japan, the Young Officers and the February 26,*

1936, Incident (Princeton: Princeton University Press, 1973).
——, 'Wartime Japan: A Military Dictatorship?' in Harold Z. Schiffrin (ed.), *Military and State in Modern Asia* (Jerusalem: Jerusalem Academic Press, 1976), pp. 61–88.
——, 'Universities and Students in Wartime Japan', *Journal of Asian Studies*, XLV, 4 (Aug. 1986), 769–87.
——, 'Friend or Foe: The Ambivalent Images of the U.S. and China in Wartime Japan', in James W. White, Michio Umegaki, and Thomas R. H. Havens (eds.), *The Ambivalence of Nationalism: Modern Japan Between East and West* (New York: University Press of America, 1990), pp. 187–212.
Shiratori, Toshio, 'Fascism versus Popular Front', *Contemporary Japan*, VI, 4 (March 1939), 581–9.
Shiroyama, Saburo, *War Criminal: The Life and Death of Hirota Koki* (Tokyo: Kodansha International, 1977).
Shyu, Lawrence, N., 'China's "Wartime Parliament": The People's Political Council, 1938–1945', in Paul K. T. Sih (ed.), *Nationalist China during the Sino-Japanese War, 1937–1945* (Hicksville: Exposition Press, 1977), pp. 273–328.
Sims, R. L. 'National Elections and Electioneering in Akita Ken, 1930–1942', in W. G. Beasley (ed.), *Modern Japan, Aspects of History, Literature and Society* (London: Allen and Unwin, 1975), pp. 89–112.
Singer, Kurt, *Mirror, Sword and Jewel*, edited with an introduction by Richard Storry (London: Croom Helm, 1973).
Smethurst, Richard J., *A Social Basis for Prewar Japanese Militarism, the Army and the Rural Community* (Berkeley: University of California Press, 1974).
Spaulding, Robert M., Jr., 'Japan's "New Bureaucrats", 1932–1945', in George M. Wilson (ed.), *Crisis Politics in Prewar Japan* (Tokyo: Sophia University, 1970), pp. 51–70
Steinhoff, Patricia Golden, 'Tenkō: Ideology and Societal Integration in Prewar Japan', Harvard University Ph.D. dissertation 1969 (microfilm).
Stimson, Henry L. and Bundy, McGeorge, *On Active Service in Peace and War* (London: Hutchinson, 1947).
Storry, Richard, *The Double Patriots, a Study of Japanese Nationalism* (London: Chatto and Windus, 1957).
Synopses of Contemporary Japanese Literature (Tokyo: Kokusai Bunka Shinkōkai, 1970).
Takagi Keiko, 'Poems of Kaneko Mitsuharu', *Japan Quarterly*, XXIII, 3 (July–Sept. 1976), 275–83.
Takahashi Makoto, 'The Development of War-Time Economic Controls', *Developing Economics*, V, 4 (Dec. 1967), 648–65.
Takaishi, Shingoro, *Japan Speaks Out* (Tokyo: The Hokuseido Press,

1938).

Talmon, J. L., *The Origins of Totalitarian Democracy* (New York: Praeger, 1961).

Tanin, O., and Yohan, E. (pseuds.), *Militarism and Fascism in Japan* (London: Martin Lawrence, 1934).

Terasaki, Gwen, *Bridge to the Sun* (Tokyo: Tuttle, 1973).

Thorne, Christopher, *The Issue of War: States, Societies, and the Far Eastern Conflict of 1941–1945* (London: Oxford University Press, 1985).

Tipton, Elise Kurashige, 'The Civil Police in the Suppression of the Prewar Japanese Left', Indiana University Ph.D. dissertation 1977 (microfilm).

Titus, David Anson, *Palace and Politics in Prewar Japan* (New York: Columbia University Press, 1974).

Togo, Shigenori, *The Cause of Japan* (New York: Simon and Schuster, 1956).

Tokayer, Marvin, and Mary Swartz, *The Fugu Plan, The Untold Story of the Japanese and the Jews During World War II* (New York: Paddington Press, 1979).

Tolischus, Otto, *Tokyo Record* (London: Hamish Hamilton, 1943).

——, *Through Japanese Eyes* (New York: Reynal and Hitchcock, 1945).

Trever-Roper, H. R., 'The Phenomenon of Fascism', in S. J. Woolf (ed.), *European Fascism* (New York: Random House, 1968), pp. 18–38.

Truman, Harry S., *Year of Decisions, 1945* (New York: Doubleday, 1955).

Tsunoda, Ryusaku et al. (eds.), *Sources of Japanese Tradition* (New York: Columbia University Press, 1958).

Tsurumi, Kazuko, *Social Change and the Individual, Japan Before and After World War II* (Princeton: Princeton University Press, 1970).

Tsurumi, Shunsuke, *An Intellectual History of Wartime Japan 1931–1945* (London: KPI, 1986).

Ubukata, Naokichi, 'Profile of Asian Minded Man, I: Tadao Yanaihara, His Colonial Studies and Religious Faith', *Developing Economies*, IV (1966), 90–105.

US Army Air Forces, Assistant Chief of Air Staff, Intelligence Headquarters, *Mission Accomplished, Interrogation of Japanese Industrial, Military, and Civil Leaders of World War II* (Washington: US Government Printing Office, 1946).

US Army, General Headquarters, Supreme Commander for the Allied Powers, Counter Intelligence Section, *The Brocade Banner: The Story of Japanese Nationalism*, 1946 (mimeographed).

US General Headquarters, Far East Command, Military Intelligence Section, Historical Division, *Statements of Japanese Officials on World War II*, 1949–50 (microfilm).

US Strategic Bombing Survey, *Japan's Struggle to End the War* (Washington: US Government Printing Office, 1946).

Ward, Robert E., (ed), *Political Development in Modern Japan* (Princeton: Princeton University Press, 1968).

Watts, Anthony J., and Gordon, Brian G., *The Imperial Japanese Navy* (Garden City: Doubleday, 1971).

Wheeler, John K., 'Rōyama Masamichi and the Search for a Middle Ground, 1932–1940', *Papers on Japan* (East Asia Research Center, Harvard University), VI (1972), 70–101.

Wilson, George M., 'A New Look at the Problem of Japanese Fascism', *Comparative Studies in Society and History*, X, 4 (July 1968), 401–13.

Woodard, William P., 'The Wartime Persecution of Nichiren Buddhism', *Transactions of the Asiatic Society of Japan*, Third Series, VII (Nov. 1959), 99–122.

Wray, Harold J., 'A Study of Contrasts, Japanese School Textbooks of 1903 and 1941–5', *Monumenta Nipponica*, XXVIII, 1 (Spring 1973), 68–86.

Yad Vashem Central Archives, Jerusalem. Testimonies of Abraham Kaufmann (03/3168), Gershom Shibolet (03/2388), Yehoshua Bram (03/3045), Shimon Bergman (03/3045), and 'Concerning Joseph Rosenstock' (01/90) (in Hebrew).

Yamamoto, Hideo, 'Profile of Asian Minded Man, III: Shiraki Tachibana', *Developing Economics*, IV (1966), 381–403.

Yamamoto, Shichihei, 'The Living God and His War Responsibility', *Japan Echo*, III, 1 (Spring 1976), 64–77.

Yanaga, Chitoshi, *Japan Since Perry* (New York: McGraw-Hill, 1949).

Yiddish Lebn in Shanghai (New York: Yiddish Scientific Institute, 1948) (in Yiddish).

Yoshida, Shigeru, *The Yoshida Memoirs* (London: Heinemann, 1961).

Yoshino, Sakuzo, 'Fascism in Japan,' *Contemporary Japan*, I, 2 (Sept. 1932), 185–97.

Index

238   *Index*

death of   80, 147; image of   145,
146, 147, 160, 161, 162
Rōyama Masamich   26, 111, 112, 121

Saionji Kimmochi, Prince   7, 8, 39, 40
Saipan, battle of: effect on government
55–6, 59, 60, 61; reported   66–7,
153
Saitō Takao: criticizes government in
Diet   17, 19; re-elected to Diet   18,
24, 27; appeals election results   35
Sakai Kōji, General   59
Sakomizu Hisatsune   52, 79
Sakonji Masazō   79
Sakurai Hyōgorō   79
Sanjōnishi, Marquis   58
Sano Manabu   120
Sasaki Nobutsuna   116
Satō Haruo   116
Satō Kenryō, Major-General   24, 46, 51
Satō Naotake   71
Satomi Ton   119
schools: reform   5; curriculum   123–4,
138–9, 141–2, 145
science, attitudes towards   137, 138,
139, 140, 141, 176
Sejima Ryūzō, Lieutenant-General   52
Serizawa Kōjirō   128
Shiga Naoya   116, 128, 134
Shiga Yoshio   120
Shigeko, emperor's daughter   39, 192 n.
13
Shigemitsu Mamoru: as foreign minister
in the Tōjō Cabinet   34, 53; as
foreign minister in the Koiso
Cabinet   69; as foreign minister in
the Higashikuni Cabinet   89; and
peace moves   58, 60, 76
Shikata Ryōji, Colonel   15
Shimada Shigetarō, Admiral: as navy
minister   54, 59, 60; supports
Tōjō   33, 53, 58; opposition to   46,
55, 56, 62, 63, 66
Shimada Toshio   69
Shimazaki Tōson   117
Shimizu Takeo   104
Shimmyō Takeo   46, 103, 104
Shimomura Hiroshi   79, 105, 118, 131
Shimomura Sadamu, General   89
Shimomura Toratarō   140, 141
Shiōden Nobutaka, General: 26, 159;
anti-Semitic views of   158–63
passim

Shirane Matsusuke, Baron   160
Shiratori Toshio   152, 159, 160
Shishi Bunroku   198 n. 13
Shizuma Katsuyuki, Major   56
Shōwa kenkyū-kai (Shōwa Research
Society)   111, 112, 125
Shōriki Matsutarō   98, 99, 105
Snow, Edgar P.   122
Sorge, Richard   13, 112, 181 n. 13
Soviet Union: relations with   6, 13, 37,
38, 59, 60, 62, 66, 72, 73, 76, 79, 85,
87, 96, 108; comparison with 11, 13,
15, 16, 125, 177; attitudes towards
120, 141, 155, 156, 157
Stalin, Joseph: comparison with   11,
173; image of   18, 156, 161;
relations with   72
Stauffenberg, Colonel Klaus   62
Stoss, Alfred   158
Streicher, Julius   159
Suetsugu Nobumasa, Admiral   55, 56
Sugihara Sempō   167
Sugimori Kojirō   114
Sugimoto Ryōkichi   200 n. 37
Sugiyama Hajime, General: and
Tōjō   10, 45, 53, 54, 63; and the
war   41, 46, 60; and Nakano
Seigō   49; and Higashikuni   58;
and Koiso   66, 68, 69; suicide
of   88
Supreme Council for the Direction of the
War (*saikō sensō shidō kaigi*)   69, 70,
85, 86
Susukida Yoshitomo   35
Suzuki Kantarō, Admiral: appointed
prime minister   77–8, 173; as prime
minister   78–90, 106; and the
decision to surrender   80, 85–90,
153
Suzuki Masabumi   123
Suzuki Shigetaka   112, 123, 140, 153
Suzuki Teiichi, Colonel   24, 46, 134, 135

Tachibana Shiraki   127
Takagi Sōkichi, Rear-Admiral   59, 124
Takahama Kiyoshi   116
Takahashi San'kichi, General   146
Takaishi Shingorō   98
Takamatsu, Prince: and the
emperor   38, 39, 58, 60, 61; and
Nakano Seigō   47, 50; and
Tōjō   57; suggests a bloc with
Germany and Russia   156; and the